LUCRETIUS
On the Nature of Things

LUCRETIUS
On the Nature of Things

Walter Englert

Reed College

Albert Keith Whitaker, Series Editor

FOCUS PHILOSOPHICAL LIBARY
FOCUS PUBLISHING
R. PULLINS COMPANY
NEWBURYPORT, MA 01950

For Mary, Francesca, and Molly

Cover: Garden with plants and birds, detail. Casa del Bracciale d'Oro, Pompeii, Italy. Copyright Scala/Art Resource, NY.

Book Team:

Publisher: *Ron Pullins*
Production Editor: *Melissa Wood*
Editorial Manager: *Cindy Zawalich*

10 9 8 7 6 5 4 3 2 1

CONTENTS

PREFACE

This translation is an attempt to render Lucretius' powerful Latin philosophic poem into an English translation that reflects the philosophic clarity and poetic power of the original. I have tried to model my translation of Lucretius' epic poem on English translations of classical and medieval poems that I greatly admire, Richmond Lattimore's translations of Homer's *Iliad* and *Odyssey*, and Allen Mandelbaum's translations of Virgil's *Aeneid* and Dante's *Divine Comedy*. I have always been struck by the way Lattimore renders the beauty and clarity of Homer while remaining so faithful to the text, and by how Mandelbaum translates Virgil and Dante with such poetic force, accuracy, and *humanitas*. When I began this project I was convinced that what was needed for Lucretius was an English translation which would bring out the inseparable poetic qualities and philosophic clarity of the poem, and which could be used by students and general readers as an accurate guide to the original.

My interest first began when I read Lucretius as an undergraduate in the Integral Liberal Arts program at St. Mary's College of California. The seminars I had on Lucretius gave me my first glimpses of the poem's power and beauty. I first read Lucretius in Latin as a graduate student with Jo-Ann Shelton at the University of California at Santa Barbara, and I learned a great deal about reading Lucretius from her. I owe a special debt to Michael Wigodsky of Stanford University, who taught a Lucretius seminar I took and was the advisor of my Stanford Dissertation, *Aristotle and Epicurus on Voluntary Action*, (1981), which I later reworked into a monograph, *Epicurus on the Swerve and Voluntary Action*, American Classical Studies 16, Atlanta, GA, 1987. Both projects involved close scrutiny of numerous passages in Lucretius (one of our chief sources of Epicurus' thought), and made me want to continue to work on the enigmatic Roman poet who put Epicurus' Greek philosophic prose into strikingly beautiful Latin verse.

In the years I worked on this translation I received help from many quarters. I want to express thanks to Reed College, which provided the sabbaticals and summer grants needed to complete the work. Thanks are also owed to my colleagues in the Reed Classics Department, Richard Tron and Nigel Nicholson, as well as colleagues and students in the Humanities 110 course at Reed who read earlier drafts of Book 1 and provided helpful feedback. I also received help from a number of Reed students who read and commented on portions of the text, including Robin Adler, Josephine Martell, Dan Harris, and Andrew Hoke. Finally, my greatest thanks go to my wife Mary and daughters Francesca and Molly. They have offered unfailing support while I worked on Lucretius, and I dedicate the translation to them with love.

REED COLLEGE
PORTLAND, OREGON
AUGUST, 2002

INTRODUCTION

Lucretius' poem *De Rerum Natura* (*On the Nature of Things*) is one of the greatest works of Latin poetry and philosophy to have come down to us. In it, Lucretius explains how the world and everything in it works in terms of the atomic theory of the Greek philosopher Epicurus. It is designed to change the lives of its readers, to replace our mistaken world views with what Lucretius argues is the only true one: Epicurus' view that everything, including gods and humans, is made up of atoms and void (empty space). Once we realize this and see what it implies, Lucretius argues, we should embrace Epicureanism, organize our lives around it, and lead a happy and blessed life freed from all our false conceptions and fears. Lucretius' task as he composed his poem in 1st century BC Rome was not an easy one. Romans were traditionally suspicious of Greek philosophy, and Italy was convulsed by a series of violent civil wars during Lucretius' lifetime. In order to understand his aims and accomplishment, it will be helpful to examine the little we know about Lucretius' life, and then discuss three important aspects of his work: what it means that he was an Epicurean, a poet, and a Roman.

A. Lucretius' Life

Little is known about Lucretius' life.[1] St. Jerome (c. 347-420 AD), making additions to the *Chronicle* of Eusebius (c. 260-339 AD), briefly characterized Lucretius' life under the year 94 BC:

> Titus Lucretius the poet was born. After being driven mad when he drank a love potion, he wrote a number of books in between periods of insanity. Cicero later edited them. He killed himself by his own hand during his 44th year of life.

Jerome's account is problematic, and none of it can be taken at face value. First, there are doubts about the years of Lucretius' birth and death. Some of the manuscripts of Jerome place the notice of Lucretius' birth under the

---

[1]   This account of Lucretius' life is based on Englert (1997).

year 96 instead of 94. Second, either date for Lucretius' death which results (53 or 51) must be balanced against the confused dating provided by Jerome's teacher, the ancient grammarian Donatus (4th c. AD), who places Lucretius' death in either 53 or 55. Given the uncertainties, scholars have been generally content with approximate dates in the 90s and 50s BC for Lucretius' birth and death. The other details of Jerome's report must be viewed with suspicion. In the past some scholars have taken the stories of the love potion, insanity, and suicide as possible and partially corroborated by passages from the poem, but now almost all scholars dismiss the stories as false and examples of anti-Epicurean polemic. Jerome's statement that Cicero, the famous Roman politician, orator, and philosopher, "edited" the *De Rerum Natura* is also controversial. Cicero refers to Lucretius once, in a letter of 54 BC ("The poems (*poemata*) of Lucretius are as you describe, full of flashes of genius, but also great artistic craft"), but there is no agreement about what, if anything, Cicero had to do with the final editing of the poem.

The *De Rerum Natura* itself provides little information about Lucretius. The poem is addressed to a person named Memmius, probably to be identified with Gaius Memmius, a Roman noble and patron of the poet Catullus (c. 84-54 BC). Lucretius was thus either known or hoping to be known in upper class Roman society. It is likely he was from the city of Rome, but other suggestions have been made, including that he was from Campania (the area around Naples), or that he was a Celtic freedman. The poem also reveals that Lucretius was well educated in both Greek and Latin literature, but we know nothing of the intellectual circles in which he moved. Some scholars have assumed that Lucretius must have been part of an Epicurean group or community like those at Herculaneum and Naples, but there is no evidence to support this. Fragments of Lucretius' poem have been tentatively identified among the charred papyrus rolls from the Epicurean library buried at Herculaneum during the eruption of Vesuvius in 79 AD.[2] If true, it would not show that Lucretius was part of an Epicurean circle around the Bay of Naples, but only that his poem made it into the Epicurean library at Herculaneum sometime before 79 AD. David Sedley has recently argued that all the evidence we can gather from Lucretius' poem shows that he worked in isolation from the main philosophical currents of his day.[3] It is also not known what contact, if any, he had with contemporary Roman poets, but his work greatly influenced Roman poets who came after him. The great Roman poet Virgil (70-19 BC) praises him at *Georgics* 2. 490-492 ("Happy he who was able to understand the causes of things and has cast beneath his feet all fears, relentless fate, and the shrieks of hungry hell."), and Ovid (43 BC - 17 AD) and Statius (c. 45 - 96 AD) mention him in their poetry.

---

[2]   Kleve (1989).

[3]   Sedley (1998) 62-93.

B. Epicurus and Epicureanism[4]

In the *De Rerum Natura*, Lucretius puts the teachings of the Greek philosopher Epicurus into Latin verse. Epicurus (341-270 BC), the founder of Epicureanism, was an Athenian citizen born on the island of Samos, off the coast of Asia Minor (modern day Turkey). He founded his school, called the Garden, in Athens around 307 BC. The school had great influence throughout antiquity, and Epicurus' work was carried on by later Epicureans down to Lucretius' time and beyond.

What were the major tenets of Epicurean philosophy that Lucretius presents in his poem? Epicurus, building on the work of the earlier Greek atomists Leucippus (5th c. BC) and Democritus (c. 460-350 BC), taught and wrote prolifically. Unfortunately, the majority of Epicurus' works have been lost. All that remains today of his writings are three "epitomes" or outlines of his teachings in the form of letters about physics (*Letter to Herodotus*), ethics (*Letter to Menoeceus*), and meteorology and astronomy (*Letter to Pythocles*), two collections of short sayings (the *Principal Doctrines* and *Vatican Sayings*), and fragments of other works, most notably his major work in thirty-seven books, *On Nature*.[5] Epicurus developed the atomic system of Leucippus and Democritus in a number of ways. It will be most convenient to outline some of his major doctrines along the lines of the standard Hellenistic division of philosophy into three parts: physics, ethics, and logic.

1. Epicurean Physics

In his physics, Epicurus was a strict materialist, teaching that nothing exists in the universe except indestructible atoms and the void (empty space). Everything else that we see around us, including ourselves, are compound bodies made up of atoms moving in the void. According to Epicurus, the universe is infinite in all directions, and there are an infinite number of variously shaped atoms moving constantly through empty space. These atoms sometimes move about separately, but at other times they come together in the void and create worlds like the one in which we live, and all of the compound bodies like water, rocks, trees, and animals that make up these worlds. Even in compound bodies, though, the atoms that compose them move around incessantly, jostling back and forth at incredible speed. Compound bodies that appear stationary to our eyes are, at the atomic level, in constant motion. All compound bodies are impermanent, coming into being and passing away. Some are relatively

---

[4] For fuller accounts of Epicurean teachings, see Rist (1972), Long (1986), Long and Sedley (1987), Mitsis (1988).

[5] Translations of Epicurus' *Letters*, *Principal Doctrines*, *Vatican Sayings*, and other fragments can be found in Inwood and Gerson (1994) and (1997). For a description of what we know about the structure and content of *On Nature*, see Sedley (1998) 94-132.

short-lived, like living creatures. Others, like rocks, the earth, and the heavenly bodies, are more durable and long-lived, but all compound bodies must eventually pass away. Only atoms and the void, Epicurus argues, are eternal and indestructible, having no beginning and no end.

Human beings too are made up of atoms. Epicurus distinguished the human body and soul, but taught that both were made up of atoms: the body of relatively large, dense atoms, and the soul, responsible for sensation and thinking, of relatively small, light, and mobile atoms. Living creatures, including human beings, perceive things when emanations flow off of physical objects and strike the sense organs. Sight, for instance, occurs when thin, swift moving images fly off of objects and strike the eyes. (Epicurus taught that all bodies are constantly shedding thin images in all directions). Thought, likewise, is caused by even thinner images that bypass the sense organs altogether and directly strike the mind, which Epicurus located in the chest in the area around the heart. When we think of someone or something, e.g., our mothers, Epicurus believed that our minds focus on thin images of our mothers that are flying around and pass through our minds located in our chests. He thus held that there are always an almost infinite number of different images flying around us at any time on which our thoughts can focus.

The soul and body come into being together, work together throughout life, and at death the soul-atoms separate from the body-atoms and scatter in different directions. Epicurus taught that there was no afterlife, since the soul does not survive as an entity after death, and held that for this reason we should have no fear of death. Epicureans believed that we can live fully blessed lives on earth, and die having no fear of punishment in the afterlife.

Finally, although strict materialists, Epicureans were not atheists. Epicurus taught that the gods existed,[6] but were completely blessed creatures who lived lives of perfect pleasure and had nothing to do with our world. Traditional tales about the gods were thus false: the gods cannot intervene in our world to help or punish humans. Epicureans taught that there was a way, however, the gods can help or harm people. If humans fail to realize the true nature of divinity, they are harmed by living in needless fear of the gods. If humans understand the gods' true nature, they are helped by taking the gods as paradigms of eternal bliss and modeling their own lives of pleasure on them. Epicureans thus advocated worshiping the gods and

---

[6] There is debate about the nature and location of the Epicurean gods. The traditional view, supported by passages in Lucretius and Cicero, is that the gods are spatial entities that live apart from our world. For a defense of this view, see Mansfeld (1993). Another view, endorsed by Long and Sedley (1987) and Obbink (1996), is that Epicurus held that the gods do not have independent spatial existence, but are thought constructs of the human mind. Purinton (2001) argues for a position that unites elements of both views.

taking part in civic religious rituals, viewing the gods not as beings directly involved in human affairs, but as paradigms of happiness to try to emulate.

2. Epicurean Ethics

In ethics, Epicurus taught that the highest form of good was pleasure, but pleasure of a particular sort. The later popular view of an "Epicurean" as a wild, profligate hedonist who seeks pleasure indiscriminately is a misleading distortion of Epicurus' views. Epicurus taught that the highest good in life is pleasure, defined as freedom from pain in the body (*aponia*), and freedom from anxiety and disturbance in the mind, a state he called *ataraxia*, literally, "untroubledness." Epicurus said there were two types of pleasure, static pleasure and kinetic pleasure. Static or "katastematic" pleasure, as Epicurus called it, is the state an organism feels when it suffers no pain or want, all its needs are met, and it is functioning well. Kinetic pleasure, or "pleasure in motion," is the pleasure an organism feels when it is physically or mentally stimulated. Kinetic pleasure apparently occurred in two ways:[7] either in the process of satisfying a want and returning an organism to its katastematic state (e.g., the pleasure an organism feels when it is thirsty and drinks until its thirst is gone), or when an organism is in a katastematic state of pleasure and its katastematic pleasure is "varied" by the addition of kinetic pleasure (e.g., when an organism is not suffering thirst, but drinks and enjoys the beverage). Epicurus taught that katastematic pleasure, when there is no physical pain or mental distress, is the highest possible for a human being. Kinetic pleasure does not increase pleasure further, but varies it.

Epicurus believed the happiest life is easy for human beings to obtain, but that human beings normally fail to obtain it because they do not see that our basic desires for food, drink, shelter, and clothing are easy to satisfy. He taught that human beings often fail to achieve happiness because they do not distinguish between three types of desires: (1) natural and necessary desires, i.e. desire for things that are necessary for life and help us avoid pain, like drinking and eating simple foods and beverages; (2) natural and non-necessary desires, i.e. desires for fine or expensive food and drink that are not necessary for life but help to "vary" our pleasure; and (3) desires that are neither natural nor necessary, i.e. desires for things like honor, fame, and political office. Epicurus advocated leading a simple, almost ascetic life, taking pleasure in easily satisfying our natural desires. He taught that almost all humans fail to see where true happiness lies, mistakenly desiring objects (fancy food, large amounts of money, honor, public office) that are difficult to obtain, increase our anxiety, and are usually harmful to our happiness. He also taught that not all pleasures should be chosen, nor all

---

[7] There has been much discussion of what exactly Epicurus meant by kinetic pleasure. I follow the account in Long and Sedley (1987) i. 112-125.

pain avoided. Humans often must give up pleasure in the present to avoid greater pain later, and choose some pain now to attain greater pleasure later. If an action promotes long term freedom from pain and anxiety, and thus our happiness, it should be chosen, if not, it should not be chosen. As Epicurus knew well, bodily pain, no matter how well humans live, is unavoidable, but he believed that pain could never threaten human happiness if it is viewed correctly. He taught techniques for maintaining mental *ataraxia* even when the body was feeling great pain, including thinking about past, present, and future pleasures. Epicurus also maintained that physical pain could always be endured, his reasoning later captured in a memorable Latin phrase: *si gravis, brevis; si longus, levis* ("It (pain) is short if it is strong, light if it is long").[8] In other words, intense pain lasts only for a short period, while pain that lasts a long time is lighter and can be endured relatively easily.

Pleasure was also the basis for evaluating virtue and ethical behavior. According to Epicurus, it is important to be courageous, just, self-controlled, and live according to the standard Greek virtues, not because they are virtues and valuable in themselves, but because the virtues are the means to the most pleasant life. Courage is more pleasurable than cowardice, self-control is necessary for the proper choice of pleasures in order to maximize one's overall pleasure, and justice is necessary not because there is anything intrinsically good about it, but to ensure the harmonious working of society, and to avoid worrying about being caught if you commit an unjust action. As Epicurus wrote in *Principal Doctrine* 34,[9] "Injustice is not a bad thing in its own right, but [only] because of the fear produced by the suspicion that one will not escape the notice of those assigned to punish such actions." In other words, justice is better than injustice because it contributes more reliably to *ataraxia* and happiness.

3. Epicurean Scientific Method

Finally, Epicurus shunned the usual philosophical category of logic, preferring instead to discuss "canonic" (from the Greek word *kanôn*, "rule, standard"), his term for his theory of knowledge which he connected closely to physics. Epicurus was an empiricist, teaching that knowledge was possible and derived from sensation. He is reported to have held that there are three criteria of truth: sensation, general concepts, and feelings.

Epicurus held that sensations were the primary criterion of truth. He taught that "all sensations are true," a claim which at first sight appears implausible, especially given the existence of optical illusions, e.g., a straight oar which appears to bend at the point where it enters the water. Epicurus, though, carefully distinguished sensations themselves from the judgments

---

[8] Cicero *De Finibus* 2.95.

[9] The translation is from Inwood and Gerson (1997): 35.

that people make about their sensations. In the case of an optical illusion like the bent oar, Epicurus would say that the image of the oar our eyes receive is true: we see an image made up of certain sizes, shapes, colors, etc. Where we may get into trouble is when we add judgments to our perceptions, such as "this is an oar", and "this oar is bent." The former statement is true, but in the case of an oar half-submerged in water, the latter is not. It is not sensation that has fooled us, but our interpretation of the sensation that has reached our eyes. Our knowledge of the world is ultimately based on sensations, and the judgments we make on the basis of sensation must be scrutinized for the many errors our minds may introduce.

One of the most important ways people can avoid making errors of judgment and attain knowledge is by attending to "general concepts." Epicurus maintained that "general concepts" or "preconceptions" (in Greek, *prolêpseis*) could function as criteria of truth. He believed that all humans from the time they are very young begin to form "general concepts" by generalizing from their sensations. After seeing a number of examples of a certain type of sensation, and hearing people refer to them as "birds," a child gradually builds up a general concept of what a bird is. After developing the concept, the child then begins to identify new examples of birds as she sees them, to form ideas about what attributes are typical of the class (two legs, wings, certain behaviors, etc.), and to distinguish birds from other types of creatures by reference to her general concepts. From such general concepts, people make statements that are true and false about objects in the world.

Epicurus' third criterion of truth was feelings (*pathê*). He taught that all of our actions must be judged by the primary feelings of pleasure and pain, and took that to be the criterion of ethical truth. All our actions must be directed to maximizing our pleasure and minimizing our pain in the long run.

Relying on these criteria of truth, Epicurus argued that we could gain knowledge not only of the visible world around us, but also of the microscopic world of atoms and the movements of the heavens above us. When investigating the visible world directly accessible to us, Epicurus taught that the way to proceed was to accept as true things that could be verified by direct and clear observation, and as false those things that could not. On the other hand, when investigating the underlying principles of matter (e.g., atoms and the void) or the heavens, realms Epicurus believed human beings do not have direct access to, he argued that we must make use of analogies with the physical world around us, and take as true those views that are "uncontested" and as false those views that are "contested".[10] For example, Epicurus argues that the only view that can

---

[10] For more on Epicurus' scientific methodology, see Long and Sedley (1987) i. 90-97 and Asmis (1983).

explain the origins and workings of the physical world around us is atomism, because it alone accounts for and does not conflict with the facts of the world as we see them. Similarly, when discussing the movements of the heavens, Epicurus posits explanations that are not contradicted by the evidence. Unlike in the discussion of the microscopic level, where the only theory that fits all the facts is atomism, in astronomy and meteorology there are often several explanations which do not contradict the phenomena. For example, Epicurus posited a number of possibilities for why the moon waxes and wanes, all of which he says may be true. Only one of the possibilities will in fact be true for our moon, but that does not stop the other explanations from being true of other similar phenomena somewhere else in the universe.

C. The *De Rerum Natura*

The *De Rerum Natura* is a poem composed of approximately 7,400 lines of Latin dactylic hexameter divided into six books. It is classified as didactic epic, a type of epic designed to instruct, and is written in a high poetic style. Lucretius was influenced by many Greek and Latin writers, including Homer, Hesiod, Euripides, Aratus, Thucydides, and Cicero, but above all by Epicurus, Empedocles, and Ennius.

From Epicurus Lucretius received his philosophical inspiration and doctrines, and Lucretius worked closely from Epicurus' writings, most of which are now lost to us. Of particular importance was Epicurus' major work, the *Peri Phuseos* (*On Nature*) in thirty-seven books. Lucretius' title *De Rerum Natura* is a Latin translation of Epicurus' Greek title *Peri Phuseos*, and many details of Lucretius' exposition probably derive from Epicurus' great work. Scholars have long debated exactly which works of Epicurus and later Epicureans Lucretius used as the main sources for his poem. Most recently, David Sedley has argued that a careful study of the structure and contents of what remains of Epicurus' *On Nature* reveals that Lucretius used it as his sole Epicurean source.[11]

Empedocles, the Greek author of a philosophical poem also titled *Peri Phuseos* (*On Nature*), was Lucretius' chief poetic inspiration for writing a philosophical poem. Epicurus had taken a dim view of writing poetry (Diogenes Laertius 10. 120). Empedocles, the great Greek philosopher and poet who lived in Acragas (Sicily) from about 492 to 432 BC, provided a model of how a philosophical poem could be written. Lucretius praises Empedocles as an inspired poet (1. 705-741), and the opening of Book 1 of Lucretius' poem, with its invocation of Venus and her opposite Mars, owes much to Empedocles' principles of love and strife. Although in Book 1 (1. 705-829) Lucretius argues against Empedocles' view that the ultimate components of our world are the four elements earth, air, fire, and water,

---

[11] Sedley (1998) 94-165.

along with the principles of love and strife, he nevertheless admired and tried to emulate Empedocles' accomplishment of writing a beautiful and powerful philosophical poem.

If Empedocles provided a model to Lucretius of how to join philosophy and poetry, the Roman poet Ennius (239-169 BC) guided Lucretius in writing an epic in Latin. Ennius had composed in many genres (including tragedy, comedy, and satire) in a variety of meters, but was most famous for his poem entitled the *Annales*. In the eighteen books of the *Annales*, Ennius told the story of Rome's history from the fall of Troy down to his own times. Ennius used the work, among other things, to update Roman epic. Earlier Roman writers had written epic poems in Latin. Livius Andronicus (3rd c. BC) had composed a Latin version of Homer's *Odyssey*, and Gnaeus Naevius (3rd c. BC) had written an epic poem on the subject of the First Punic War (Rome's first war with her great rival Carthage). Both poets composed their poems in Saturnian verse, a meter the Romans also used in the 3rd and 2nd centuries for some inscriptions and epitaphs. For the *Annales*, Ennius rejected Saturnian verse and instead adapted the meter known as dactylic hexameter from Homer and other Greek epic poets to Latin. Lucretius' poetic style was much influenced by Ennius, especially in his choice of meter (dactylic hexameter), use of alliteration, word play, and use of compound and archaic Latin words. Lucretius mentions Ennius early in his poem (1. 112-126), praising him as a great Roman poet ("He was the first to bring down/ a crown of everlasting foliage from lovely Mount Helicon/ to become famous throughout the Italian tribes of people." 1.117-119). But Lucretius also sees him as a poetic rival to be surpassed, largely because his view of the world was wrong. At the beginning of the *Annales*, Ennius had related how the shade of the poet Homer appeared to him and told him that he, Ennius, was the reincarnation of Homer. As Lucretius writes (1.124-126), "(Ennius) recalls how from that region the shade of Homer, forever/ blooming, rose before him and began to shed salty/ tears, setting out in words the nature of things." The last phrase of these verses, "setting out in words the nature of things," is important. As he makes clear, Lucretius saw the "nature of things" that Ennius and Homer are here reporting as false, and he is composing his poem, *On the Nature of Things*, to set out the true nature of things.

The six books of the poem fall into three groups of two: (1) Books 1 and 2 treat the nature of the atom, (2) Books 3 and 4 the nature of the soul, and (3) Books 5 and 6 the nature of the world. Book 1 opens with an invocation to Venus as mother of the Roman race, generating force of nature, and personification of Epicurean pleasure. It includes an address to Memmius (the main addressee of the poem), an attack on religion, the setting out of basic philosophical principles, the existence of void and atoms, a critique of earlier philosophers (Heraclitus, Empedocles, Anaxagoras), and the infinite nature of matter, space, and the universe. Book 2 begins by praising Epicurean philosophy, and is devoted to the motions, shapes, and characteristics of atoms, and explains the birth and death of worlds including our own. Book 3 starts by praising Epicurus' accomplishments, and then sets out the nature of the soul in atomic terms, arguing that the soul is mortal. It concludes with a diatribe against the fear of death. Lucretius begins Book 4 by describing his poetic mission, and then explains some psychological matters: the nature of atomic images, their role in perception and thinking, the processes of digestion, movement, sleeping, and dreaming. He ends with a spirited diatribe against the passion of love. Book 5 praises Epicurus as the savior of mankind, discusses the birth and growth of our world, argues against divine agency, discusses the heavenly bodies, and describes the origin and growth of life and human society on earth. Book 6, too, begins with praise for Epicurus, and discusses meteorological and geological topics, including thunder and lightning, clouds and rain, earthquakes, volcanoes, magnets, and plagues. Book 6 ends with an account of the great plague at Athens based on a passage from the historian Thucydides.

As the summary of contents reveals, the poem deals primarily with Epicurean physical theory. Lucretius does not provide an extended account of Epicurean ethical theory in the poem, but his chief purpose in laying out the tenets of Epicurean physics is ethical. He hopes to dispel the fears people have of the gods and death by providing a clear and persuasive account of how the world works in atomic terms. The poem is unfinished, although scholars disagree on to what extent. Some suggest that Lucretius intended to add to the poem, fulfilling his promise at 5. 155 to write more about the gods, clearing up the many repetitions found throughout the work, and perhaps ending the poem on a different note than with the account of the plague at Athens. Others have argued that the poem is substantially finished, and that the repetitions and ending serve intended philosophical purposes.

D. The *De Rerum Natura* and the Roman World

In what sense is Lucretius' poem a Roman work? As we have seen, Lucretius took the writings of the Greek philosopher Epicurus and, using the philosophical poetry of Empedocles and Ennius' *Annales* as models, created his own Latin philosophical epic. Lucretius knew his task was not an easy one. The Roman people had not embraced Greek philosophy easily. They saw philosophy, correctly, as a Greek invention, and viewed it with suspicion. In the century before Lucretius many philosophers, including Epicureans, had been expelled from the city of Rome.[12] Roman doubts about the value of philosophy continued into the 1st century BC, but some

---

[12] For an account of the tension between the Romans and Greek philosophers in the 2nd c. BC, see Gruen (1990).

members of the Roman upper classes began to see it as an important part of the education of elite young men. Many wealthy Roman men in their late teens and twenties traveled to Athens and other Greek cities for training in rhetoric and philosophy, and Greek rhetoricians and philosophers came to Rome to teach as well. As a result, Romans began to accept some of the teachings of Greek philosophy and adapt them for their own uses,[13] and some writers even began to write philosophical works in Latin for their fellow countrymen.[14]   The philosophy that most successfully adapted to the world of the Roman upper classes was Stoicism, the chief philosophic rival of Epicureanism. Stoicism stressed, among other things, taking an active part in political life, cultivating the Stoic moral virtues that mapped onto the traditional Roman virtues, and acknowledging a divine providence and fate that ruled the universe rationally and that could be made to fit the Roman view that they had been fated by the gods to rule the world. Epicureanism, by contrast, urged its adherents to avoid politics, seek their own pleasure as the highest good, and taught that the world was impersonal and not under the influence of fate or divine direction.

Lucretius wrote his poem to try to convert his Roman audience to what looked like the very un-Roman ideals of Epicureanism. In the poem he asks that his fellow Romans give up many of their beliefs about what makes life valuable: wealth, honor, power, high office, traditional public and private worship of the gods, and the pride that they feel at being part of a powerful empire, and adopt in their place a vision of the world that is strangely double (the atomic level and the visible level) and which demonstrates that happiness is to be found in freedom from pain and anxiety, in semi-retirement from society, in the company of Epicurean friends. Was life not better, he seems to ask in the poem, with atoms and void in a random universe where the Epicurean could control his or her own happiness, than in the seemingly random political order of the late Roman Republic, where stability and true happiness seemed impossible to obtain?

The *De Rerum Natura* is Lucretius' attempt to make Greek philosophy relevant to his fellow Romans. Lucretius says he is presenting the doctrines of Epicurus faithfully, and as far as we can tell all of the philosophical doctrines he presents in the poem are those of his master Epicurus, not his own. What is his own is the way Lucretius presents Epicurus' ideas.

---

[13] For an interesting account of what Roman philosophy meant to members of the Roman upper class, see Griffin (1989).

[14] Including the Epicurean writers Amafinius, Rabirius, and Catius, about whom very little is known. For more on the philosophical and intellectual climate of Lucretius' time, see Rawson (1985). The most famous example of a Roman who tried to adapt Greek philosophy for his fellow citizens was Cicero, who wrote a series of philosophical works, most of which are still extant.

In order to reach his Roman audience, he abandons the dense Greek prose of Epicurus and creates a Latin poem of great power and beauty.   To convert his readers to Epicureanism, he begins in Book I with the invocation to Venus, the mother of the Roman race, and with the Roman world of false values, and gradually replaces that false world with a true picture of the universe, with its atoms, void, worlds, compound bodies, death, and true happiness.[15] How successful was Lucretius in converting Roman readers to Epicureanism? It is hard to say, since our evidence for the reception of his work is rather slim. Judging from the poem he wrote, though, we can say that Lucretius set out Epicureanism for his fellow Romans in as accurate, sympathetic, and persuasive an account as he could.

E. Note on the Translation

Because the *De Rerum Natura* is a philosophical poem, I felt it was important that my English translation be in poetic form. My chief aim in this translation is accuracy, while at the same time keeping as much of the character of Lucretius' Latin poetry as I could in English. As noted above, the meter Lucretius wrote in is dactylic hexameter, the usual meter in Greek and Latin verse for Epic poetry, including the works of Homer, Hesiod, Ennius' *Annales*, Virgil's *Aeneid*, and Ovid's *Metamorphoses*. It is a verse composed of six[16] "feet" or metrical units, and each foot is either a dactyl ($^-$ $^\smile$ $^\smile$ = one long and two short syllables), or a spondee ($^-$ $^-$ = two long syllables). A dactyl and a spondee are metrically equivalent because one long syllable ($^-$) is equal to two short syllables ($^\smile$ $^\smile$). Here are the first five lines of the poem in Latin, with the scansion noted above each syllable.

> Āenĕădūm gĕnĕtrīx, hŏmĭnūm dīvōmquĕ vŏlūptăs
> ālmă Vĕnūs, cāelī sūbtēr lābēntĭă sīgnă
> quāe mărĕ nāvĭgĕrūm, quāe tērrās frūgĭfĕrēntīs
> cōncĕlĕbrās, pēr tē quŏnĭām gĕnŭs ōmnē͡ānĭmāntŭm
> cōncĭpĭtūr vīsītque͡exōrtūm lūmĭnă sōlĭs.

As some help towards pronouncing the Latin and experiencing the dactylic rhythm, here are the same five lines, written with the long syllables in UPPERCASE letters and the short syllables in lowercase letters. I have also separated words into syllables with a dash (-), and used a (/) to divide the six feet that make up each line.

---

[15] For insightful accounts of the way Lucretius adapts Epicureanism for his Roman audience, see Clay (1983), Gale (1994), and Sedley (1998).

[16] "hex" is the Greek word for "six."

AE-ne-a-/DUM ge-ne-/TRIX, ho-mi-/NUM DI-/VOM-que vo-/LUP-tas
AL-ma Ve-/NUS, CAE-/LI SUB-/TER LA-/BEN-ti-a /SIG-na
QUAE ma-re/ NA-vi-ge-/RUM, QUAE/ TER-RAS/ FRU-gi-fe-/REN-TIS
CON-ce-le/BRAS PER /TE quo-ni-/AM ge-nus/OM-na-ni-/MAN-tum
CON-ci-pi-/TUR VI-/SIT-QUEX-/OR-TUM /LU-mi-na /SO-lis.

    I have not tried to duplicate Lucretius' dactylic hexameters in my English translation, but instead have used a rough five or six beat line to suggest some of their movement. The length of such lines is well suited for rendering Lucetius' hexameters into English, and allowed me to do a line-by-line translation. Here, for the sake of example, are the first five lines of my translation corresponding to the lines of Lucretius just quoted. I have placed an accent mark (´) over each syllable that is stressed in English, and except in rare instances in the translation, each line is intended to have five or six stresses.

Móther of the descéndants of Aenéas, pleásure of húmans and góds,
lífegiving Vénus, it is yoú who beneáth the glíding sígns
of heáven makes the shíp-bearing seá and the fruítful eárth
teem with lífe, since through yoú the whóle ráce of líving creátures
is conceíved, bórn, and gázes on the líght of the sún.

    Other features of Lucretius' poetic style that are particularly noticeable, and which I have tried to capture in the translation, are his use of compound words, neologisms (invention of new words), and alliteration (a series of words that all begin with the same letter or sound). To translate Lucretius' Latin compound words, I have used a compound or hyphenated word in English (e.g., in line 3 Lucretius uses the word *navigerum*, derived from the roots *navis* (ship) and *gero* (carry), which is thus translated "ship-bearing"). Lucretius was also inclined to invent new words when an exact Latin equivalent for what he was trying to say did not exist, or when he wanted to add extra emphasis. Since very little Latin before or contemporary with Lucretius has survived, we cannot always be sure that a word that occurs only in Lucretius was coined by him, but there are so many words that occur for the first or only time in Latin in Lucretius' text that it seems likely many are his own invention. In the case of many of these neologisms I have taken the liberty of coining English words to translate them in order to call Lucretius' practice to the attention of the reader. When I have done this, I have marked it in a footnote. A good example occurs at 2.498, where Lucretius uses the Latin word *maximitate*, a word found nowhere else in Latin. I have translated *maximitate* with the made up English word "maxitude" ("Otherwise you would force some seeds to be of enormous maxitude...") to indicate to the reader that Lucretius has apparently made up the word in Latin. Finally, where possible I have tried to capture examples of Lucretius' use of alliteration in my translation. For example, at 4.88 Lucretius writes *quae volgo volitant subtili praedita filo* with an alliteration of the v's beginning the words *volgo volitant*. I have translated the line as "which freely fly around endowed with subtle texture", capturing Lucretius' v-sounds with the f-sounds in the phrase "freely fly."

No translation, especially of poetry, can be completely transparent, allowing all of the nuances of the original text to appear in the translation. I have been constantly aware of this as I struggled to find English equivalents for Lucretius' words, phrases, and poetic devices. I have also benefited greatly from consulting other English translations of Lucretius, especially those of Bailey (1947), Humphries (1968), Rouse and Smith (1982), Latham and Godwin (1994), Esolen (1995), Melville (1997), and M.F. Smith (2001). The number of recent translations reflects the increased study of Hellenistic and Roman philosophy in the past few decades, and Lucretius' central role in that scholarly renaissance. I hope that readers of this translation will begin to develop a love of Lucretius' poetry and Epicurean philosophy, and that they are inspired to take up the study of Latin in order to experience the full and powerful beauty of the *De Rerum Natura* first hand.

SELECT BIBLIOGRAPHY

Algra, K., Koenen, M., and Schrijvers, P. (1997) (eds.) *Lucretius and His Intellectual Background*. (Amsterdam, Oxford, New York, Tokyo).

Annas, J. (1992). *Hellenistic Philosophy of Mind*. (Berkeley, Los Angeles, and Oxford).

Asmis, E. (1984). *Epicurus' Scientific Method* (Ithaca and London).

Bailey, C. (1947). *Lucretius: De Rerum Natura libri sex, edited with prolegomena, critical apparatus, translation, and commentary*. (Oxford).

Boyancé, P. (1963). *Lucrèce et l'épicurisme*. (Paris).

Clay, D. (1983). *Lucretius and Epicurus*. (Ithaca and London).

Conte, G.B. (1994) "Lucretius" in *Latin Literature: A History*. (Baltimore and London), 155-174.

Costa, C.D.N. (1984). *De Rerum Natura Liber V*. (Oxford).

Diogenes Laertius. (1925). *Lives of Eminent Philosophers*, Vol. II. R.D. Hicks (tr.), Loeb Classical Library. (Cambridge, Mass. and London).

Dudley, D.R. , ed. (1965). *Lucretius*. (London).

Englert, W. (1987). *Epicurus on the Swerve and Voluntary Action*. American Classical Studies 16. (Atlanta).

—— (1997). "Lucretius" in the *Encyclopedia of Classical Philosophy*. D.J. Zeyl, ed. (Westport, CT), 309-311.

Esolen, A. tr. (1995). *Lucretius On the Nature of Things, De rerum natura*. (Baltimore and London).

Fowler, D.P. (2002) *Lucretius on Atomic Motion. A Commentary on De rerum natura 2.1-332*. (Oxford).

Fowler, P.G. and D.P. (1996). "Lucretius", in *The Oxford Classical Dictionary*, 3rd ed. (Oxford), 888-890.

Furley, D.J. (1967). *Two Studies in the Greek Atomists*. (Princeton).

Gale, M. (1994). *Myth and Poetry in Lucretius*. (Cambridge).

—— (2001). *Lucretius and Didactic Epic*. (London).

Giussani, C. (1896-98). *T. Lucreti Cari De Rerum Natura Libri Sex*. 4 volumes. (Torino).

Godwin, J. (1991). *De Rerum Natura VI*. (Warminster).

Griffin, M. "Philosophy, Politics, and Politicians at Rome." In M. Griffin and J. Barnes, eds., *Philosophia Togata: Essays on Philosophy and Roman Society*. (Oxford): 1-37.

Gruen, E. (1990). *Studies in Greek Culture and Roman Policy*, Chapter 5: "Philosophy, Rhetoric, and Roman Anxieties." (Berkeley, Los Angeles, London). 158-192.

Humphries, R. tr. (1968). *Lucretius: The Way Things Are*. (Bloomington).

Inwood, B. and Gerson, L.P. (1994). (eds.) *The Epicurus Reader: Selected Writings and Testimonia*. (Indianapolis and Cambridge).

—— (1997). (eds.) *Hellenistic Philosophy: Introductory Readings*. 2nd ed. (Indianapolis and Cambridge).

Johnson, W.R. (2000). *Lucretius and the Modern World*. (London).

Kenney, E.J. (1971). *Lucretius, De Rerum Natura Book III*. (Cambridge).

—— (1977). *Lucretius. Greece and Rome, New Surveys in the Classics*, 11. (Oxford).

Kleve, K. (1989). "Lucretius in Herculaneum", *Cronache Ercolanesi* 19: 5-27.

Latham, R. and Godwin, J. trs. (1994). *Lucretius: On the Nature of the Universe*. (Harmondsworth).

Long, A.A. (1974). *Hellenistic Philosophy*. (London and New York). 2nd ed. 1986.

—— and Sedley, D.N. (1987). *The Hellenistic Philosophers*. 2 vol. (Cambridge).

Mansfeld, J. (1993). "Aspects of Epicurean Theology." *Mnemosyne* 46: 172-210.

Melville, R. tr. (1997). *Lucretius: On the Nature of the Universe*. (Oxford).

Minadeo, R. (1969). *The Lyre of Science: Form and Meaning in Lucretius' De Rerum Natura*. (Detroit).

Minyard, J.D. (1985). *Lucretius and the Late Republic: An Essay in Roman Intellectual History. Mnemosyne Supplement* 90. (Leiden).

Mitsis, P. (1988). *Epicurus' Ethical Theory: The Pleasures of Invulnerability*. (Ithaca).

Nisbet, R. (1986). "Lucretius" in "The Poets of the Late Republic", in J. Boardman, J. Griffin, and O. Murray (eds.) *The Oxford History of the Classical World*, (Oxford), 479-487.

Nussbaum, M. (1994). *The Therapy of Desire: Theory and Practice in Hellenistic Ethics*. (Princeton).

Obbink, D. (1996). *Philodemus On Piety, Part I: Critical Text with Commentary*. (Oxford).

Patin, M. (1868). "L'anti-Lucrèce chez Lucrèce", in *Études sur la poésie latine*, vol. 1. (Paris).

Purinton, J.S. (1999). "Epicurus on 'Free Volition' and the Atomic Swerve." *Phronesis* 44: 253-299.

—— (2001). "Epicurus on the Nature of the Gods." *Oxford Studies in Ancient Philosophy* 21:181-231.

Rawson, E. (1985). *Intellectual Life in the Late Roman Republic*. (Baltimore).

Rist, J. (1972) *Epicurus: An Introduction*. (Cambridge).

Rouse, W.H.D. and Smith, M.F., trs. (1982). *Lucretius: De Rerum Natura*. 2nd Editon. (Cambridge, Mass. and London).

Santayana, G. (1910). *Three Philosophical Poets*. (Cambridge, Mass.).

Sedley, D. (1998). *Lucretius and the Transformation of Greek Wisdom*. (Cambridge).

—— (1999). "Epicureanism", in R. Audi (ed.) *The Cambridge Dictionary of Philosophy*. 2nd edition. (Cambridge), 269-271.

Segal, C. (1990). *Lucretius on Death and Anxiety*. (Princeton).

Smith, M.F., tr. (2001). *Lucretius: On the Nature of Things*. (Indianapolis and Cambridge).

Wallach, B.P. (1976). *Lucretius and the Diatribe against the Fear of Death: De Rerum Natura III. 830-1094. Mnemosyne Supplement* 40 . (Leiden).

West, D. A. (1969). *The Imagery and Poetry of Lucretius*. (Edinburgh).

OUTLINE OF THE POEM

Book One

A. Proem (1-148)

    1. Invocation to Venus (1-49)
    2. Appeal to Memmius (50-61)
    3. Praise of Epicurus and attack on religion (62-135)
    4. Difficulty of Lucretius' task (136-148)

B. Fundamental principles of atomism (149-482)

    1. Nothing is created out of nothing through divine intervention (149-214)
    2. Nothing is destroyed into nothing (215-264)
    3. Matter exists in the form of unseen particles (265-328)
    4. Void or empty space exists (329-417)
    5. Everything else is a property or accident of atoms and void (418-482)

C. The atoms are solid, eternal, and indivisible (483-634)

D. Criticism of earlier theories (635-920)

    1. Criticism of Heraclitus (635-704)
    2. Criticism of Empedocles (705-829)
    3. Criticism of Anaxagoras (830-920)

E. Lucretius' mission (921-950)

F. Infinity of the universe, matter, and space (951-1117)

    1. Infinity of the universe (951-1001)
    2. Infinity of space (1002-1007)
    3. Infinity of matter (1008-1051)
    4. Universe has no center (1052-1113)
    5. Conclusion (1114-1117)

Book Two

A. Proem: the blessings of Epicureanism (1-61)

B. The motions of atoms (62-332)
1. Introduction (62-79)
2. Atoms are in constant motion (80-141)
3. Velocity of atomic motion (142-166)
4. Arguments against divine control (167-183)
5. Weight of atoms causes downward motion (184-215)
6. Swerve of atoms (216-293)
7. Matter and motion the same through all time (294-307)
8. Atoms constantly move in compounds that are at rest (308-332)

C. The shapes of atoms (333-729)
1. Variety of atomic shapes and the effects they produce (333-477)
2. Finite number of atomic shapes (478-580)
3. Atomic compounds (581-729)

D. Atoms lack secondary qualities (730-1022)
1. Atoms lack color (730-841)
2. Atoms lack other secondary qualities (842-864)
3. Atoms lack sensation (865-990)
4. Summary (991-1022)

E. Infinite worlds and the vastness of the Universe (1023-1174)
1. Introduction (1023-1047)
2. Proofs that other worlds exist (1048-1089)
3. Attack on the theological view (1090-1104)
4. Growth and decline of worlds (1105-1174)

Book Three

A. Introduction (1-93)
1. Proem: Praise of Epicurus (1-30)
2. Wretchedness of those who fear death (31-93)

B. Nature and structure of the mind and soul (94-416)
1. Soul is corporeal and not a type of harmony (94-135)
2. Unity of the mind (*animus, mens*) and soul (*anima*) (136-160)
3. Mind and soul are corporeal (161-176)
4. Fineness of the mind's and soul's atoms (177-230)

5. Four types of mind and soul atoms (231-322)
6. Unity of the soul and body (323-416)

C. Proofs of the mortality of the soul (417-829)

1. Introduction (417-424)
2. Proofs based on the atomic structure of the soul (425-444)
3. Proofs based on the shared life of soul and body (445-547)
4. Proofs based on the physical connection of body and soul (548-669)
5. The soul does not exist before the body (670-783)
6. Other proofs that the soul is mortal (784-829)

D. No need to fear death (830-1094)

1. Death is nothing to us, because we lose all sensation (830-869)
2. Refutation of false assumptions about the nature of death (870-930)
3. Rebuke by Nature herself (931-77)
4. Real hell is the hell humans create within themselves (978-1023)
5. Death happens to everyone, even the great (1024-1052)
6. Causes of human unhappiness in life (1053-1075)
7. Conclusion: death is not to be feared (1076-1094)

Book Four

A. Proem: Lucretius' mission (1-25)

B. Existence and nature of images (*simulacra*) (26-215)

1. Existence of images (26-109)
2. Thinness of images (110-128)
3. Spontaneous production of images (129-142)
4. Quickness of image production (143-175)
5. Rapid movement of images (176-215)

C. Sensation and thought (216-822)

1. Sight and images (216-378)
2. Optical illusions and false mental inferences (379-468)
3. Arguments against skepticism (469-521)
4. The other senses (522-721)
    a. Sound and hearing (522-614)
    b. Taste (615-672)
    c. Smell (673-705)
    d. Animals affected differently by sensations (706-721)

ON THE NATURE OF THINGS

VENUS

BOOK I

Mother of the descendants of Aeneas,[1] pleasure of humans and gods,
lifegiving Venus, it is you who beneath the gliding signs
of heaven makes the ship-bearing sea and the fruitful earth
teem with life, since through you the whole race of living creatures
is conceived, born, and gazes on the light of the sun.   5
You, goddess, you the winds flee, you the clouds
of the sky flee at your coming, for you earth the artificer
sends up her sweet flowers, for you the expanses of the sea smile,
and the heavens, now peaceful, shine with diffused light.
For as soon as the sight of a spring day is revealed,   10
and the life-bringing breeze of the west wind is released and blows,
the birds of the air are the first to announce you and your arrival,
o goddess, overpowered in their hearts by your force.
Next wild beasts and flocks prance about their glad pastures
and swim across rushing streams. So taken by delight   15
each follows you eagerly wherever you proceed to lead them.
Then through the seas and mountains and fast-clutching rivers,
through the leaf-thronged home of birds and the verdant plains,
you strike, injecting sweet love into the hearts of all,
and make them eagerly create their offspring, each according to kind. 20
Since you alone guide the nature of things
and without you nothing emerges into the sunlit shores
of light, nothing glad or lovely comes into being,
I am eagerly striving for you to be my ally in writing these verses

you
alone

---

[1] The "descendants of Aeneas" are the Romans. According to legend,
Aeneas was a Trojan hero who, after the fall of Troy to the Greeks, led a
group of Trojans to Italy and founded a city. His descendants eventually
founded the city of Rome. The story of Aeneas' journey to Italy and
actions there are told in Virgil's *Aeneid*, written thirty to forty years after
Lucretius' poem.

nature of gods = free from anxiety

25   that I am trying to set out about the nature of things
for our illustrious son of the Memmii,[2] whom you, goddess, on every
occasion have wished to be preeminent, adorned with every blessing.
All the more endow these words with everlasting charm, goddess.
Meanwhile, make it so that the savage claims of war

30   are put to sleep and lie quiet throughout every sea and land.
For you alone have the power to bring aid to mortals
with tranquil peace, since Mars, strong in arms, rules
the savage claims of war, and he often lets himself sink
into your lap, completely overcome by the unceasing wound of love.

35   And so gazing upwards, bending back his smooth neck,
he gapes at you, goddess, and feeds his hungry eyes with love.
And as he lies there, his breath hangs on your lips.
Goddess, with your blessed body flow down around him
as he reclines, and pour forth sweet words from your mouth,

40   o glorious one, seeking gentle peace for the Romans.
For neither can I perform my task with a tranquil mind
when our country is in trouble, nor can the shining offspring of the
    Memmii
fail to attend to the safety of the state at such times.
For it must be that the entire nature of the gods

45   spends everlasting time enjoying perfect peace,
far removed and long separated from our concerns.
For free from all anxiety, free from dangers,
powerful in its own resources, having no need of us,
it is not won over by the good things we do nor touched by anger.[3]

50   For the rest, turn open ears and a sharp mind
set free from cares to the true system of philosophy,
so that you do not despise and abandon my gifts to you,
set out with constant eagerness, before they are understood.
For I am beginning to set out for you the deepest workings
of the heavens and the gods, and to reveal the first beginnings[4] of

55   things
out of which nature creates all things, and increases and maintains
    them,
and into which nature dissolves them again once they have perished.
These we are accustomed, in setting forth our account, to call
"matter" and "the generating bodies of things" and to name them

---

2   The poem is addressed to a Roman named Memmius, probably Gaius
Memmius, the patron of the Roman poet Catullus.

3   1.44-49 = 2.646-651.

4   "The first beginnings" = *primordia*, one of the Latin terms Lucretius uses
for "atoms." Lucretius never uses the Greek term *atomoi* ("atoms") in
the poem.

"the seeds of things," and to use the term "first bodies" for them,   **60**
because all things exist from these first beginnings.[5]
It used to be that human life, polluted, was lying
in the dirt before our eyes, crushed by the weight of religion,
which stretched out its head on display from the regions of heaven,
threatening mortals from above with its horrible-looking face.   **65**
It was a Greek man[6] who first dared to raise his mortal eyes
against religion, and who first fought back against it.
Neither the stories about the gods, nor thunderbolts, nor the sky
with its threatening rumbles held him back, but provoked
all the more the fierce sharpness of his mind, so that he desired   **70**
to be the first to shatter the imprisoning bolts of the gates of nature.
As a result the vital force of his mind was victorious,
and he traveled far beyond the flaming walls of the world
and trekked throughout the measureless universe in mind and spirit.
As victor he brings back from there the knowledge of what can come to
     be,   **75**
what cannot, in short, by what process each thing
has its power limited, and its deep-set boundary stone.
And so the tables are turned. Religion lies crushed
beneath our feet, and his victory raises us to the sky.
I am afraid of one thing in all this: that you might think   **80**
that you are starting on the first steps of an unholy system of thought,
and are walking the path of crime. On the contrary, it has happened too
     often
that this so-called religion has produced criminal and unholy actions.
Thus was the case at Aulis when the chosen leaders of the Greeks,
the first among men, foully defiled the altar   **85**
of the virgin goddess of the crossroads[7] with the blood of Iphianassa.[8]
As soon as the sacrificial headband was wreathed about her virgin
     locks
with its streamers flowing down equally from both her cheeks,

ΣΡΙϹШΡͷϚ

---

[5] As just noted, Lucretius does not transliterate Epicurus' Greek term for
     atom (*atomos*, literally "unable to be cut") into Latin, but instead uses a
     number of different Latin terms to get at the idea.

[6] Epicurus (341-271 BC), the founder of Epicureanism and the
     philosophical hero of Lucretius' poem.

[7] "Virgin goddess of the crossroads" = Diana (Artemis in Greek).

[8] Iphianassa is the name Homer used for Iphigenia, the daughter of
     Agamemnon and Clytemnestra. Artemis forced Agamemnon and the
     Greeks to sacrifice Iphigenia before the Greeks could sail to Troy at the
     beginning of the Trojan War. The story of her sacrifice was retold in
     many 5th c. BC Greek tragedies, including Euripides' *Iphigenia at Aulis*,
     and Aeschylus' *Agamemnon*.

and as soon as she saw her father standing in mourning before the
    altar,
90 with his attendants beside him concealing the iron blade,
and the citizens pouring forth tears at the sight of her,
speechless with fear she sank in her knees and fell to the ground.
Nor was it a help to the wretched girl at such a moment
that she had been the first child to call the king "father."
95 She was lifted up by men's hands and led trembling
to the altar, not so that she might be greeted by the loud-ringing
marriage hymn when the solemn wedding rite was finished,
but that the chaste girl might be slaughtered unchastely at the very
    point
of marriage, a grieving victim, by the sacrificial stroke of her father.
All this so that a happy and auspicious departure might be granted to
100   the fleet.
Such great evils could religion make seem advisable.
Even you today at some time or other will be overcome
by the fearful words of seers and try to desert us.
Why not, since so many are the dreams they can now
105 invent for you which can overturn the guiding principles of your life
and throw all your fortunes into complete confusion with fear!
And deservedly so. For if people saw that there is a fixed limit
to oppressive cares, with some reason they would be strong enough
to fight back against religious beliefs and the threats of seers.
110 As it is, there is no means of resisting, no power,
since death must bring with it the fear of eternal punishment.
For people do not know what the nature of the soul is.
Is it born, or does it work its way into us as we are being born?
Does it perish when we do, torn apart by death,
115 or does it go to see the shades of Orcus[9] and its desolate pits?
Or does it work its way by divine aid into other creatures,
as our Ennius[10] proclaimed? He was the first to bring down
a crown of everlasting foliage from lovely Mount Helicon[11]
to become famous throughout the Italian tribes of people.
120 And yet moreover Ennius still sets forth
in his everlasting verses that there really are regions of Acheron,
where neither our souls nor our bodies remain,
but certain kinds of shades pale in wondrous ways.
He recalls how from that region the shade of Homer, forever

---

[9] "The shades of Orcus" = the underworld.

[10] Ennius (239-169 BC) was one of the greatest early Roman poets. For
Ennius, see Introduction p. xix.

[11] Mt. Helicon, located in Boeotia in Greece, was the home of the Muses.

law of nature

blooming, rose before him and began to shed salty   **125**
tears, setting out in words the nature of things.
Therefore we must not only give a correct account of celestial
matters, explaining in what way the wanderings of the sun
and moon occur and by what power things happen on earth.
We must also take special care and employ keen reasoning   **130**
to see where the soul and the nature of the mind come from,
and what it is that meets our minds and terrifies us when
we are awake and suffering from disease, and when we are buried in
      sleep,
so that we seem to hear and see face to face people
who have already met death and whose bones the earth embraces.   **135**
Nor does it escape my thought that it is difficult to throw light
upon the obscure discoveries of the Greeks in Latin verses,
especially since we must use new words for many things
because of the poverty of our language and the newness of the subject
      matter.
But still it is your excellence and the pleasure of the sweet friendship **140**
I hope to have with you that urges me to undergo hardship
however great and to keep my watch in the quiet of the night
as I try to find the right words and poem with which at last
I might be able to hold a clear light up to your mind
that will allow you to see deeply into obscure matters.   **145**
Therefore this fear and darkness of the mind must be shattered
apart not by the rays of the sun and the clear shafts
of the day but by the external appearance and inner law of nature.[12]
Its first principle will take its starting point for us as follows:
nothing ever comes to be from nothing through divine intervention.[13]   **150**
The reason that fear so dominates all mortals is
because they see many things happen on earth and in the heavens
the causes of whose activities they are able in no way
to understand, and they imagine they take place through divine power.
For which reason, when we see that nothing can be created from
      nothing,   **155**
then we will more correctly perceive what we are after:
the source from which each thing is created, and the way
each thing happens without divine intervention.
For if things came to be from nothing, every kind of thing

---

12   1.146-148 = 3.91-93.

13   This is the first major law of Epicurean physics: Nothing can come to be
     out of nothing. Cf. Epicurus' *Letter to Herodotus* 38 ("First, nothing
     comes into being out of what does not exist"). Lucretius' words in 150,
     "through divine intervention," appear to be his own addition.

each thing is born

160 could be born from all things, and nothing would need a seed.
Men might sprout from the sea and the scaly race
of fishes from the earth, and birds might hatch from the sky.
Cattle and other livestock, and every kind of beast,
with uncertain birth would inhabit farms and wilderness alike.
165 Trees would not consistently produce the same fruit,
but they would change, and all trees could bear all fruit.
Since there would not be generating bodies for each thing,
how could there be a fixed and constant mother for things?
But now, since all things are created from fixed seeds,
170 each thing is born and emerges into the shores of light
from the source of the matter and first bodies of each thing.
And thus all things are unable to be born from all things,
because there is a separate power present in fixed things.
And why do we see roses in the spring, grain in the heat,
175 or vines bursting forth in response to autumn's call?
Is it not because whatever is created becomes visible
in its own time when fixed seeds have flowed together,
while favorable seasons are at hand and the lively earth safely
brings forth tender things into the shores of light?
180 But if they came to be from nothing, they would suddenly spring forth
at random periods of time and during unsuitable parts of the year,
seeing that there would be no first beginnings which would be able
to be kept apart from generating union at an unfavorable time.
Nor further, in order for things to increase, would there need to be time
185 for seeds to come together, if they were able to grow from nothing.
For tiny babies would suddenly become young adults,
and trees would rise up and leap from the earth in an instant.
It is obvious that none of these things happens, since everything
increases little by little, as is fitting for fixed seed,
190 and preserves their kind as they increase. Thus you can recognize
that each thing grows and is nourished from its own matter.
In addition, without dependable rains each year
the earth is unable to produce its joy-bringing crops,
nor is the nature of living creatures, if deprived of food,
195 able to reproduce its race and safeguard its life.
You should thus believe all the more that many bodies are common
to many things, as we see letters are common to words,
rather than that anything is able to exist without first beginnings.
Next, why was nature unable to produce men
so large that they could cross the ocean by walking through the
200   shallows,
rip apart huge mountains with their bare hands,
and succeed in living through many ages of living creatures,
unless it is because fixed matter has been assigned to things

for their growth, from which it is determined what is able to come to be?
So it must be confessed that nothing is able to come from nothing,   **205**
since things have a need for seed by which they all can,
when created, be brought forth into the soft breezes of the air.
Finally, since we see that cultivated lands are better than uncultivated,
and produce better crops when they are cared for by our hands,
it is clear that there exist in the earth the first beginnings of things   **210**
which we stir into being when we turn over the fertile clods
with a plough and work the soil of the earth from deep down.
But if there were not first beginnings, you would see everything
come to be much better on its own without our efforts.
Next is this: nature dissolves each thing back   **215**
into its particles and does not destroy things into nothing.[14]
For if anything were mortal in all its parts, each thing
would perish by being snatched suddenly from before our eyes.
For no need would exist for a force that was able to arrange
the destruction of the parts of each thing and dissolve its structure.   **220**
But as it is, since each thing is composed out of eternal seed,
until a force is present that hammers apart the thing with a blow
or penetrates within through empty spaces and dissolves it,
nature does not allow the destruction of anything to be seen.
And if time annihilates whatever it removes through the aging process,   **225**
consuming all the matter, from where would Venus restore
the living race each according to kind, or from where
does earth the sweet artificer nourish and increase them
once restored, providing them with food each according to kind?
From where would internal springs and external, far-off rivers   **230**
supply the sea? From where would the sky feed the stars?
For infinite time gone by and the passing days
ought to have consumed everything that has a mortal structure.
But if in this duration and time gone by there have been
things from which this sum of things is restored and exists,   **235**
they are without any doubt endowed with an immortal nature.
Therefore everything cannot be changed back into nothing.
Next, the same force and cause would destroy everything
indiscriminately, unless they were held together by an eternal stuff
entangled to a lesser or greater degree in its interconnections with itself.   **240**
Indeed a mere touch would undoubtedly be a sufficient cause

---

[14] This is the second major law of Epicurean physics: Nothing can be destroyed into nothing, or everything would cease to be. Cf. Epicurus' *Letter to Herodotus* 39 ("And if what disappears had perished into what is not, all things would have perished, since what they were dissolved into does not exist.").

of death, especially seeing that there would be nothing with eternal
    body
whose texture a special force would be required to dissolve.
But as things are, since there are various interconnections
245 of the first beginnings with themselves and matter is everlasting,
things persist with their bodies sound, until a force found
sufficiently strong to overcome their textures meets them.
Thus not one thing returns to nothing, but all things
when they split apart return to the first bodies of matter.
250 Lastly, the rains pass away, when father sky
sends them down into the lap of mother earth.
But glistening crops erupt and branches turn green on trees,
while the trees themselves grow and are weighed down by fruit.
Hence further our race and the race of beasts are fed,
255 hence we see glad cities flower with children
and lush forests everywhere sing with young birds.
Hence cows exhausted by their fat lay their bodies
down on the joyful pasture and the glistening moisture of milk
drips from their distended udders. Hence new calves
260 play and frolic on shaky limbs in the soft grass,
their tender young minds drunk on pure milk.
Thus all things that are visible do not perish completely,
since nature remakes one thing from another, nor does she allow
anything to be born unless it is aided by another's death.
Come now, since I have shown that things cannot be created from
265   nothing,
and likewise that once created they cannot be reduced to nothing,
lest by any chance you still begin to doubt my words,
since you cannot see the first beginnings of things with your eyes,
let me remind you besides that there are bodies which you must admit
270 exist in things and yet are not able to be seen.
First, when the force of the wind is whipped up it lashes
at the sea, overwhelming huge ships and scattering the clouds.
Rushing along at times with a quick whirlwind it strews
the plains with great trees and attacks the mountain tops
275 with forest-cracking blasts. So the wind with its shrill howling
rages wildly, shrieking savagely and moaning with menace.
It is therefore beyond doubt that there are invisible bodies of wind
which sweep over the sea, the lands, and the clouds of the sky,
buffeting them and snatching them up in a sudden whirlwind.
280 They flow along and breed destruction in the same way
as when the soothing nature of water is carried off suddenly
in an overflowing river, when it has been swollen after heavy rains
by a tremendous rush of water coming off the high mountains.
It tosses shattered branches from the forests and whole trees,

and not even sturdy bridges can withstand the sudden force   **285**
of the approaching water. Stirred up by the heavy rains,
the river rushes against the pilings with effective force.
It wreaks a deafening havoc and beneath its waves it rolls
huge rocks, rushing against whatever opposes its flow.
Therefore so too should the blasts of wind be carried along,   **290**
which, whenever they have spread out in any direction
like a powerful river, drive things before them and rush at them
with constant force, and now and then in a twisting gust
they seize them and quickly carry them off in a spinning whirlwind.
Therefore again and again there are invisible bodies of wind,   **295**
since they have been found to rival mighty rivers in what
they do and in how they act, and rivers have bodies we can see.
Second, we experience the different kinds of smells things have,
but nonetheless we never see the smells coming to our noses.
We do not see warm heat, nor can we apprehend   **300**
cold with our eyes, nor are we in the habit of seeing voices.
But it must be that all these things are bodily
by nature, since they are able to set the sense organs in motion.
For nothing is able to touch or be touched except body.
Third, clothes hung along the wave-beaten shore   **305**
grow damp, but they dry when spread out in the sun.
But we neither see how the dampness of the water settled on them,
nor again how it was forced out owing to the heat.
This shows that the moisture is split up into small
particles that the eye is in no way able to see.   **310**
Fourth, as the sun completes its journey year after year
a ring on the finger grows thinner beneath with wear,
the fall of water-drops hollows out a stone, the curved
iron plow of a farmer shrinks imperceptibly in the fields,
and we see that people's feet today are wearing down   **315**
the stone surfaces of the street. Then too near the gates of the city
bronze statues extend right hands thinned
by the frequent touch of those who pass by and greet them.
These then we see diminish, since they have been worn away.
But the jealous nature of vision blocks our seeing which   **320**
bodies move away at any given time.
Finally, whatever time and nature gradually add
to things, compelling them to grow in due measure,
no sharpness of vision, no matter how it strains, is able to see.
Moreover, neither when things age by the wasting of time,   **325**
nor when rocks overhanging the sea are eaten away by the devouring
salt are you able to see at the time what they are losing.
This is proof that nature conducts her business with invisible bodies.
But all things are not held packed tightly

330 together everywhere by the nature of body, for there is void in things.
Understanding this will be useful to you in many matters.
It will prevent you from wandering around, always doubting and
    seeking
after the nature of reality, and from lacking faith in my words.
Therefore there exists intangible space, void, and emptiness.
335 If void did not exist, there is no way things
would be able to move. For that which is the natural role[15] of body,
to roll in the way and obstruct, would be present at all times
for all things. Therefore nothing would be able
to move forward, because nothing would provide a beginning of
    yielding.
340 Yet now through the oceans and lands and the heights of heaven
we see before our eyes many things move by many
means and in various ways. If void did not exist,
these things would not only be deprived of and lack
restless motion, but would never have been brought to birth at all,
345 since everywhere matter would be still, packed tightly together.
Besides, however solid things might be thought to be,
nevertheless you may tell their bodies are loose-knit from this:
in rocks in caves the liquid moisture of water seeps
and trickles through, and everything weeps with plentiful drops.
350 Food is distributed into every part of an animal's body.
Trees grow and bear fruit at the proper time,
because food is distributed throughout all the parts of trees,
from the deepest roots, through the trunks, and throughout all the
    branches.
Voices travel through walls and fly across closed-off
355 rooms in houses, stiffening cold penetrates to the bone.
These things you would never see happen in any way
unless there were empty spaces through which individual bodies pass.
And next, why do we see that some things exceed
others in weight, although they are no different in size?
360 For if there is the same amount of body in a ball of wool
as there is in a ball of lead, it is fair to suppose they weigh
the same, since it is the role of body to press everything downward.
But in contrast it is the nature of the void to persist without weight.
Therefore whatever is equal in size but is observed to be lighter
365 without doubt shows that it possesses more void.
But in contrast the heavier thing declares that there is more body in it
and that it has within much less empty space.

---

[15] "Role...roll" is an attempt to get at Lucretius' play on words with *officium*
("duty, function, job, role") and *officere* ("to block, get in the way").

Therefore it is certain that what we have been searching for with keen
reasoning, what we call void, exists, mixed in things.
In order that what some assert in these matters not be able   370
to lead you from the truth, I feel compelled to outstrip their argument.
They say that water yields to scaly creatures as they strive
and opens fluid paths, because fish leave spaces
behind them where the waters as they yield are able to flow together.
So too they say that other things are able to move   375
among themselves and change place, although all is full.
This all has of course been accepted on false reasoning.
For where can the scaly creatures go forward after all,
if water does not give space? Furthermore where will the waves
be able to give place, when the fish will not be able to go?   380
Therefore either all bodies must be deprived of motion,
or it must be admitted that void is mixed in things, from which
source each thing takes its first beginning of motion.
Finally, if two broad bodies suddenly leap
apart from their union, it is of course necessary that air fill   385
up all the void which is created between the bodies.
Yet however fast the breezes circulate with which the air
flows together, still the entire space would never be able
to be filled up at one time. For the air must
occupy each space in succession, before all are occupied.   390
But if someone by chance should happen to think that this occurs
when the bodies leap apart because the air compresses itself,
he errs. For then a vacuum is created which did not exist
before and likewise a vacuum is filled which existed before,
nor is air able to be condensed in any such way   395
nor, if it could, could it, I think, without void
contract into itself and gather its parts into one.
Wherefore although you delay by raising many objections,
it is nevertheless necessary to admit that void is present in things.
And moreover by relating many arguments to you I am able   400
to scrape together trust in these words of mine.
But these little traces are enough for a keen intellect,
and by their means you are able to discover the rest on your own.
For just as dogs often find with their noses the resting places,
covered by foliage, of a wild beast that roams the mountains,   405
as soon as they set to work on the sure traces of its path,
so you yourself on your own will be able in such cases
to see one thing from another and to work your way into every
dark hiding place and drag back the truth from them.
But if you show hesitation or turn aside a little from your task,   410
I am able to promise this clearly to you, Memmius:
such large draughts from deep fountains will my sweet

tongue pour out from my well-stocked mind
that I am afraid that slow-moving old age will creep
415 through our limbs and dissolve the bonds of life in both of us
before the whole abundant supply of arguments in my poem
on any particular point has been sent flying through your ears.
But now to return to weave in words what I have begun:
the nature of the universe, then, as it is in itself, is made
420 up of two things; for there are bodies and void.
Bodies are located in the void and move in it this way and that.
For ordinary perception declares by itself that body exists.
Unless trust in perception is firmly founded and flourishes,
in the case of hidden things there will be nothing to which we can refer
425 to prove anything at all with the reasoning power of the mind.
Then again if there were no place and space, which we call void,
bodies would never be able to have location nor to travel
at all in this way and that in any direction.
This is what I have already showed you a little while ago.[16]
In addition to this, there is nothing you are able to name which is
430   distinct
and separated off apart from all body and the void,
which can be discovered to be some third type of nature.
For whatever will exist, this will have to be something itself.
Now if it will be subject to touch, no matter how light and tiny,   **(435)**
435 it will, by an increase either great or at least small, if it does exist,   **(434)**
increase the number of body and be part of the sum of the whole.
But if it will not be subject to touch, and is able from no side
to stop anything which is traveling from passing through it,
it will of course be what we call empty void.
440 In addition, whatever will exist by itself either will act on something
or will have to suffer other things acting upon it,
or will be such that things are able to exist and move in it.
But nothing is able to act or be acted upon without body,
nor again to provide place unless what is void and empty.
445 Therefore besides void and bodies there can remain by itself
among the number of things no third nature
that could come and make contact with our senses at any time
or that anyone might be able to grasp with the reasoning power of the
       mind.
For all things that have a name, either you will find that they are
       properties
450 of these two things or you will see that they are accidents of them.
A property is that which is never able to be disjoined

---

[16] 1.335-345, 370-383.

and separated off without a fatally harmful disintegration,
as weight is to rocks, heat to fire, fluidity is to water,
tangibility to all bodies, and intangibility to void.
Slavery, on the other hand, and poverty and wealth,   **455**
freedom, war, peace, and other things at whose
arrival and departure the nature of things remains unharmed,
we are accustomed to call, as is right, accidents.
Time likewise does not exist independently, but from things themselves
comes a sense of what has happened in ages past, then what   **460**
thing looms before us, and then further what will follow.
No one, it must be confessed, senses time through itself,
separated off from the motion and the quiet immobility of things.
Indeed when they say the daughter of Tyndareus[17] was raped and the
    Trojan
peoples were subdued in war, we must beware that they do not
    accidentally   **465**
force us to admit that these things exist on their own
just because an age which is past and can't be called back
took away these races of men, whose accidents these were.
For whatever will have happened will be able to be called an accident,
on the one hand of the lands, on the other of the regions of space
    themselves.   **470**
Indeed if there had been no material for things, nor place
and space, in which all things are carried out,
never would the fire, fanned by love for the beautiful shape
of Tyndareus' daughter, glistening in the Phrygian heart of Alexander,
have ignited the glowing contests of savage war,   **475**
nor unbeknownst to the Trojans would the wooden horse have set fire
to Pergama by giving birth to Greeks at night.
You can see, then, that absolutely all things that occur
never are nor exist through themselves as body does,
nor are they spoken of in the same sense as void is,   **480**
but rather so that you can rightly call them events
of body and place, in which all things are carried on.
Bodies, moreover, are partly the first beginnings of things,
partly the things that are formed by the assemblage of first beginnings.
But those that are the first beginnings of things, no force is strong
    enough   **485**
to destroy. For with solid body they are victorious in the end.[18]
And yet it seems difficult to believe that anything

---

[17] Helen of Troy.

[18] i.e., the first beginnings are so strong and solid that nothing can destroy
    them.

can be found with solid body among things that exist.
For lightning from heaven makes its way through the walls of houses,
490 as do shouts and voices. Iron glows with heat in the fire,
and rocks burst apart because of fierce blazing heat.
The unyielding hardness of gold is loosened and dissolved by heat,
and the ice of bronze is overcome by flame and melts.
Heat and penetrating cold seep through silver,
495 seeing that we have felt both as we solemnly hold our cups
in hand and the dew of water is poured in from above.
To such an extent does there seem to be no solidity in things.
But nevertheless because true reason and the nature of things
compels us, stand by me, until I explain in a few verses
500 that there are things which exist with solid and eternal body,
which we are demonstrating to be the seeds and first beginnings of
      things,
from where now exists the entire created sum of things.
First, since the twofold nature of the two
things has been found to exist far different,
505 that is of body and of place, in which all things occur,
each must be in and for itself, and unmixed.
For wherever there is empty space, which we call void,
there is no body. And wherever body is located,
there empty space will never exist.
510 Therefore the first bodies are solid and without void.
Moreover, since void is present in created things,
it must be that solid matter exists around it.
And there is nothing that can be shown by true reasoning
to conceal void with its body and to have it within,
515 unless you admit that what holds it in is solid.
Now that thing can be nothing except an assemblage
of matter, which is able to contain the void in things.
Matter, therefore, which exists with a solid body,
is able to be eternal, when all other bodies are dissolved.
520 Then further, if there were nothing which was empty void,
all would be solid. In contrast, unless there were definite bodies
which fill up whatever places they hold,
all that is would exist as vacant and empty space.
Therefore without doubt body has been alternately marked off
525 from void, since the universe is neither completely full
nor yet empty. There are, therefore, definite bodies
which are able to mark off empty from occupied space.
These bodies cannot be struck and dissolved by external
blows, nor can they be penetrated and undone from deep within.
530 Nor can they be attacked and grow weak in another way,

as I demonstrated to you above a little while ago.[19]
For it seems clear that unless a thing has void in it
it cannot be crushed, broken, or split by being cut in two,
nor can it take in water, seeping cold,
and penetrating fire, by which all things are destroyed.   535
And the more void each thing contains within,
the more it is attacked by these things deep within and is weakened.
Therefore if the primary bodies are solid and are without void,
just as I have demonstrated, they must necessarily be eternal.
Moreover, unless matter had been eternal, before now   540
all things would have been completely reduced to nothing
and whatever we see would have been born again from nothing.
But since I have shown above that nothing is able to be created
from nothing and that what has been made cannot be recalled to nothing,
the first beginnings must be endowed with immortal bodies,   545
into which all things can be dissolved in their final moments,
so that matter can be supplied for the re-creation of things.
Therefore primary bodies exist in their solid singleness,
for in no other way can they be kept safe forever
from an infinite time past and recreate things again.   550
In addition, if nature had established no end
to the breaking apart of things, the bodies of matter now
would have been reduced to such a state by the breakage of earlier ages
that nothing could be conceived from them within a fixed amount
of time and reach the full limit of its age.   555
For we see that anything can be dissolved more quickly
than it can be rebuilt. Therefore whatever the infinitely long
span of days of all time that has gone before
had broken apart up until now by demolishing and dissolving,
never could it have been created again in the time that remains.   560
But of course a limit of breaking apart has been established
and remains fixed, since we see that each thing is recreated
and that a finite amount of time for each generation of things
exists, in which they are able to attain the flower of their life.
In addition, although the bodies of matter are totally solid,   565
it is still possible to explain how all those things
which are made soft (air, water, earth, and fires)[20]
are made and by what force they are all borne along,
when once void has been mixed up in things.
But on the contrary, if the first bodies of things were soft,   570

---

[19] 1.215-264, 485-502

[20] These are the four elements of the Presocratic philosopher Empedocles.
    Lucretius argues against Empedocles below in lines 716-829.

from what source strong flints and iron were created,
no explanation could be given. For all nature
will completely lack the starting point for a foundation.
Therefore the primary bodies are solid, powerful in their singleness.
575 Through a more tightly condensed union of them, all things
can be riveted together and display impressive strength.
Further, if no end has been appointed to the breaking apart
of bodies, yet it is necessary that from time eternal bodies
of each kind of thing survive even now,
580 which have not yet been attacked by any danger.
But since they exist endowed with a fragile nature,
it is inconsistent to think that they have been able to survive for all time
when they have been buffeted by innumerable blows throughout the
ages.
Next, since there has been appointed for things, each according
585 to their kind, a limit of growth and of remaining alive,
and seeing that what they each are capable of by the laws of nature,
and further what they are incapable of, stand ordained,
and since nothing is changed, but all things remain constant
to such an extent that all the different kinds of birds
590 in their order show the markings of their kind on their bodies,
they ought doubtless also to have a body of unchanging
matter. For if the first beginnings of things
are able to be mastered and changed in any way,
it would also be uncertain what can come to be,
595 what cannot, in short, by what process each thing
has its power limited and its deep-set boundary stone,
nor could the generations according to their kinds so often recall
the nature, behavior, way of life, and movements of their parents.
Then further, since there is an extreme point in each case
600 on that body our senses are no longer able to discern,
each point is undoubtedly without parts
and is endowed with the smallest nature possible, nor did it ever exist
separately by itself, nor will it ever have the power to do
so afterwards, since it is itself a primary and single part of another.
605 Thence more and more similar parts in their order
fill out the nature of the atom in a tight mass.
Since these points are unable to exist by themselves, they must
be fixed fast so that they can in no way be pulled away.
Therefore primary bodies exist in their solid singleness,
610 closely packed and tightly bound in their minimal parts.[21]

---

[21] Unlike many other ancient philosophers, Epicurus held that both space
and time were not infinitely divisible and that there were minimal units

They were not assembled from a collection of minimal parts,
but rather they are powerfully strong in their eternal singleness,
and from them nature, keeping safe the seeds of things,
has never allowed anything to be pulled away or diminished.
Moreover, unless a minimum exists, all the tiniest   **615**
bodies will be made up of an infinite number of parts,
since in that case the half of a half will always have
a half, nor will there be anything to set a limit.
Therefore what difference will there be between the sum of things
and the least of things? There will be none. For although the whole sum   **620**
of things be completely infinite, nevertheless, those things
that are tiniest will equally be made up out of infinite parts.
But since true reasoning shouts back and denies
that the mind can believe this, you should give in and admit
that these things now exist possessing no parts   **625**
and endowed with a minimal nature. And since they exist,
you must also admit that the atoms are solid and eternal.
Finally, if nature, the creator of things, had been accustomed to compel
all things to be dissolved into their minimal parts,
it would not now be able to create anything from them,   **630**
because things that are not augmented by any parts
are unable to have those things which generating matter
ought to have: different connections, weight, blows,
meetings, motions, through which all things take place.
Therefore those who think that the primary substance of things   **635**
is fire, and that the sum of things consists of fire alone,
are seen to have fallen far from true reasoning.
Heraclitus[22] was the first to enter the fray as their leader.
He was famous on account of his obscure language more among the foolish
than those thoughtful Greeks who seek the truth.   **640**
For stupid people find more impressive and attractive
all things that they see hidden beneath twisted words,
and they judge those things true which can caress
their ears prettily and which are colored with delightful sound.

---

of space and time beyond which space and time could not be further divided. He taught that atoms were made up of "minimal parts" that could neither be physically nor conceptually divided. He also argued that atoms could never be split up into their component minimal parts. For more on minimal parts, see Epicurus' *Letter to Herodotus* 55-59.

[22] Heraclitus of Ephesus lived in the 6th to 5th century BC, and was one of the most famous Presocratic philosophers. He taught that all things that existed were made up of different forms of fire.

645 For how are things able to be so varied, I ask,
    if they are created from pure fire alone?
    For it would be no help for hot fire to become dense
    or to be rarified, if the parts of fire had the same nature
    that fire taken as a whole has as well.
650 For the heat would be more intense when its parts were condensed,
    and weaker when they were pulled apart and dispersed.
    Beyond this there is nothing you can imagine happening
    under such conditions, still less that such a great variety
    of things could exist because of condensed and rarified fire.
655 This too: If they were to assume that void is mixed
    in things, fire will become dense or be left rarified.
    But since they see many things that go against them,
    and flee from allowing there to be pure void in things,
    while they fear the steep path, they lose the true one,
660 nor again do they see that if void is removed from things,
    everything is condensed and one body is created from all.
    This body could not speed anything from itself,
    like warming fire sends out light and heat,
    so that you see that it is not composed of closely packed parts.
665 But if by chance they believe that fire can in some other way
    be extinguished in its union and change its substance,
    of course if they do not refrain from doing this in any part,
    doubtless all heat will perish completely into nothing,
    and all things that are created would come to be from nothing.
670 For whatever is changed and departs from its own limits,
    this is immediately the death of that which it was before.[23]
    Accordingly it is necessary that something be preserved safe for things,
    or else you would see all things return completely to nothing
    and from nothing the supply of things would be reborn and grow.
675 Now therefore since there are certain most definite bodies,
    which always preserve the same nature,
    by whose departure or arrival, and changed ordering,
    things change their nature and bodies transform themselves,
    you can be sure that these bodies of things are not made out of fire.
680 For it would make no difference that certain things separate and leave,
    and others are added, and certain others change their ordering,
    if all of them still retained the nature of fire.
    For whatever they would create would in all ways be fire.
    The truth, as I think, is this: there are certain bodies,
    whose coming-togethers, movements, order, positions, and
685   configurations

---

23   1.670-671 = 1.792-793, 2.753-754, 3.519-520.

create fire. When their order is changed, they change a thing's
nature, and they are not like fire nor any other
thing which is able to send off bodies
to our sense organs and touch our touch by its contact.
Further, to say that all things are fire   690
and that nothing real exists in the number of things except fire,
as this same man[24] does, seems to be completely crazy.
For he himself fought back against his senses with his senses,
and thereby undermined the source on which all his beliefs depend,
and the source of his knowing that fire which he names.   695
For he believes that the senses truly perceive fire,
but not other things, which are no less clear.
This seems to me to be both silly and crazy.
What other criterion can we use? What can be more certain to us
than our senses themselves, by which we distinguish true and false? 700
Besides, why would anyone exclude everything else
and desire to leave only the nature of fire,
anymore than to deny the existence of fire, while admitting the existence
of something else? It seems to be equal madness to say either.
Therefore those who think that the primary substance of things   705
is fire, and that the sum of things can consist of fire,
and those who have made air the first principle for the creation
of things,[25] and whoever has thought that water
alone by itself fabricates things[26] or that earth creates
all things and is changed into all the natures of things,[27]   710
seem to have wandered very far from the truth.
Add, too, those who double the first beginnings of things,
joining air to fire[28] and earth to water,[29]
and those who think that all things are able to develop
from four things: fire, earth, air, and water.[30]   715
Foremost among such men is Empedocles of Acragas,
whom an island[31] bore within the three-cornered shores of its lands.
The Ionian sea flows around this island with its great

---

[24] Heraclitus.

[25] Anaximenes of Miletus (c. 585-525 BC) and Diogenes of Apollonia (5th
        century BC).

[26] Thales of Miletus (c. 6th century BC)

[27] The reference is uncertain.

[28] The reference is uncertain.

[29] Xenophanes of Colophon (c. 570-478 BC).

[30] Empedocles of Acragas (Sicily) (c.492-432 BC)

[31] Sicily

inlets and sprays salty brine from its green waves.

720 In its narrow strait the rushing sea divides with its waves
the shores of the lands of Aeolia[32] from the boundaries of Sicily.
Here is destructive Charybdis[33] and here the rumblings of Etna[34]
threaten to gather the anger of its flames together again,
so that its violence might once again spew forth flames

725 from its jaws and again launch shafts of fire to the sky.
Although this region seems great and marvelous in many
ways to the races of men, and is said to be worth seeing,
rich in good things, and protected by the great force of its men,
nevertheless it seems to have had in it nothing more outstanding

730 than this man, nor holier, more wondrous, and precious.
Nay indeed the poems from his divine mind
shout aloud and set out his outstanding discoveries,
so that he seems scarcely to have been created from human stock.
Nevertheless he and those I mentioned above, ranked

735 far below him in many ways and lesser by far,
although they made many fine and divine discoveries,
and issued responses from, so to speak, the shrine of their hearts
with more holiness and with much more certain reasoning than
the Pythia[35] who speaks from the tripod and laurel of Apollo,
nevertheless about the first beginnings of things, they have come

740   crashing down,
and though great, with a great fall they fell there mightily.[36]
First because although they take away void from things,
they posit motion and leave things soft and porous:
air, sun, rain, earth, animals, fruits,

745 and yet they do not mix void into the bodies of these things.
Next because they establish no limit at all for dividing
bodies nor any cessation for the breaking up of things,
nor further does any minimum in things exist for them,
although we see that there is for each thing

750 that extreme point which to our senses appears to be a minimum,
so that from this you can infer that the extreme point in those things
which you cannot see exists as a minimum in them.
In addition, since they have made the primary elements

---

[32] Southern Italy.

[33] A famous narrow whirlpool located in the straits of Messina between Sicily and the Italian mainland.

[34] Etna = Mt. Etna, located in Eastern Sicily and the highest active volcano in Europe.

[35] The Pythia was the priestess at the oracle of Delphi in Greece.

[36] This line imitates Homer *Iliad* 16.776.

of things soft, things which we see are born
and endowed with mortal body, the whole sum of things   **755**
ought now to return completely to nothing,
and the supply of things ought to be reborn from nothing and thrive.
And how far each of these is from the truth you will understand by
    now.
Next, these elements are in many ways hostile and like poison
themselves to themselves among themselves. Therefore if they meet   **760**
either they will perish, or scatter just as, when a storm has gathered,
we see thunderbolts, rain, and the winds scatter apart.
Again, if all things are created from four elements
and all are dissolved into these things again, how
can these elements be called the first beginnings of things any more
    than   **765**
on the contrary things be called the first beginnings of the elements,
our thought reversed? For they are begotten in alternation and change
    color
and their whole nature among themselves for all time.
[we see thunderbolts, rain, and the winds scatter apart.][37]
But if by chance you think that fire and the body of earth   **770**
and airy breezes and the dew of water come together
in a way that none of them changes its nature in the compound,
you will find that nothing will be able to be created from them,
not a living thing, nor one with a lifeless body, like a tree.
For each thing combined in a discordant heap will display   **775**
its own nature, and air will be seen to be mixed
together with earth, and fire to stand with water.
But the first beginnings in creating things must
of necessity possess a nature that is secret and invisible,
so that nothing can show forth which would fight against and hinder **780**
whatever is created from being able to exist with its own character.
And furthermore, they[38] begin from the heaven and its fires
and maintain that fire first turns itself into the breezes
of the air, and then rain is produced, and then that earth is created
from rain, and that all things are changed back again from earth: **785**
first water, afterwards air, and finally heat,
and that these things never cease changing among themselves,
and travel from heaven to earth, from earth to the stars of the firmament.
First beginnings ought never to do this in any way.
For something unchangeable must necessarily remain,   **790**

---

[37] This line was repeated here from 763 by a copyist's error.

[38] Who "they" are is unclear. Some scholars think Lucretius is attacking
    the Stoics, but others disagree and have suggested different possibilities.

so that all things not be completely reduced to nothing.
For whatever is changed and departs from its own limits,
this is immediately the death of that which it was before.
Therefore since those things which I have just mentioned above
795   undergo change, they must be made up
of other things, which can never change, or else
you would see all things return completely to nothing.
Why not rather posit certain bodies endowed with such a nature
that if they created, say, fire, these same bodies
800   would be able, with a few of them taken away and a few of them added,
and with their ordering and movement changed, to create the breezes
    of the air,
and in this way all other things could be changed into others?
"But," you say, "it is a plain and obvious fact that all
things are nourished and grow from the earth into the breezes of the
    air;
805   and unless the weather gives free play at the right time
to the rains, so that by the melting of the clouds the trees may sway,
and unless the sun for its part cradles and warms them,
crops, trees, and living creatures cannot grow."
Yes, and unless we have the benefit of dry food and soft
810   liquid, our flesh would soon be lost and all life
too would be released from all our sinews and bones.
Beyond a shadow of a doubt we are helped along and nourished
by specific things, as are other things by other specific things.
Doubtless because many first beginnings, common
815   in many ways to many things, are mixed in things,
so different things are nourished by different things.
And it often makes a great difference with these same
first beginnings with what and in what position they are held,
and what motions they impart and receive among themselves.
820   For sky, sea, earth, rivers, and sun are composed
of the same things, and so too crops, trees, and animals,
but they are mixed with different things and are moved in different
    ways.
And furthermore, here and there in our verses themselves
you see many letters shared by many words,
825   although it is still necessary to admit that the verses and words[39]
differ among themselves in meaning and in the sounding of their
    sounds.
So much can letters accomplish with only a change in ordering.
But the first beginnings of things can bring more differences into play,

---

[39]   1.823-825 = 2.688-690.

from which the various things in their several kinds can be created.
Now let us also examine Anaxagoras' "homoeomeria," [40]   **830**
as the Greeks call it, which the poverty of our native speech
does not allow us to name in our own language,
but nevertheless it is easy to explain the thing itself in words.
First, as to what he calls the homoeomeria of things,
he clearly thinks that bones are made of small and tiny   **835**
bones, and that flesh is made from small and tiny
pieces of flesh, and that blood is created when many
drops of blood intermingle with one another,
and that from flecks of gold there can be built up
gold, and that from small pieces of earth earth can grow,   **840**
and that fires can be from fires, and water from waters,
and he imagines and thinks of other things in the same way.
And nevertheless he does not allow that void is present in things
in any part, nor that there is an end to dividing bodies.
Therefore in both of these reasonings he seems to have made   **845**
the same errors as those people whom I discussed above. [41]
Add that he makes the first beginnings too weak,
if they are first beginnings at all which are endowed with a nature
similar to the things themselves and suffer in the same way
and perish, nor does anything hold them back from destruction.   **850**
For which of them will endure when they are heavily crushed,
so that they can escape death, when they are in the very teeth of
  destruction?
Will it be fire? Water? Air? Which of these? Blood? Bones?
None of these, I think, when everything will be as equally and completely
mortal as the clearly perceptible things we see   **855**
with our own eyes perish when they are overcome by some force.
But I appeal to the things we have proved before, that nothing
can sink into nothingness nor again grow from nothing.
Moreover, since food increases and nourishes the body,
we are able to know that veins and blood and bones   **860**
<and sinews are composed of parts different in kind;> [42]
or if they say that all foods are mixed in body
and have in themselves small bodies of sinews,
and bones and veins besides, and parts of blood,

---

[40] Anaxagoras was a Presocratic philosopher from Clazomenae (c.500-428
    BC). Lucretius uses the Greek term "homoeomeria" (ho-moi-o-MER-i-
    a, literally "having like parts") as the name for Anaxagoras' doctrine
    that there is a bit of everything in everything.

[41] Heraclitus and Empedocles.

[42] The text is corrupt here. I have translated Lambinus' suggested addition.

it will happen that all food itself, both dry and liquid,
865 will be supposed to be made out of things unlike itself,
with bones and sinews and gore and blood mixed in.
Moreover if whatever bodies grow from the earth,
are in the earth, the earth must necessarily consist of
things unlike itself which arise from the earth.
870 Take another case, and you may use the same words.
If flame lies hidden in logs, and smoke and ashes,
logs must consist of things unlike themselves,
873 of things unlike themselves which arise from the logs.   (874)
874 Moreover whatever bodies earth nourishes and increases[43]   (873)

            *   *   *   *   *   *   *   *   *   *   *   *   *

875 There remains here some slight means of escaping detection,
which Anaxagoras took for himself, that he thinks that all things
are mixed with all things and escape detection, but that one
thing is visible, whose particles have been mixed in the greatest
        numbers
and are more visible and located right up front.
880 But this is far removed from true reasoning.
For it would be natural also for grains of wheat, when they are broken
under the oppressive strength of stone, to release a trace
of blood or something of those things which are nourished in our body.
When we rub with stone on stone, the blood should ooze out.
885 In a similar way it would be right for grass, too, and water
often to release sweet drops which are similar in taste
to the richness of the milk of wool-bearing sheep.
Yes, and it would be right, when clods of earth are crumbled up,
for types of grasses and wheat and foliage often to be seen
890 to lie hidden dispersed in tiny portions within the earth,
and finally it would be right, when logs would be broken open,
for ashes and smoke, and tiny fires, to be seen to be hidden.
Since the plain facts show that none of this happens,
we may know that things are not mixed in things in this way,
895 but rather that seeds, mixed up in many ways, and common
to many things, must lie hidden in things.
"But," you will object, "it often happens on great mountains
that the neighboring tops of high trees are rubbed together
among themselves when a strong south wind forces them
900 to do this until they burst and flash into a flower of flames."
And nevertheless fire is not implanted in firs, of course,
but there are many seeds of fire which when they flow together
by rubbing create fiery destruction in the woods.

---

[43] There is a lacuna in the text after line 874.

Free the mind from religion

But if there were fully formed flames hidden in the woods,
fires would not be able to be contained for a moment;   905
they would destroy woods everywhere, they would incinerate orchards.
Now then, do you see, as we said a little earlier,[44]
that it often is very important with these same first beginnings
with what and in what position they are held,
and what motions they impart and receive among themselves,   910
and that the same things, a little changed among themselves, create
both fires and fir? This is the way even with words themselves
when the letters are changed around a little among themselves,
since we designate firs and fires by a change in sound.[45]
Finally, if you think that whatever you see in things   915
that are visible cannot be created unless you posit
bodies of matter endowed with a nature like the whole,
by this reasoning the first beginnings perish on you.
The first beginnings will rock with rolling laughter, howl
aloud, and with salty tears drench their faces and cheeks.[46]   920
Now come, understand what remains and hear more clearly.
I am very aware how obscure these things are. But great
hope for praise strikes my heart with a sharp thyrsus[47]
and at the same time strikes into my breast sweet love
for the Muses. Now roused by this in my lively mind   925
I am traversing the remote places of the Pierides,[48] untrodden by the
     sole
of anyone before. It is a joy to approach pure springs
and to drink from them, and it is a joy to pick new flowers
and to seek a preeminent crown for my head from that place
whence the Muses had wreathed the temples of no one before;[49]   930
first because I am teaching about great things and proceeding
to free the mind from the narrow bonds of religion,
next because I am writing so clear a poem about so obscure
a subject, touching everything with the charm of the Muses.
For this too seems to be not without reason.   935
But just as when physicians try to give loathsome wormwood
to children, they first touch the rim of the cup all

---

[44] Lines 817-819.

[45] Lucretius uses the Latin terms *ligna* ("wood, firs") and *ignis* ("fires").

[46] 1.919-920 are nearly identical to 2.976-977.

[47] A thyrsus was a wand whose tip was wrapped with ivy or vine leaves.
     It was a symbol of the worship of Dionysus and poetic inspiration.

[48] Pierides = the daughters of Pierus, i.e. , the Muses.

[49] Lucretius claims to be the first Roman to write a philosophic poem.

around with the sweet, golden liquid of honey,
so that the unsuspecting age of children may be tricked as far
940 as their lips, and so that meanwhile the child might drink down
the bitter wormwood juice and though deceived, be not deceased,
but rather by such means be restored and become well,
so I now, since this system seems for the most part to be
too bitter to those who have not tried it and
945 the common people shrink back from it, I wanted to explain
our system to you in sweet-spoken Pierian[50] song
and touch it, so to speak, with the sweet honey of the Muses.
I have done so in the hope I might in this way be able to hold
your attention in our verses, until you look into the whole
950 nature of things, with what shape it is endowed and exists.[51]
But since I have shown that the most solid bodies of matter
are indestructible and fly around forever without stopping,
now come, let us unfold whether there is a limit to their sum
or not; and likewise that which has been discovered to be void
955 or place or space, in which all things take place,
let us consider whether it is all at bottom bounded, or whether
it stretches out, limitless in extent and immensely deep.
Therefore all that exists is bounded in no direction
of its ways; for in that case it would have to have an end point.
960 And, moreover, it seems that there cannot be an endpoint for anything,
unless there is something beyond it which limits it, so that there is seen
    to be
a place beyond which this nature of our senses cannot follow.
Now since it must be confessed that there is nothing outside the universe,
it does not have an endpoint, and therefore lacks boundary and limit.
965 It does not matter in what region of the universe you place yourself;
so true is it that whatever place anyone occupies, he leaves
the universe infinite in all directions to the same extent.
Besides, suppose now that the totality of space
were to be limited: if someone were to run all the way
970 to its final boundaries and hurl a flying spear,
do you prefer to think that, spun with great strength,
it would go where it was sent, and fly far,
or do you think that something would be able to stop and block it?
For you must admit and accept one of the two alternatives.
975 Either choice will prevent your escape and force you
to concede that the universe stretches forth without limit.
For whether there is something that stops it and makes it so

---

[50] i.e. , sacred to the Muses.

[51] 1.926-950 = 4.1-25, with a few minor differences.

that it cannot go where it was sent and reach its goal, or whether
it travels beyond, it did not set out from the end of the universe.
In this way I will proceed and, wherever you place the ultimate   **980**
boundaries, I will ask, "What finally happens to the spear?"
It will turn out that an end of the universe cannot be fixed,
and that an opportunity for flight always extends the flight.
Besides, if the whole space of the entire sum of things
had been shut in and were fixed with certain boundaries,   **985**
and had been enclosed, by now the supply of matter would everywhere
have flowed to the bottom because of its solidity and weight.
Nothing could move beneath the cover of the sky,
nor would there be a sky at all nor light of the sun,
since all matter would lie gathered in a heap,   **990**
having by now sunk down in infinite time.
But as things are, of course, no rest has been given to the bodies
of the first beginnings, since there is absolutely no bottom
where they could flow together, so to speak, and take their places.
All things are always being carried along   **995**
in constant motion on all sides, and bodies of matter
are supplied from below, speeding out of infinite space.
Finally, before our eyes one thing is seen to limit
another: the air hedges in hills, and mountains the air.
Land bounds the sea, and sea, in return, bounds all lands,   **1000**
whereas truly there is nothing which could limit the universe from the
        outside.
Therefore the nature of place and the space of the abyss
is such that neither could shining thunderbolts traverse it on their
        endless
journey, gliding on through an eternal tract of time,
nor, further, by their travelling make it so that there remained any less
        to go,   **1005**
such an immense supply of space extends everywhere for things,
with no limits anywhere in any direction.
Moreover, nature insures that the sum of things cannot
on its own set a limit to itself, and forces body
to be bounded by void, and what is void to be bounded by body,   **1010**
so that it thus renders the universe infinite by their alternation,
or else one of the two, if the other of them does not bound it,
in its single nature extends nevertheless without limit.[52]
<But if the void were limited, the infinite atoms would not
have a place to exist; and if matter were limited>

---

[52] There is a lacuna after 1013. Following Diels' suggestion, I have supplied
      a possible rendering of what might be missing.

neither the sea nor the land nor the bright regions of the sky
1015 nor the human race nor the holy bodies of the gods
would be able to exist for even a small fraction of an hour.
For the supply of matter, wrenched apart from its union,
would have been dissolved and carried along through the great void,
or, more accurately, it never would have come together and created
1020 anything, since in its scattered state it could not have been brought
together.
For certainly not by design did the first beginnings of things
arrange themselves in their order with keen intent, nor surely
did they reach an agreement about what motions each would take.
But since many of them are moved in many ways throughout the
1025   universe
and from endless time are stirred up and excited by collisions,
by trying motions and unions of every kind
they finally arrive at arrangements like those
which produce and maintain this sum of things.[53]
And it too, preserved for many great years
1030 when once it had been cast into suitable motions,
insures that rivers replenish the greedy sea with the abundant
waves of their streams, and that the earth, nurtured by the sun's heat,
renews its offspring, and that the race of living things is bred
and flourishes, and that the gliding fires of heaven live on.
1035 In no way would they do this, unless a supply
of matter could rise up from the infinite, from which they are accustomed
to make up all that is lost in due time.
For just as the nature of living things, when deprived of food,
loses bulk and fades, so all things ought
1040 to be dissolved as soon as matter fails to be supplied
when it is for whatever reason diverted from its course.
Nor are blows from the outside in all directions able
to maintain every world that has been gathered together.
Indeed they can repeatedly pound and preserve a part,
1045 until others arrive and the sum is able to be supplied.
But sometimes they are forced to spring back, and in so doing
provide for the first beginnings of things the space and opportunity
for escape, so that they can be free and move away from their unions.
Wherefore again and again it is necessary that many things
1050 be provided, and yet in order that even blows too be present,
it is necessary that the supply of matter be everywhere infinite.
In these matters flee far from believing, Memmius,

---

[53] "This sum of things" = "our world"

what some say:[54] that everything tends to the center of the universe,
and that thus the nature of the world stands firm without any
external blows, and that top and bottom cannot be undone   1055
in any direction, because all things tend toward the center
(if you can believe that anything is able to stand on itself!).
And they say that all heavy things that are under the earth
press upwards and rest on the earth upside down,
just like the images of things we now see in water.   1060
And in a similar way they maintain that animals wander around
upside down, and cannot fall from the earth
to the regions of space below, anymore than our bodies
of their own accord can fly off into regions of the sky.
And that when they see the sun, we gaze upon the stars   1065
of the night, and that they share with us in alternation
the seasons of the sky, and have nights equal to our days.
But empty <error has commended> these false things to fools,[55]
because they have tackled <the problem with twisted reasoning.>
For there can be no center, <since the universe is>   1070
infinite. Nor indeed, if there now <were a center,>
would anything be able to rest for all that, rather
than <be driven> far away for any other reason.
For all place and space, which <we call> void,
whether at the center or not at the center, <must> yield   1075
equally to heavy bodies, wherever their movements tend.
Nor is there any place where when bodies reach it
the power of weight is lost and they stand still in the void.
Nor ought that which is void hold up anything,
but must, as its own nature requires, hasten to yield.   1080
Therefore not at all in this manner can things be held
together in union, overcome by a longing for the center.
Moreover, since they posit that not all bodies
tend to the center, but those of earth and water,
the moisture of the sea and the great waters from the mountains,[56] **(1086) 1085**
and the things which are contained in an earthly body, so to
       speak;   **(1085)**
but on the contrary they explain that the light breezes of the air
and hot fires are carried away together from the center,

---

[54] Lucretius probably has the Aristotelian and perhaps Stoic conceptions
of the world in mind.

[55] The text of lines 1068-1075 is damaged. I have translated the lines with
Munro's suggested additions.

[56] The text is uncertain. I have followed editors who transpose lines 1085
and 1086.

and so the entire aether[57] twinkles all around with stars
1090 and the flames of the sun are fed in the sky-blue sky,
      because all heat, fleeing from the center, collects there,
      nor further could the highest branches of trees leaf out,
      unless each is fed little by little from the earth...[58]

    *   *   *   *   *   *   *   *   *   *   *   *   *

1102 lest, in the winged way of flames the walls of the world
      suddenly fly away and dissolve in the great void,
      and lest other things follow in a similar way,
1105 lest the thundering regions of the sky rush upwards,
      the earth suddenly snatch itself from under our feet,
      and all of it, among the scattered ruins of things and sky
      that have let their bodies go, depart through the vast void,
      so that in an instant of time nothing remains behind
1110 except empty space and invisible first beginnings.
      For from whatever part you will first decide bodies are missing,
      this part will be the door of death for things,
      and by it the whole throng of matter will make its exit.
      Thus you will learn these things, led with little effort.
1115 For one thing will be clarified by another, nor will dark night
      deprive you of your way, until you see deeply into the ultimate
      principles of nature: so things will illuminate other things.

---

[57] "Aether" = the upper air.
[58] Lines 1094-1101 are lost.

ON THE NATURE OF THINGS

BOOK II

Sweet it is, when the wind whips the water on the great sea,
to gaze from the land upon the great struggles of another,
not because it is a delightful pleasure for anyone to be distressed,
but because it is sweet to observe those evils which you lack yourself.
Sweet, too, to gaze upon the great contests of war   **(6) 5**
staged on the plains, when you are free from all danger.   **(5)**
But nothing is more delightful than to possess sanctuaries
which are lofty, peaceful, and well fortified by the teachings of the
    wise.
From there you can look down upon others and see them lose
their way here and there and wander, seeking a road through life,   **10**
struggling with their wits, striving with their high birth,
exerting themselves night and day with outstanding effort
to rise to the level of the greatest wealth and to have mastery over things.
O wretched minds of men, o blind hearts!
In what darkness of life and in what great dangers   **15**
this little span of time is spent! Don't you see
that nature cries out for nothing except that somehow
pain be separated and absent from the body, and that she enjoy in the
    mind
pleasant feelings, and be far from care and fear?
Therefore we see that there is need for very little   **20**
for our bodily nature, just enough to take away pain
and also to spread out many delights before us;
nor does nature itself ever ask for anything more pleasing,
if there are no golden statues of youths in the halls,
holding fire-bearing torches in their right hands,   **25**
so illumination can be supplied for banquets at nighttime,[1]
if the house does not gleam with silver and shine with gold,
and if the gilded and paneled roof timbers do not resound with the
    lyre,

---

[1] Lines 24-26 echo Homer, *Odyssey* VII. 100-102.

when nevertheless people lie in groups on the soft grass
30 beside a stream of water beneath the branches of a tall tree
and at little expense delightfully tend to their bodies,
especially when the weather smiles and the seasons of the year
sprinkle the green-growing grass with flowers.
Nor do hot fevers leave the body more quickly,
35 if you lie on embroidered cloth and blushing purple sheets,
than if you have to recuperate under common cloth.
Wherefore since neither wealth nor high birth nor the glory of ruling
do our body any good at all, so it remains,
that they cannot be thought to benefit our mind at all either.
40 Unless by chance when you see your legions seething about
on the Campus Martius[2] as they rouse pretend images of war,
well supported by reinforcements and a force of cavalry,
decked out in arms and all equally spirited,[3]
then these things chase fear-produced and frightened
45 religious superstitions from the mind, and fears of death
then leave your heart unoccupied and free from care.
But if we see that these things are ridiculous and frivolous,
and in truth the fears of men and the cares that follow them
neither fear the clash of arms nor fierce weapons,
50 and boldly walk among kings and those who have power over things,
and do not stand in awe of the gleam of gold
nor the shining brilliance of a purple-colored garment,
why do you doubt that all of this power belongs to reason,
especially since all life struggles in the darkness?
55 For just like children who tremble and fear everything
in the dark night, so we are afraid in the light sometimes
of things that ought to be no more feared than
the things that children tremble at and imagine will happen.
Therefore this fear and darkness of the mind must be shattered
60 apart not by the rays of the sun and the clear shafts
of the day but by the external appearance and inner law of nature.[4]
Now come, I will explain with what motion the generating bodies
of matter generate different things, and destroy what has been
    generated,
and by what force they are compelled to do this, and what

---

[2] The phrase *per loca campi*, literally "throughout the surface of the plain,"
    probably refers to the Campus Martius ("Field of Mars"), a large field
    by the Tiber River in Rome that the Romans used for exercise and military
    practice.

[3] There are textual difficulties with both lines 42 and 43.

[4] 2.55-61 = 3.87-93, 6.35-41; 2.59-61 = 1.146-148.

velocity of voyaging through the vast void has been assigned to them. **65**
You remember to give yourself over to my words.
For certainly matter does not cohere to itself close-packed,
since we see each thing decrease and observe all
things flowing away, so to speak, with the length of time,
and old age taking them away from our sight. **70**
But nevertheless the sum of things is seen to remain safe,
because whatever bodies are lost from one thing
diminish what they depart, and increase that to which they have come.
They force the former to deteriorate, but the latter on the contrary to
    flourish,
nor do they remain there. So the sum of things is renewed **75**
always, and mortal creatures live by mutual exchange.
Some races increase, others are diminished,
and in a short time the generations of living creatures change
and like runners pass on the torch of life.
If you think that the first beginnings of things can stop **80**
and by stopping produce new motions among things,
you are wandering astray, far from true reasoning.
For since the first beginnings wander through the void,
they must all be borne along by their own weight
or by chance by the blow of another. For when, hastening, they often **85**
have met and collided, it happens that they leap apart suddenly
in different directions. Nor is this so amazing, since they are extremely
hard in their solid weight, and nothing blocks them from behind.
And so that you may perceive all the more that all the bodies of matter
are tossed around, remember that there is no bottom at all **90**
in the sum of the whole, nor do the first bodies have a place
to sit and rest, since space is without limit and bounds,
and I have shown with many words that it is immense and lies open
everywhere in all directions, and have proved it by sure reasoning.
Since this is the case, doubtless no rest **95**
has been granted to the first bodies throughout the deep void.
Rather, driven on in continuous and varied motion,
some are pressed together and then leap apart at great intervals,
others move violently at small distances after the blow.
And whichever ones in their more tightly condensed union **100**
meet and leap back at tiny intervals,
and are themselves tangled together in their intricate shapes,
these make up the strong roots of rock
and the brute bodies of iron, and others of this type.
Of the others which wander farther through the great void, **105**
a few leap far apart and rebound from afar
at great distances. These supply us
with thin air and the brilliant light of the sun.

And many, moreover, wander through the great void,
which have been cast back from the unions which make things, nor
110   could
they ever be incorporated and unite their motions, too.
Of this process, as I recall, a model and image
always exists and is present before our eyes.
For gaze closely, whenever the rays of the sun enter
115   and pour their light through the dark places of houses.
You will see many minute bodies mixed in many ways
through empty space in the very light of the rays,
and, as if in an unending struggle, giving rise to battles
and fights, struggling in squadrons and never taking a rest,
120   driven on by their frequent meetings and partings.
So you can conjecture from this how the first beginnings of things
are always tossed about in the great void,
at least in so far as a small thing is able to provide
a model of great things and the traces of a concept.[5]
125   It is even more important that you turn your attention to these bodies
that are seen to create disturbances in the rays of the sun,
because such disturbances indicate that there are also motions
of matter lurking below, hidden and unseen.
For you will see many of them there, struck by invisible blows,
130   change direction and, beaten back again, be turned
now this way, now that, everywhere in all directions.
Of course this wandering of all of them comes from the first beginnings.
For first the first bodies of things are moved by themselves;
next those bodies, which are composed of small compounds
135   and are so to speak nearest to the strength of the first beginnings,
are struck by their invisible blows and moved, and they themselves
in their turn stir up bodies that are slightly bigger.
So motion arises from the first beginnings and gradually reaches
the level of our senses, so that those things are moved
140   also which we are able to see in the light of the sun,
yet by what blows they do this is not readily apparent.
Now what speed has been given to the bodies of matter
you can learn in a few words from this, Memmius:
First, when dawn sprinkles the earth with new light
145   and many kinds of birds, flying through remote groves
through the soft air, fill the places with flowing voices,
how suddenly the sun, rising at this time, is accustomed

---

[5] With the word "concept" (*notitia*), Lucretius here refers to the Epicurean
doctrine of "general concept" or "preconception" (in Greek, *prolêpsis*).
For more on this doctrine, see Introduction p. xvii.

to pour forth and clothe everything with its light,
we see is plain and obvious to everybody.
But that heat and glad light which the sun emits   **150**
does not travel through empty void. It is forced to go
more slowly, while it beats aside, so to speak, the waves of air.
Nor do the particles of heat travel one by one,
but rather entangled and crowded together among themselves.
Therefore at the same time they are restrained by one another   **155**
and are hindered from the outside, so that they are forced to travel more
   slowly.
But the primary bodies which exist in their solid singleness,
when they travel through the empty void, and nothing delays them
    from without
and they, themselves forming a unity from their own parts,
are carried along in haste in the one direction in which   **160**
they began to move, ought of course to surpass in speed
and be carried along much more quickly than the light of the sun,
and cover many times the extent of space in the same
time in which the flashing light of the sun spreads across the sky.[6]

         *   *   *   *   *   *   *   *   *   *   *   *   *

nor to pursue the first beginnings of things one by one,   **165**
to see in what way each is borne along.
But in opposition to this, certain people,[7] ignorant about matter,
believe that without the power of the gods nature is unable,
in ways so suitable to the needs of human beings,
to change the seasons of the years and to produce crops   **170**
and other things too, which divine pleasure, the guide of life,
persuades mortals to approach, herself leading them
and through the affairs of Venus persuading them to propagate their
    generations,
so that the human race does not go extinct. When they imagine that the
    gods
have arranged everything for the sake of human beings, in every   **175**
respect they are seen to have fallen far from true reasoning.
For even though I were ignorant about what first bodies of things are,
this nevertheless I would dare to prove from the very ways
of the sky and establish from many other things:
that the nature of the world has in no way been created for us   **180**
by the gods, so great are the faults with which it stands endowed.
These I will make clear to you later,[8] Memmius.

---

[6] There is a lacuna in the text after line 164.

[7] Although Lucretius does not name them, this group could include the
    Academics, Peripatetics, and Stoics.

[8] 5.195–234.

Now I will explain that which remains concerning motion.
Now is the place, I think, in these matters to prove
185 to you this, too: that nothing corporeal is able
by its own force to be borne upwards and move upwards.
Don't let bodies of fire deceive you in this respect.
For upwards flames arise and grow larger,
and upwards grow shining crops and trees, although all things
190 with weight, in so far as in them lies, are borne downwards.
Nor, when fires leap up on the roofs of houses
and with quick flames have a taste of beams and rafters,
should we think that they act on their own, shot up without force.
It is the same when blood, sent from our body, shoots out
195 leaping on high and spatters its red drops around.
And don't you also see with what great force fluid water
spits out beams and rafters? For the deeper many of us have pushed
     them
straight down and pressed with great force and effort,
all the more eagerly does it throw them up and send them back,
200 so that they leap up and come more than half way out.
Nor yet do we doubt, I think, that all these, in so far
as in them lies, are borne downward through the empty void.
In the same way, therefore, flames also must be able
to ascend squeezed upwards through the breezes of the air, although
205 their weights, in so far as in them lies, fight to lead them downwards.
Don't you see at night in the sky that shooting stars,
flying on high, trail long stretches of flames
in whatever direction nature provides a passage?
Don't you perceive that stars and constellations fall to earth?
210 The sun, too, from the top of the sky distributes its heat
in all directions and sows the fields with light;
thus too is the heat of the sun turned to earth.
And you perceive that bolts of lightning fly crosswise through the rain,
as now here and now there fire bursts out of the clouds
215 and speeds about. The fiery force falls commonly to earth.
In this matter there is this, too, that I want you to understand,
that when the first bodies are moving straight downward through the
     void
by their own weight, at times completely undetermined
and in undetermined places they swerve a little from their course,
220 but only so much as you could call a change of motion.[9]

---

[9] Lucretius here introduces Epicurus' controversial doctrine of the random
"swerve" of atoms. This passage (216-293) is the most detailed account
of the swerve we have. No mention of it has been found in the works of
Epicurus that have survived, but passages in other authors

SWERVE

Because unless they were accustomed to swerving, all would fall
downwards like drops of rain through the deep void,
nor would a collision occur, nor would a blow be produced
by the first beginnings. Thus nature would never have created anything.
But if by chance anyone believes that heavier bodies,   **225**
because they are carried along more quickly straight through the void,
fall upon lighter ones from above and so produce
the blows which are able to supply generating motions,
he goes astray, far from true reasoning.
For whatever things fall through water and insubstantial air   **230**
must hasten their falls in proportion to their weight,
since the body of water and the thin nature of air
are not at all able to delay each thing equally,
but yield more quickly when they are overcome by heavier things.
But on the other hand neither on any side nor at any   **235**
time can empty void hold up anything,
but must, as its nature requires, hasten to give way.
Therefore all must be borne on through the peaceful void
moved at equal rates, though not of equal weights.
Thus heavier bodies will never be able to fall on lighter   **240**
ones from above nor on their own to cause collisions which produce
the various motions through which nature accomplishes things.
Wherefore again and again it is necessary that bodies
swerve a little, but no more than a minimum,[10] lest we seem
to be inventing oblique motions, and the true facts refute it.   **245**
For we see that this is clear and manifest, that weights,
in so far as in them lies, cannot travel obliquely,
when they fall from above, as far as you can perceive.
But that it does not make itself swerve at all
from the straight direction of its path, who is there who can perceive? **250**
And next if every motion is always linked,

(including Cicero, Philodemus, Plutarch, Diogenes of Oenoanda, and
Plotinus) discuss it. How exactly Epicurus thought the swerve helped to
preserve "free will" (*libera voluntas* in Lucretius' Latin phrase) has been a
source of great controversy. For further discussion and bibliography,
see Furley (1967), Englert (1987), Long and Sedley (1987), Annas (1992),
and Purinton (1999).

[10] With the term "minimum," Lucretius refers to the Epicurean doctrine
that both space and time were not infinitely divisible and that there
were minimal units of space and time beyond which space and time
could not be further divided. Thus when Lucretius says that atoms
swerve "no more than a minimum," he means that they swerve no
more than one "minimum," i.e., the smallest possible unit of space. For
more on the Epicurean doctrine of the minimum see Long and Sedley
(1987) I.39-44.

and a new one always arises from an old one in sure succession,
and if by declining the primary bodies do not make
a certain beginning of motion to burst the laws of fate,
255 so that cause does not follow cause from infinity,
from where does there arise for living creatures throughout the world,
from where, I say, is this free will, torn from fate,
by which we go wherever pleasure leads each of us,
and likewise decline our motions at no fixed time
260 or fixed region of space, but where the mind itself carries us?
For doubtless one's own will provides for each a beginning
of these things, and from it motions stream through the limbs.
For don't you also see that while the starting gates drop in an instant,
the desirous force of the horses is nevertheless not able
265 to burst forth as suddenly as the mind itself desires?
For the entire store of matter throughout the whole body has
to be stimulated to motion, so that once it is stimulated and has exerted
        itself
throughout every limb it can follow the mind's eagerness.
So you can see that a beginning of motion is created in the heart,
270 and comes forth first from the will of the mind,
and then is conveyed through the whole body and limbs.
Nor is it similar to when we are struck by a blow and travel forward
by the great strength and great constraint of another.
For then it is clear that the whole matter of our entire
275 body moves and is seized against our will,
until the will reins it in throughout the limbs.
Now you see, don't you, that although an external force pushes many,
and often forces them to move forward and to be thrown headlong
against their will, there is nevertheless something in our breast
280 which is able to offer resistance and fight back?
And at its bidding too the store of matter
is sometimes forced to change direction through the limbs and joints,
and although it is pushed forward, it is checked and again comes to
        rest.
Wherefore it is also necessary to admit that there is likewise in the
        atoms
285 another cause of motions besides collisions and weight,
from which comes this innate power in us,
since we see that nothing can come into being from nothing.
For weight prevents everything from happening by blows
as if by external force. But so that the mind itself
290 has no internal necessity in performing all its actions,
and is not forced as if conquered to bear and suffer,
the tiny swerve of the atoms at no fixed region
of space nor fixed time brings it about.

Nor was the supply of matter ever more tightly packed,
nor set apart at greater intervals, either.   **295**
For neither does anything add to it, nor does anything perish from it.
Wherefore with whatever motions the bodies of the first beginnings
now move, they moved with the same motions in ages past,
and in the future they will always be carried along in a similar way,
and whatever things usually arise will arise under the same   **300**
conditions and will exist and grow and flourish in their strength,
in so far as it is granted to each through the laws of nature.
Nor is any force capable of changing the sum of things.
For neither is there anything outside the universe to which   ●
any kind of matter can flee, nor is there a place where   **305**
a new force can arise and burst into the universe and change
the whole nature of things and alter its motions.
In these matters the following is not to be wondered at:
why, when all the first beginnings of things are in motion,
yet the sum total seems to stand totally at rest,   **310**
except if something is moved with its own body.
For the whole nature of the primary bodies lies far below
our senses. Therefore, since you cannot now see
the primary bodies themselves, they abscond with their motions, too,
especially when even those things we can see often conceal   **315**
their motions, if they are separated from us by a great distance.
For often on the hillside, cropping their glad pastures,
wool-bearing flocks creep on wherever the grass, sparkling
with fresh dew, calls out and invites each of them,
and the lambs, now full, play and gently butt their heads.   **320**
All these things appear blurred to us from a distance,
and stand still like a white blotch on a green hillside.
Moreover, when great legions fill places on the plains
with their marching, stirring up pretend images of war,
and the gleam raises itself to the sky and all the earth around   **325**
glitters back with bronze and beneath from the force of the men
noise rises from their feet, and the mountains, struck by their shouting,
hurl back their voices to the stars of heaven,
and the horsemen dart about and suddenly charge across
the middle of the plain, shaking it with their mighty attack —   **330**
and nevertheless there is a certain place on the tall mountains, from
    which
they appear to be still and remain unmoved as a gleam on the plains.
Now come, see next of what kinds are the first beginnings
of all things, and how far different they are
in form, how varied they are in their many kinds of shapes.   **335**
Not that only a few are endowed with similar shape,
but that they are not everywhere all like all.

And no wonder: For since the supply of them is so great,
that there is neither a limit, as I have shown,[11] nor any total,
340 they doubtless all should not be precisely equal
in form to all, nor furnished with a similar shape.
Besides, the human race, and the mute, swimming schools
of scaly fish, and the glad flocks and wild beasts,
and the different kinds of birds which throng the gladdening watering
345 places around river banks, springs, and lakes,
and which frequent and frequently fly through remote groves —
go ahead, choose anyone you want from any kind —
still you will find that they differ from each other in shape.
Nor in any other way could an offspring recognize its mother,
nor a mother its offspring. But we see that they can, and that they
350   appear
to be recognized by one another no less than people are.
For often before the esteemed shrines of the gods a calf
is sacrificed and falls beside the incense-burning altars,
breathing out a hot river of blood from its breast.
But its mother, bereft of her child, and wandering about the green
355   pasture,
looks for its footprints pressed into the ground by its cloven hoofs,
searching every place with her eyes, if she might only be able
to see her lost young, and halting she fills
the leafy grove with her wailing and frequently returns
360 to the stable, pierced through with longing for her calf.
Neither tender willows, nor the grass enlivened by the dew,
nor any rivers gliding along on full banks
are able to soothe her mind and remove her sudden care,
nor are the appearances of other calves in the glad pastures
365 able to divert her mind and ease her care.
So unceasingly does she seek a thing that is her own and known to her.
Besides, young kids with their tremulous voices
recognize their horned mothers, and the butting lambs
the flocks of bleating sheep. So, as nature requires,
370 they usually all run to their own udders of milk.
Finally, choose any kind of grain, and you will still see
that each is not identical to others in its own class,
but that certain differences of form run throughout.
And in the same way we see the class of shells
375 paint the bosom of the earth, where with soft waves
the sea pounds the thirsty sand on the curving shoreline.
Wherefore again and again in the same way it is necessary,
since the first beginnings of things exist by nature and were not

---

[11] l. 921-1117.

made by hand after the fixed form of one thing,
that some of them fly around with shapes which differ from each other. **380**
It is very easy by the reasoning power of the mind for us
to explain why the fire of lightning is much more penetrating
than our fire that arises from terrestrial timber.
For you can say that the heavenly fire of lightning
is more subtle and is made up of small shapes **385**
and so passes through openings which our fire,
arising from wood and made from timber, cannot.
Besides, light passes through horn, but rain
is repelled. And why, unless those bodies of light were smaller
than those which make up the refreshing liquid of water? **390**
And we see wine flow as quickly as you want through a colander,
but in contrast slow olive oil takes its time,
either because no doubt it is made up of elements which are larger,
or more hooked and entangled with one another,
and so it happens that the individual first beginnings **395**
cannot be so suddenly separated from each other
and ooze out through their own individual openings.
In addition, the liquids of honey and milk produce
a pleasant sensation on the tongue as they are rolled in the mouth,
but in contrast the foul nature of wormwood and wild **400**
centaury[12] contorts the mouth with a horrible taste.
Thus you may easily recognize that those things which can touch
the senses pleasantly are made up of smooth and round atoms,
but in contrast whatever things seem bitter and harsh are held
entangled with one another by atoms which are more hooked, **405**
and consequently they are accustomed to tear open paths
into our senses and burst through the body by their entrance.
Finally, all things that are good and bad for the senses
to touch fight with one another, made from different shapes;
lest by chance you should think the sharp shudder **410**
of a shrieking saw is made up of atoms as smooth
as musical melodies which musicians awaken and shape
on the strings with their agile fingers, and lest you think
the first beginnings penetrate people's noses
with similar shapes when they burn foul corpses, **415**
as when the stage has just been sprinkled with Cilician saffron[13]
and the altar nearby breathes scents from Panchaea,[14]

---

[12] Centaury was a plant used to treat various ailments.

[13] Before a performance the Roman stage was sprinkled with a saffron solution to make it smell good. The best saffron came from Cilicia (Turkey).

[14] Panchaea was a mythical island supposedly located east of Arabia.

and lest you decide that the soothing colors of things
which can feed the eyes are made up of seeds like those
420 which sting the pupil and force it to tears,
or appear awful and foul with a horrible appearance.
For every shape that delights the senses has not
been created without some smoothness in the first beginnings.
But, in contrast, whatever shape is annoying and harsh,
425 has been found to be not without some roughness in its matter.
And there are those first beginnings, too, which in their turn are thought
rightly neither to be smooth nor completely hooked with curved points,
but rather with angles projecting out a little, the sort which
would tickle the senses rather than cause them any harm.
430 Now of this sort are wine lees and the taste of elecampane.[15]
And next, that hot fires and cold frost
are toothed in different ways to sting the senses
of the body, the touch of each of them indicates to us.
For touch, yes touch, by the holy powers of the gods,
435 is a sense of the body, either when a thing works itself
in from the outside, or when what arises in the body harms it,
or gives delight as it exits through the generating acts of Venus,
or after a blow when the seeds create a disturbance in the body itself
and, stirred up by one another, confuse the senses,
440 as if by chance you yourself were now to hit
some part of your body and were to see what it was like.
Therefore it is necessary that the shapes of the first beginnings should
differ greatly, since they can produce various sensations.
Next, the things which seem hard and dense to us
445 must be held together and joined deep within by first beginnings
that are more hooked to one another and branch-like.
Now in this group especially adamantine rocks stand
in the front ranks, accustomed as they are to defy blows,
and mighty flint-stones and the strength of hard iron,
450 and bronze fixtures that squeal as they withstand the door bolts.
And those things ought to be made of lighter and rounder
first beginnings, which are liquid and have a fluid body.
For it is just as easy to scoop poppy seeds as water;
the individual globules are not hindered by each other,
455 and a poppy seed, when struck, rolls just as easily downhill.
Finally, all things which you see fly apart
in an instant, like smoke, clouds, and flames, even if they are not
composed entirely out of smooth and round first beginnings,
nevertheless must still not be hampered by entangled first beginnings,

---

[15] Elecampane is a plant with a tart and bitter flavor.

so that they are able to sting the body and penetrate rocks,   **460**
and nevertheless not cling together. Thus you may be able
to recognize easily that whatever we see to be spiked to the senses
are made up not of entangled, but sharp, first beginnings.
But that you see that the same things are fluid and bitter,
like the brine of the sea, ought in no way to seem remarkable;   **465**
For because it is fluid, it is composed of smooth and round particles,
and rough bodies of pain are mixed in with them.
Nor nevertheless must these bodies be held hooked together.
And it is clear nevertheless that they are spherical, although they are
     rough,
so that they can roll along and at the same time hurt the senses.   **470**
And so that you think all the more that rough first beginnings
are mixed with smooth and create the bitter body of Neptune,[16]
there is a means of separating them and observing how
sweet water, when it is filtered through earth a number
of times, flows into a pit and becomes fresh.   **475**
For it leaves above the elements of foul brine,
since the rough elements can get stuck more easily in the earth.
Because I have shown this, [17] I will go on to subjoin a principle
which is connected to this and is therefore convincing, that the first
     elements
of things differ in shape in a limited number of ways.[18]   **480**
For if it were not so, once again then certain seeds
will have to possess bodies of unlimited size.
For in the same single smallness of any first body
shapes cannot vary much from one to another.
For imagine that the first bodies are composed of three minimal   **485**
parts, or make them larger by adding a few more.
Certainly when you have tried all those parts of one body,
placing them at top and bottom, interchanging right and left,
investigating in every way what appearance of form
of its whole body each arrangement produces,   **490**
beyond that, if by chance you want to vary the shapes,
other minimal parts will have to be added. From which it will follow,
that by similar reasoning the order will require other minimal

---

[16] The "bitter body of Neptune" = seawater.

[17] It is hard to see to what Lucretius is here referring. Some editors
(including Brieger and Giussani) think a passage has dropped out; others,
like Bailey, think that Lucretius refers to a proof that there is a limit to
the size of atoms which he intended to write but never got around to
including in the poem.

[18] Cf. Epicurus, *Letter to Herodotus* 42.

parts, if by chance you want to vary the shapes again.
495 Therefore increase in bulk is an immediate consequence of
novelty of forms. Wherefore there is no way that you are able
to believe that the seeds differ infinitely in form.
Otherwise you would force some seeds to be of enormous maxitude, [19]
which I have already shown above can never win approval.
500 For then, let me tell you, oriental garments and shining Meliboean[20]
purple tinged with the color of Thessalian shells,
and the golden races of peacocks imbued with laughing grace,
would lie vanquished by the new colors of things,
and the fragrance of myrrh and the flavor of honey would be spurned.
505 The singing of swans, and the songs of Phoebus skillfully played
on the strings, would be defeated and silenced in a similar way.
For one thing would always be arising more outstanding than the rest.
And likewise everything could decline in the other direction into a
     worse
state, just as we said they might into a better state.
510 For, in contrast, one thing would always be more offensive than the rest
to noses, ears, eyes, and the taste of the mouth.
Since this is not so, but a fixed limit has been assigned to things
and controls the range at both ends, it must be admitted
that matter too differs in its shapes to a limited degree.
515 Next, from fires all the way up to the cold frosts of winter
there is a limit, and it is measured back again in the same way.
For all heat and cold and levels of warmth in the middle
lie between two extremes, and cover the range in succession.
Therefore created things differ in limited ways,
520 since they are marked at both extremes by sharp points,
beset on the one side by flames, and on the other by stiff frosts.
Because I have shown this, I will proceed to subjoin a principle
which is connected to this and is therefore convincing, that the first
     elements
of things which have been made with shape similar to one another
525 are infinite in number.[21] For since the difference between forms
is finite, it is necessary that those forms which are similar
be infinite in number, or the sum total of matter
will be finite, which I have proved[22] not to be the case,
showing in my verses that the tiny bodies of matter

---

[19] The word "maxitude" translates Lucretius' *maximitate*, a word he
apparently coined to replace the metrically inadmissible *magnitudine*.

[20] Meliboea was a town on the coast of Thessaly in Greece.

[21] Cf. Epicurus *Letter to Herodotus* 42.

[22] 1.1008-1051.

from the infinite continue to hold together the totality   **530**
of things by a continual harness-team of blows from all sides.
For whereas you see that certain animals are rather rare,
and perceive that there is in them a less fertile nature,
still in another region and place, and in remote lands,
there may be many of this kind that replenish the number.[23]   **535**
So we see this especially among four footed beasts
in the case of snake-handed elephants. India is protected
by an ivory wall of many thousands of these,
so that it can never be deeply penetrated by an attack, so great
is the supply of those beasts of which we see so few examples.   **540**
But yet if I concede this, too — let there be something
as unique as you want, all alone with the body it was born with,
which nothing in the whole wide world resembles —
still, unless there is an infinite supply of matter,
from which it can be conceived and brought to birth, it will not   **545**
be able to be created, nor, what is more, to grow and be nourished.
For indeed if I assume this, too — that the bodies which generate
this one thing were finite, tossed about through the universe —
whence, where, by what force, and how will they meet
and congregate in such a great ocean and foreign throng of matter?   **550**
They do not have, I believe, a way of uniting,
but, just as when many great shipwrecks have occurred,
the great sea habitually scatters the transoms, ribs,
sail-yards, prow, masts, and oars as they bob along,
so that the stern-fittings, floating to all the lands' shores,   **555**
make their appearance and issue their warning to mortals,
so that they resolve to shun the traps, power, and treachery
of the faithless sea, and not trust it at any time
when the deceptive allure of the serene sea smiles:
so if you once decide that certain first beginnings   **560**
are finite in number, currents of matter moving in different
directions ought to scatter and sprinkle them through all time,
so that never could they be pressed together and united in union,
nor remain in union, nor be added to and grow.
That both of these things happen obvious facts make plain: **565**
that things are born and, once generated, are able to increase.
Therefore it is clear that the first beginnings of things of each

---

[23] Lucretius here refers to the Epicurean doctrine of *isonomia*, or "equal distribution," "equilibrium." According to Cicero in *On the Nature of the Gods* 1.19.50, Epicurus taught that there was an equal distribution of things in the universe. If some things seem rarer in one part of the universe, there must be more of them in other parts of the universe to balance things out.

kind are infinite, and from them all things are composed.
And therefore neither can destructive motions prevail
570 forever and eternally entomb the forces of preservation,
nor further are the motions which generate and make things increase
able to keep created things forever safe.
Thus a war is waged with a well-balanced contest
of the first beginnings, carried on throughout infinite time.
575 Now here and now there the vital principles of things conquer
and are conquered in the same way. Funeral rites are intermingled
with the cries babies raise when they gaze upon the shores of light.
Nor has any night followed day or dawn followed night,
which has not heard mixed with the weak wailing of babies
580 the lamentations which accompany death and dark funeral rites.
This point also in these matters it is good to keep
tightly sealed and to hold it in mind melded to memory,
that there is not one thing whose nature is manifest to our sight
which is composed of only one type of first beginning,
585 nor is there anything which is not made from well-mixed seed.
And whatever possesses many more capacities and powers
in itself, shows thereby that there are very many types
and varying shapes of first beginnings in it.
First, the earth has first bodies in it,
590 from which fountains churning up frigid water continually renew
the boundless sea, and has first bodies, from which fires arise.
For in many places the earth's topsoil has a fiery glow,
while from its innermost depths Mt. Etna's[24] onslaught rages with fire.
Then too it has particles in it from which it can send forth
595 shining crops and glad trees for the races of men,
from which, too, it can offer streams, leafy branches,
and glad food to the mountain-roaming race of wild beasts.
Thus the earth alone is called the Great Mother of the gods,[25]
the mother of wild beasts, and the generating source of our bodies.
600 The ancient, learned poets of the Greeks sang that she
from her throne on a chariot drives two yoked lions,
thus teaching that the great earth hangs in a stretch
of air and that earth cannot sit upon earth.

---

[24] Mt. Etna is a volcano in Sicily, famous in antiquity for its violent eruptions.

[25] Lucretius here refers to Cybele, the great mother-goddess of Anatolia (in Turkey), an important deity whose worship was introduced to Rome in 205/204 BC. She was worshiped annually with public games during the festival of the Megalensia. She was often represented, as here, with lions and wearing a crown in the shape of city walls.

They attached the wild beasts, because however wild an offspring is,
it ought to be subdued and softened by the kindness of its parents. 605
They encircled the top of her head with a crown in the shape of a wall,
because she is fortified in excellent locations and upholds cities.
Endowed with this emblem, the image of the divine mother
is now carried with horrifying effect throughout the great earth.
The different races in accordance with the ancient practice of her sacred 610
rites call her the Idaean[26] mother and give her bands of Phrygians
as her attendants, because they declare that it is from these borders[27]
that crops first began to be produced for the whole world.
They bestow the Galli[28] upon her, because they wished to signify
that those who do violence to the divinity of their mother and have
been found 615
to be ungrateful to their parents must be thought unworthy
to bring forth living offspring into the shores of light.
Taut tambourines thunder under their palms and concave cymbals
clang around her, trumpets threaten with their hoarse-sounding song,
the hollow flute excites minds with the Phrygian mode,[29] 620
and they brandish weapons, symbols of their violent madness,
which have the power to terrify the unappreciative minds and unholy
hearts of ordinary people with fear by the power of the goddess.
Therefore as soon as she is carried through great cities
and silently blesses mortals with a voiceless greeting, 625
with silver and gold they strew the entire parade route,
enriching her with bountificial[30] alms, and they snow over her
with rose petals, providing shade to the mother and her band of
followers.
Here an armed band, whom the Greeks call by the name
"Curetes,"[31] whenever they play among the bands of Phrygians 630

---

[26] She is called "Idaean" after Mt. Ida in Phrygia (in Turkey).

[27] i.e., the borders of Phrygia.

[28] The Galli were priests of the Great Mother who became eunuchs through self-mutilation.

[29] The Phrygian mode of music was characterized in antiquity as "frenzied and emotional" (Aristotle *Politics* 1342b).

[30] "Bountificial" translates *largifica*, a word Lucretius apparently coined.

[31] As Lucretius goes on to explain, the Curetes were mythological male warriors of Crete who helped the goddess Rhea hide the infant Zeus (Jupiter) from his father Cronos (Saturn) on Mt. Dicte, covering up Zeus' crying by clashing their metal shields together. The Curetes were often identified or confused with the Corybantes, followers of the great mother goddess Cybele.

and leap up and down in measured time, gladdened by blood,
shaking their terrifying helmet-crests with a nod of their heads,
recall to mind the Dictaean Curetes, who are said
to have concealed once the famous wailing of Jupiter on Crete,
635 when as boys around a baby boy with agile dance[32]
637 in armor they beat bronze against bronze in measured time,
so that Saturn[33] might not get him and chew him in his jaws,
and produce an everlasting wound in his Mother's heart.
640 That is why they accompany the Great Mother with their arms,
or else it is because they signify that the goddess bids them
to be willing to defend their fatherland with arms and courage
and to be an apparent protection and ornament for their parents.
Although this is set forth and related well and excellently,
645 nevertheless it is far removed from true reasoning.
For it must be that the entire nature of the gods
spends everlasting time enjoying perfect peace,
far removed and long separated from our concerns.
For free from all anxiety, free from dangers,
650 powerful in its own resources, having no need of us,
it is not won over by good things we do nor touched by anger.[34]
Truly, the earth lacks feeling at all times,
and because it possesses the first beginnings of many things,
it bears much in many ways into the light of the sun.
655 Here if anyone decides to call the sea "Neptune"
and crops "Ceres," and prefers to misuse the name "Bacchus"
rather than to employ the real name of the liquid,[35]
let us allow him to declare that the earth is the mother of the gods,
659 as long as, nevertheless, he himself really
660 refrains from defiling his mind with base religious superstition.[36] **(680)**
And so oftentimes, cropping grass from a single field,
wool-bearing sheep and the offspring of horses, fierce in war,
and the ox-horned herds, beneath the same expanse of sky,
slaking their thirst from a single stream of water,
live their lives with different appearances and retain their parents'
665   nature
and imitate their ways of acting each after its own kind.   **(665)**

---

[32] Line 636 in the manuscripts is a partial conflation of lines 635 and 637, and makes little sense. I have followed most editors and omitted it.

[33] Saturn (Cronos to the Greeks) was Jupiter's father. He was in the habit of eating his children as soon as his wife Rhea gave birth to them.

[34] 2.646-651 = 1.44-49.

[35] "Real name of the liquid" = wine.

[36] Line 680 was transferred here by Lachmann.

So great is the difference of matter in whatever
type of grass, so great in every stream.
So too each living creature of them all
is composed of bones, blood, veins, warmth, moisture,   670
flesh, and sinews, which are also all very different,   (670)
formed by different shapes of the first beginnings.
Then too whatever things are burned by fire and combust
preserve in their bodies, if nothing else, those things
which enable them to burst into flames and give off light   675
and throw sparks and scatter embers in all directions.   (675)
If you examine other things in a similar frame of mind
you will then find that they conceal seeds of many things
in their body and contain many kinds of shapes.   679
Next, you see many things on which color and taste   (679) 680
are bestowed together with scent, like most fruits.[37]   681
Therefore these ought to be composed of many kinds of shapes.
For smell penetrates our limbs where color does not,
and likewise color separately, and separately taste, winds its way
into the senses. Thus you can recognize they differ in their primary
        shapes.   685
Therefore different shapes are assembled in a single globule
and things are made up of mixed seed.
And furthermore, here and there in our verses themselves
you see many letters shared by many words,
although it is still necessary to admit that the verses and words[38]   690
are composed among themselves as different words from different
        letters.
It is not that only a few letters commonly recur,
nor that no two among them are made of letters
all the same, but that they are not everywhere all like all.
So in other things likewise, although many first beginnings   695
are common to many things, still truly they are able
to make up among themselves very different wholes.
And so it said deservedly that the human race and crops
and glad trees are composed of different particles.
But it must not be thought that all particles can be connected in all   700
ways. For then you would see monstrosities commonly occurring,
and the forms of men half-beast[39] appearing, and from time to time

---

[37] "Fruits" is a translation of *poma*, an emendation by Bruno of the mss.
   dona, "gifts, offerings." It is possible one or more lines has dropped out
   after 681.

[38] 2.688-690 = 1.823-825.

[39] By "the forms of men half-beast" Lucretius probably is referring to
   centaurs.

tall boughs exsprouting[40] from living body,
and many terrestrial limbs joined to marine creatures,
705 and then nature pasturing Chimaeras breathing fire
from their foul mouths throughout lands which produce everything.
It is obvious that none of these things happens, since we can
see that all things, created from fixed seeds
and a fixed mother, preserve their kind as they grow.
710 Doubtless this happens for a fixed reason.
For particles appropriate to each are passed from all kinds of foods
within into their limbs, and once connected produce
suitable motions. But, in contrast, we see that nature discards
foreign matter back onto the earth, and many things
715 with invisible bodies flee from the body after being blasted by blows.
These things were neither able to be connected to any place nor
to harmonize with and imitate the live-giving motions within.
But lest by chance you think that animals alone are bound
by these laws, the same account puts limits on all things.
720 For just as in their nature all things that have been created
differ among themselves, so it is necessary that each
be made up of differently shaped first beginnings;
It is not that only a few are endowed with similar shape,
but that it is uncommon that all are equal to all.
725 Since, furthermore, the seeds are different, there must be differences in
spacings, paths, connections, weight, blows,
meetings, and motions. These things not only separate
living bodies, but sunder the earth and the entire sea
and keep the whole sky away from the earth.
730 Now come, heed words won by my sweet labor,
so that you do not think that these white things which you see
shining before your eyes are made out of white first beginnings,
or that these things which are black arise from black seed.
Nor should you believe that those things which are imbued
735 with whatever other color have this color because
the bodies of matter are tinged with a color which matches it.
For the first bodies of matter have absolutely no color
at all, neither the same as visible bodies nor dissimilar either.
If by chance you think that there can be no mental focusing[41]

---

[40] "Exsprouting" translates *egigni*, a word Lucretius apparently coined.

[41] "Mental focusing" is a translation of *animi iniectus*, literally, "projection of the mind." This is a reference to Epicurus' doctrine of *epibolê tês dianoias*, "focusing of the mind," " application of the mind," an act the mind makes when it focuses on a thought (in the form of a mental image). Epicurus placed great importance on this mental faculty, and Diogenes Laertius reports (10.31) that later Epicureans included it as a

on bodies like these,[42] you are wandering far from the true path.   **740**
For since the blind-born,[43] who have never gazed upon
the light of the sun, nevertheless recognize bodies by touch
which from day one have been associated with no color,
you may also know that we are able to conceive in our minds
the notion of bodies daubed with no hue.   **745**
Again, we ourselves touch things in the blinding darkness,
but in no way do we perceive that they are tinged with any color.
Since I establish that this is the case, now I will show that   **748**
[the first bodies] are [forever deprived of all color].[44]   **[748a]**
For every color undergoes complete change, and all   **749**
[things which change color change themselves.]   **[749a]**
First beginnings ought never to do this in any   **750**
way. For something unchangeable must remain,
so that all things not be completely reduced to nothing.
For whatever is changed and departs from its own limits,
this is immediately the death of that which it was before.[45]
Consequently be careful not to color the seeds of things,   **755**
or else you would see everything return completely to nothing.
Moreover, if the quality of color is not assigned to the first
beginnings, and yet they are endowed with different shapes
from which they produce and vary colors of every kind
(because it makes a great difference in the case of all the   **760**
seeds with what and in what position they are held,
and what motions they impart and receive among themselves),
easily and immediately you would be able to render a reason
why those things which a short while ago were dark-colored
are able to change to a marble-white sheen so suddenly,   **765**
as the sea, when great winds have stirred up its surface,
is turned into white waves with marble-white sheen.
For you could explain that what we often see to be dark-colored,
when its constituent material is thoroughly mixed and the arrangement
of its first beginnings is changed and some are added and some
          subtracted,   **770**
immediately it happens that it appears shining and white.

---

fourth criterion of truth alongside Epicurus' three other criteria
(sensations, preconceptions, and feelings).

[42] i.e., atoms without any color.

[43] "Blind-born" translates *caecigeni*, a word Lucretius apparently coined.

[44] There are textual difficulties in lines 748-750. I follow Bailey and other
editors who think that several lines have dropped out, and translate
Bailey's suggested supplements.

[45] 2.753-754 = 1.670-671, 1.792-793, 3.519-520.

But if the level surface of the sea were composed of dark blue-green
atoms, there is no way they would be able to turn white.
For in whatever way you would stir up things which are dark
775   blue-green, never can they change their color to marble-white.
But if the atoms which produce the sea's single, pure gleam
are tinged one with one color and another with another,
just as often from other forms and differing shapes
there is produced something square and of uniform shape,
780   it would be natural, just as we see that in a square there exist
different shapes, to see in the level surface of the sea,
or in any other single, pure gleam,
colors varied and far different from one another.
Moreover not at all do the different shapes hurt
785   and hinder the whole from being square on the outside,
but the different colors of things impede and prohibit
the whole thing from being able to be one gleaming color.
Then further, the reasoning which leads and misleads us to attribute
at times colors to the first beginnings of things
790   collapses, since white things are not created from white,
nor things recognized as black from black, but from different colors.
For indeed much more easily will white things arise
and originate from no color rather than from black color
or from any other color, which would fight back and resist.
795   Moreover, since colors cannot exist without light,
and the first beginnings of things do not emerge into the light,
one can know that they are not covered with any color.
For what sort of color will there be in the blinding darkness?
Nay, even by light itself color is changed in so far as
800   it is struck by direct or oblique light and reflects it back,
in the way the plumage of pigeons appears in the sun,
the plumage which is located around the nape and encircles the neck.
For at one time it happens that it is red with bright garnet,
sometimes from a certain angle it happens to appear
805   to mix lapis lazuli among green emeralds.
And the peacock's tail, when it is filled with great light,
changes colors in the same way as it turns around.
Since colors are created by a certain blow of light,
one can realize that colors must not be thought to be made without it.
810   And since the pupil of the eye receives into itself a certain type
of blow when it is said to perceive white color,
and yet another type, when it perceives black and other colors,
and since it makes no difference what color the things you touch happen
to be, but rather with what sort of shape they are furnished,
815   you can be certain that the first beginnings have no need of colors,
but by their different shapes they produce different kinds of touch.

Moreover since the nature of color is not fixed with fixed
shapes and all formamations[46] of first beginnings
are able to be any color you want, why are
those things which are made up of them not equally   820
drenched with colors of every type in every type?
For it would be natural often even for crows as they flew about
to throw off white color from their white feathers
and for black swans[47] to be made of black seed
or of any other color, either solid or varied.   825
Nay rather also, the more anything is pulled
into tiny parts, the more it happens that you can see
the color little by little vanish and fade away.
So it happens when purple cloth is torn into small parts.
Purple or Phoenician scarlet, by far the brightest color,   830
is completely lost when it is pulled apart strand by strand.
From this you can realize that all color is breathed out
of particles before they reach the level of the seeds of things.
Finally, since you admit that not all bodies
give off noise and smell, it is therefore the case   835
that you do not attribute sounds and smells to all things.
Thus, since we cannot make out everything with our eyes,
we can be sure that some things exist bereft of color
as some things exist without smell or far removed from sound,
and that a sharp mind can grasp these things no less   840
than it can take note of those deprived of other things.
But lest by chance you think that the primary bodies exist
lacking only color, they are also deprived of warmth
and cold and boiling heat in every respect,
and they are carried along stripped of sound and starved of moisture, 845
nor do they throw off any odor of their own from their body.
For just as when you begin to make the pleasant liquid of marjoram
and myrrh oil, and the flowery fragrance of nard, which breathes
nectar to the nostrils, it is right to seek above all,
in so far as you may and can find it, olive oil which is odorless   850
by nature, which will transmit no scent to the nostrils,
so that it can as little as possible taint and spoil with its strong flavor
the scents mixed and cooked in its substance,
so for the same reason, the first beginnings of things should
not attach their smell to things as they are created,   855

---

[46] "Formamations" is a translation of a word *formamenta* that Lucretius
apparently invented.

[47] Lucretius and other Romans only knew white swans, and had no idea
that black swans existed in Australia.

nor their sound, since they can give off nothing from themselves,
nor, for a similar reason, any flavor at all,
nor cold nor likewise warmth or boiling heat, and the rest.
Since these qualities are nevertheless such as to be mortal, (pliability
860 being associated with a soft body, fragility with a crumbly one,
and hollowness with one of loose texture), all must be disjoined
from the first beginnings if we want to lay immortal foundations
for things, upon which depends the sum of life, or else
you would see all things return completely to nothing.
865 Now it is necessary to admit that whatever things we see to possess
sensation are nevertheless all made from first beginnings
which lack sensation. Neither do the phenomena refute this
nor do they contradict it. They are things plainly known.
Rather, they lead us by the hand and compel us to believe that living
870 creatures arise, as I say, from things that lack sensation.
Indeed you can watch worms emerge alive from stinking
dung when the earth, damp from unseasonably heavy
rains, turns rotten,[48] and you can, besides,
see all things change themselves in the same way.
875 Brooks, branches, and glad pastures turn themselves
into cattle, and cattle change their nature into our bodies,
and from our body often the living force of wild
animals and the bodies of the powerful-of-wing[49] increase.
So nature turns all foods into living bodies
880 and from this source produces all the sensations of animals,
not much differently at all than she unravels dry
wood into flames and turns them all into fires.
Don't you therefore see that it makes a great difference
in what order all the first beginnings of things are arranged,
and with which they are mixed together when they give and receive
885   motions?
Then further, what is it that moves and strikes the mind itself,
which moves it and forces it to display different feelings,
so that you do not believe that the sensible arises from insensibles?
No doubt it is that rocks and wood and earth, when mixed into one,
890 still cannot give rise to life-giving sensation.
It will be helpful in these matters to remember the following:
I am not saying that sensations arise immediately from absolutely
all things which produce sensible things, but rather

---

48 A number of ancient philosophers besides the Epicureans also believed
in spontaneous generation.

49 i.e., birds. "Powerful-of-wing" translates *pennipotentum*, a word Lucretius
apparently coined.

that it makes a great difference, first, how small the bodies are
that produce a sensible thing,[50] and with what shape they are endowed, **895**
and secondly, what motions, arrangements, and positions they have.
We can see none of these conditions in wood and dirt clods.
And nevertheless these same items, when they are rotted out, so to
    speak,
by rain, give birth to little worms, because the bodies of matter
are disrupted from their original motions by a new condition   **900**
and are brought together so that living things are bound to be produced.
Next, those[51] who maintain that the sensible can be created from sensible
    things
which themselves in turn were accustomed to gain sensations from
    others   **903**
<these make the seeds of sensation mortal>[52]   **(903a)**
when they make them soft. For every sensation is linked   **904**
to internal organs, sinews, and veins, all of which   **905**
we see are soft and created from perishable body.
But nevertheless let it be granted that these things can exist forever.
Yet surely they ought to have the sensation of a part,
or be thought to be like whole living creatures.
But it is impossible that parts are able to have sensation by themselves, **910**
for every sensation of the parts looks to something else,[53]
and neither can the hand nor any other part of the body, when separated
from us, maintain any hold on sensation by itself.
The other option remains: that they are like whole animals.
Thus likewise it is necessary that they feel what we feel[54]   **(923) 915**
so that they can feel along with us the life-giving feelings all over. **(915)**
How then could they be called the first beginnings of things   **(916)**
and escape the ways of death, when they are living things,   **(917)**
and living things are one and the same as mortal things?   **(918)**
Yet grant that they can do this. Still by their coming together and
    meeting   **(919) 920**
they will create nothing except a mob and throng of living things, **(920)**

---

[50] As Lucretius makes clear in Book 3, the soul atoms that produce life in
living creatures are smaller and more mobile than other kinds of atoms.

[51] The argument here is probably directed at Anaxagoras and others who
say living things must be produced from other living things.

[52] There is a lacuna in the text here of one or more lines. I have translated
along the lines suggested by Bailey.

[53] The text of this line is very uncertain. I have translated Lachmann's
suggested emendations.

[54] I have followed most editors and translators and accepted Bernays'
transposition of line 923. The passage would make little sense otherwise.

just as to be sure men, cattle, and wild animals cannot   (921)
produce anything else among themselves by their associating
    together.   (922)
But if by chance they lose their own sensation from their body
925 and take another,[55] what need was there for that which was removed
to be assigned to them? Then moreover, as to what we alluded to before,
since we see the eggs of birds turn into living chicks,
and worms seethe up out of the ground
which has turned rotten from unseasonably heavy rains,
930 you can know that sensations are able to arise from non-sensations.
But if by chance someone will say that at any rate
sensation can arise from non-sensation by a process of change,
or by some kind of birth, so to speak, by which it is brought forth,[56]
it will be sufficient to make this plain to him and to prove
935 that birth cannot happen unless a union has occurred before,
nor is anything changed without a union being involved.
First, sensations can belong to no body at all
before the nature of the living creature has itself been generated,
and no wonder, since its substance is kept scattered about
940 in the air, in rivers, in the earth, and in the things created from the earth,
nor has it come together yet and assembled the appropriate
interactive live-giving motions, by means of which the all-watching
senses, once kindled, watch over every living creature.
Moreover, in the case of any animal whatsoever, a blow which is greater
945 than its nature can endure quickly flattens it and proceeds
to confound all its senses, both of body and of mind.
For the arrangements of the first beginnings are dissolved
and deep within the life-giving motions are obstructed,
until the substance is shaken throughout every limb,
950 releases the life-giving knots of the soul from the body,
and scatters and expels the soul outside through every pore.
For what more do we think a blow is able to do
when inflicted than to dash away and destroy each thing?
It happens too that when a blow is inflicted less sharply
955 the remaining life-giving motions often win out,
win out and quiet the great disturbances from the blow
and recall each part back again to its own movements,
and dash away death's motion which now is gaining mastery,
so to speak, in the body, and ignite the senses which are nearly lost.

---

[55] That is, if the supposition is that these living parts give up their own
sensations and take on the sensations of the whole they now form.

[56] It is unclear who the opponents are against whom Lucretius is arguing.
Many earlier editors identified the opponents as Stoic, but this seems
unlikely.

For in what other way can living creatures collect   960
their minds and return to life from the very threshold of death
instead of passing to the point where it almost ran and passing away?
Moreover, since there is pain when the bodies of matter
are disturbed by some force throughout the living flesh
and limbs and they shake within in their dwelling places,   965
and when they return to their place, alluring pleasure arises,
one can realize that the primary bodies cannot be assailed
by any pain, nor can they take any pleasure from themselves,
since they are not composed of any bodies of first beginnings,
by the strangeness of whose motion they might be afflicted   970
or take any enjoyment of refreshing sweetness.
Thus in no way ought they be endowed with any sensation.
Next, if sensation must now be attributed to their own first
beginnings so that all living creatures can possess sensation,
what about those from which the human race is specially increased? 975
And of course the first beginnings rock with rolling laughter,
howl, and with dewy tears sprinkle their faces and cheeks,[57]
and are practiced in discussing at length the make-up of things
and further, they seek out what their own first beginnings are!
Since indeed they resemble whole mortal creatures,   980
they themselves must also consist of other elements,
and after that those from others, so that you do not dare stop.
In fact I will proceed: whatever you will say speaks and laughs
and thinks must be composed of other things which can do the same.
But if we see that this whole idea is stark raving mad,   985
and it is possible to laugh without being made out of laughing bodies,
and to think and engage in argument using learned language
without being made out of seeds that think and are fluent,
why are those things which we see have sensation any
less able to be blended from seeds that completely lack sensation? 990
Next, we have all sprung from the sky's seed.[58]
This same one is the father of all. When bountiful mother
earth receives from him the wet drops of moisture,
she conceives and gives birth to shining crops and glad trees
and the human race, she gives birth to all the races of wild beasts, 995
when she furnishes them food, on which all creatures maintain

---

[57] 2.976-977 are nearly identical to 1.919-920.

[58] 2. 991-1022 form the conclusion of the section on the secondary qualities
     of atoms and sensation which began at line 730. The opening lines of
     this section are based on lines from a play of Euripides, the *Chrysippus*,
     which survives only in fragments. Euripides, in turn, had been influenced
     in that play by the Presocratic philosophers Anaxagoras and Empedocles.

their bodies, lead a sweet life, and propagate progeny.
For this reason she has deservedly received the name of mother.
Likewise what was from the earth before falls back again
1000 into the earth, and what was sent from the shores of heaven
the regions of sky take back again when it is given back.
Nor does death destroy things so much that it does
away with the bodies of matter, but it disperses their union.
Then it joins one thing to others and brings it about
1005 that all things transpose shapes and change colors
and experience sensations and lose them in an instant of time,
so you may know that it matters greatly with the same first beginnings
   of things
with what and in what position they are held,
and what motions they impart and receive among themselves,[59]
1010 and may not think that what we see flowing across the surface
of things and at times being born and then suddenly perishing
can remain in the possession of eternal primary bodies.[60]
Nay rather also it matters in our verses themselves
with what and in what kind of order they are placed.
1015 For the same letters signify the sky, sea, earth,
likewise rivers, sun, crops, trees, and animals.
If not all are similar, by far the greatest part
are: truly it is by position that things are differentiated.
1019 So in things themselves likewise once the coming-togethers,[61]
1021 movements, order, positions, and configurations of their matter
are completely changed, the things also ought to be changed.
Now turn your mind for me to true reasoning.
For a radically new thing struggles to gain access to your ears,
1025 and a new appearance of things to reveal itself.
But no thing is ever so easy, that it is not at first
rather difficult to believe, and likewise
there is nothing that is so great or so wondrous
that little by little all do not decrease their wonder at it.
1030 First of all, take the bright, pure color of the sky and all
that it holds within it, the planets wandering here and there,
the moon and the gleam of the sun with its luminous light.
If all of these were now for the first time presented to mortals,
if unexpectedly they were suddenly presented to them, what would be
   more

---

[59] 2.1008-1009 = 2. 761-762, 1. 818-819, 1. 909-910.

[60] Lucretius restates in very poetic language the principle that the colors of objects that we see do not belong to the atoms, but are the results of the arrangement and position of the atoms.

[61] I have omitted line 1020, which almost all modern editors delete.

wondrous to tell of than these things, or which the nations   1035
would before have dared less to believe would come to be?
Nothing, I suppose: so wondrous would this sight have been.
Yet consider how nobody now, jaded by seeing it so much,
thinks it worth gazing up into the brilliant regions of the sky!
Therefore stop being scared off by newness alone.   1040
Don't spit reason from your mind, but rather with sharp
judgment weigh things carefully, and if they seem true to you,
put up your hands,[62] if it is false, take up arms against it.
For the mind, since the totality of space is infinite outside beyond
these walls of the world, seeks an explanation about what lies   1045
beyond there, out where the mind desires to see,
and where the projection of the mind[63] flies alone and free.
First, in every direction around us,
on either side, above, and below throughout the universe
there is no limit. So I have demonstrated.[64] The very facts   1050
speak for themselves, and the nature of the heavenly depths is apparent.
Now in no way must it be thought to be like the truth —
since everywhere infinite space lies empty
and seeds numberless in their number in the totality of the heavenly
       depths
fly around in many ways driven on by eternal motion —   1055
that this was the only world and heavens created,
and that beyond it those many bodies of matter do nothing at all:
especially because this world was made by nature, and the seeds
of things, colliding on their own, automatically, by chance, were driven
together in many ways, senselessly, purposelessly, vainly.   1060
But at last those seeds coalesced which, suddenly thrown together,
might on each occasion become the beginnings of great things:
of the world, sea, sky, and the race of living creatures.
Wherefore again and again it is necessary to admit
that there are other groupings of matter in other locations   1065
like the one here which the aether holds in its greedy embrace.
Moreover, when much matter is on hand,
and when space is present and neither substance nor any cause is a
       hindrance,
things ought of course to be carried out and created.
And now if there is such a great supply of seeds that an entire age   1070
of living creatures is unable to count them, and if the same force
and nature continues on which has the power to throw together

---

[62] i.e., surrender.

[63] See note on line 739 above.

[64] 1. 951-1001.

the seeds of things each into its place in the same way
as they have been thrown together in this world, it must
1075 be admitted that there are other worlds in other regions,
as well as different races of men and breeds of wild beasts.
In addition, in the sum total of things there is nothing singular,
which is born unique and grows unique and alone;
it instead belongs to some class, and there are very many of the same
1080 kind. In the first place, turn your mind to animals.
You will find that the mountain-roaming family of wild beasts are thus,
thus the twin offspring[65] of humans, thus too the silent
herds of scaly fish and all bodies of flying creatures.
Wherefore by similar reasoning it must be admitted
1085 that both the earth and sun, the moon, the sea and others that exist
are not unique, but rather innumerable in number;
since indeed the deeply driven boundary stone of life
equally waits for them, and they are equally endowed with a natural
     body,
as every class which abounds after its own kind here on earth.
1090 If you learn these things well and hold on to them, nature appears,
liberated at once and freed from haughty masters,
to do everything herself by herself on her own without the gods.
For by the gods' sacred hearts, which in tranquil peace
pass their placid age and serene life: Who
1095 is powerful enough to rule the totality of the boundless universe,
who to hold fast in hand the powerful reins of the deep,
who to rotate all the heavens at once and to warm
all the fertile worlds with ethereal fires,
or to be present in all places at all times,
1100 so as to create darkness with clouds and shake the clear expanses
of the sky with thunder, and then hurl lightning and often demolish
his own temples, and as he retires to desolate places,
vent his rage by practicing with his weapon, which often passes by
the guilty and deprives the innocent and undeserving of life?
1105 And since the time of the earth's generation and the first birthday
of the sea and earth and the original rising of the sun,
many bodies have been added from without, many seeds have been
     added
around, which the great universe has tossed and brought together.
From these the sea and lands might increase and from these
1110 the sky's home might acquire space and lift its lofty
ceiling far from the lands, and the air might rise up.
For all bodies from all places are apportioned off by blows,

---

[65] "Twin offspring" probably refers to "male and female offspring."

each to its own, and draw back into their own classes:
moisture goes to moisture, from earthy body earth
grows, and fires forge fire, and aether aether, **1115**
until nature, the perfecting and creative mother of things,
has led all to the final limit of growth.
Thus it happens, when nothing more is put into
the life-giving veins than what flows out and draws back.
Here development ought to stop for all things, **1120**
here nature forcefully reins in growth.
For whatever you see growing bigger with giddy increase
and gradually ascending the steps of adulthood
take in many more bodies for themselves than they emit from themselves,
as long as food flows easily into all its veins and as long as **1125**
things are not so widely spread out that they release a lot
and spend more than their life makes use of.
For surely you must put up your hands and admit that many bodies
flow out and draw back from things; but more ought
to be added on until they reach the highest pinnacle of growth. **1130**
Then age slowly breaks down vigor and adult
strength, and life melts away into its worse stage.
Indeed the bigger a thing is, once it stops growing,
and the wider it is, the more bodies it scatters everywhere
in all directions and sends out from itself: **1135**
neither is food easily distributed to all its veins,
nor is there enough, considering what great surges it surges out,
from which a sufficient amount can arise and be at hand.
Justly then do things perish, when they have let things flow
away and have become rarefied, and when they all succumb to external
    blows, **1140**
since in the end nourishment fails old age,
and bodies do not stop pounding on anything
from the outside, destroying and violently subduing it by blows.
So too, therefore, will the walls of the wide world be assailed
on all sides and sink into crumbling ruins. **1145**
For it is nourishment which must renew and make everything whole,
    nourishment
which must prop up, nourishment which must support, all things.
But in vain, since neither do the veins allow in
what is sufficient, nor does nature provide what is needed.
Why even now its life is shattered, and the exhausted earth **1150**
scarcely can produce little animals,[66] although it once produced
all breeds and gave birth to the enormous bodies of wild beasts.

---

[66] i.e., like the spontaneously generated worms of lines 2. 871 ff.

For it was no golden rope, [67] I think, that lowered from heaven above
the races of mortal creatures onto the fields below,

1155 neither was it the sea nor the waves splashing on the rocks that created
          them,
but the same earth generated them that now nourishes them from herself.
Moreover in the beginning, she herself on her own produced
shining crops and glad vineyards for mortal creatures,
she herself provided sweet fruit and glad pastures,

1160 which now even with all our hard work scarcely grow at all.
And we grind down oxen and the energy of farmers,
we wear out iron plows and scarcely get enough from the fields,
so miserly are they with fruit and so demanding of our effort.
Now the aged plowman shakes his head and sighs

1165 too frequently that his great efforts have come to no purpose,
and when he compares present times to times
gone by, he often praises the fortunes of his parent.
Sadly too the planter of the old wrinkled vine
lashes out at the tendency of the times and drones on about the age,

1170 and mutters about how earlier times were filled with piety
and had easily supported life with narrow farm boundaries,
when the amount of land allotted to each man was far less.
He does not grasp that all things gradually waste away
and go to the grave, exhausted by the long space of time.

---

[67] The image of the golden rope is found in Homer, *Iliad* 8. 19, where Zeus
says that all the gods and goddesses together could not pull him down
from heaven with a golden rope. Philosophers, including the Stoics,
allegorized the episode in various ways.

"You are our father"

ON THE NATURE OF THINGS

BOOK III

From shadows so sheer you[1] were the first who was able to cast
such clear light and illuminate all that makes life worthwhile:
it is you I follow, O glory of the Greek race, and now
in the tracks you have laid down I fix my firm footprints,
not so much eager to compete with you, but because from love   5
I desire to imitate you. For why would a swallow contend with
swans, or what can young goats with their shaky legs
accomplish in a race to match the powerful energy of a horse?
You are our father, the discover of how things are, you supply us
with a father's precepts, and from your pages, o illustrious one,   10
just as bees sample everything in the flower-strewn meadow,
so we too feed upon all of your golden words,
golden they are, and always worthy of eternal life.
For as soon as your philosophy, sprung from your divine mind,
begins to give voice to the nature of things,   15
the mind's terrors dissipate, the walls of the world
dissolve, I see things carried along through the whole void.
The divinity of the gods appears, and their quiet dwelling-places,
which neither winds buffet nor clouds soak with violent
rains, nor does snow formed from biting frost, falling   20
white, disturb them, but an always cloudless atmosphere
spreads over them and smiles with light diffused in all directions.[2]
Nature, moreover, supplies all their needs, nor does anything
nibble away at their peace of mind[3] at any time.

---

[1] Lucretius addresses Epicurus.

[2] Lucretius' description of the residences of the gods are based on Homer, *Odyssey* 6.42-46.

[3] "Peace of mind" is a translation of *animi pacem*, the Latin translation of the Greek *ataraxia*, the goal of Epicurean philosophy. On *ataraxia*, see Introduction, pp. xv-xvi.

63

25 But in contrast, never do the regions of Acheron appear,[4]
    nor does the earth prevent from being seen all the things
    which are carried along through the void below beneath our feet.
    Then, from these things a kind of divine rapture
    and shivering awe seizes me, because in this way nature
30 by your power has been uncovered and laid open in all directions.
    And since I have shown of what sort are the beginnings
    of all things,[5] and how, differing in their various shapes,
    they fly around on their own, stirred up by eternal motion,
    and how from them all things are able to be created,
35 next after these things it appears that the nature of the mind
    and soul[6] must now be made clear in my verses,
    and the fear of Acheron must be thrown violently out the door.
    This fear throws human life into deep and utter confusion,
    staining everything with the black darkness of death,
40 and leaves no pleasure clear and pure.
    For although people often assert that sickness and a bad reputation
    are more to be feared than the infernal regions of death,
    and that they know the nature of the mind is made up of blood,
    or maybe of wind, if by chance they want it that way,   (46)
45 and further, that they have no need at all of our philosophy,   (44)
    you can tell from the following that they proclaim all this to gain (45)
    praise rather than because the idea itself is thought to be true:
    These same people, exiled from their country and banished far
    from the sight of humans, befouled by some awful crime,
50 inflicted in short with every trouble, continue living,
    and wherever these wretched people go they sacrifice to their ancestors,
    and slaughter black cattle and send down offerings
    to the shades below, and in intense situations turn
    their minds much more intensely to religion.
55 Wherefore it is more effective to gauge a person in times
    of doubt and danger, and to learn what they are like in adversity.
    For then at last real voices are extracted from the bottom
    of the heart and the mask is ripped off: reality remains.
    So too, greed and blind burning after elected office,
60 which coerce wretched people to go beyond the boundaries
    of what is right, and at times as allies in crime and accomplices
    they exert themselves night and day with outstanding effort
    to rise to the level of the greatest wealth—these lacerations of life

---

[4] "Regions of Acheron" = "hell." Acheron was one of the rivers of hell.

[5] "Beginnings of all things" = atoms.

[6] "Mind" = *mens*, "soul" = *anima*. Lucretius distinguishes the mind and
    the soul in his account. See lines 94-116 below.

are nourished in no small way by the fear of death.
For low social standing and bitter poverty nearly always   **65**
seem to be far removed from a calm and pleasant life,
and to be a kind of loitering, so to speak, before the gates of death.
This is why people, attacked by false fears,
desiring to escape far away and to withdraw themselves far away,
amass wealth through civil bloodshed and in their greed double   **70**
their riches, piling up slaughter on slaughter.
Unmercifully they rejoice in the sad death of a brother
and they disdain and fear eating with their relatives.[7]
In a similar way, often as a result of the same fear,
envy taunts them that before their very eyes he is powerful,   **75**
he is the center of attention, who parades in official glory,[8]
while they whine that they themselves are mired in obscurity.
Some perish to acquire a statue or good name.
And often through fear of death such a great hatred of life
and of seeing the light grabs hold of human beings,   **80**
that they inflict death on themselves with a sad heart,
forgetting that this fear is the source of their cares.
It convinces one to abuse honor, another to burst
the ties of friendship, and in short to abandon responsible conduct.[9]
For these days people often betray their country   **85**
and dear parents, trying to escape the regions of Acheron.
For just like children who tremble and fear everything
in the dark night, so we are afraid in the light sometimes
of things that ought to be no more feared than
the things that children tremble at and imagine will happen.   **90**
Therefore this fear and darkness of the mind must be shattered
apart not by the rays of the sun and the clear shafts
of the day but by the external appearance and inner law of nature.[10]
First, I say that the mind, which we often call the intellect,
in which the rational and guiding principle of life is located,   **95**
is part of a person no less than a hand and a foot
and eyes are parts of the whole living creature.
<However certain philosophers have thought>[11]
that the mind's power of sensation is not located in a particular part,

---

[7] i.e., they are afraid of being poisoned.

[8] The reference in "official glory" is to the dress of Roman magistrates.

[9] "Responsible conduct" = *pietas*, a key Roman virtue, which meant
    something like "the care and duty one owed to one's parents, family,
    friends, and state."

[10] 3.87-93 = 2.55-61, 6.35-41. 3. 91-93 = 1.146-148

[11] There is a lacuna here where one or more lines have been lost.

Harmony

but is a certain state of the body that produces life,
100   which the Greeks call a "harmony,"[12] something which gives us
life and sensation, although there is no intellect in any part —
as when often the body is said to possess good health,
and yet this health is no part of the healthy person.
They thus do not locate the mind's consciousness in a particular part;
105   in this they seem to me to wander seriously astray.
And so the body, which is plainly visible, is often sick,
although we still feel pleasure in another part unseen.
And on the contrary it happens that the opposite is often true in turn,
when one troubled in mind feels pleasure throughout the entire body.
110   This is no different than if, when a sick person's foot felt pain,
the head, meanwhile, happened to be in no pain.
Moreover when the limbs are given over to soft sleep
and the body lies sprawled out, heavy and senseless,
there is nevertheless something in us which during this time
115   is stirred in many ways and receives into itself all
the motions of joy and empty cares of the heart.
Now so that you can understand that the soul also is present
in the limbs and that it is not by harmony that the body secures
        sensation,
first it happens that when a large portion of the body is dragged
120   away, often life still remains in our limbs.
And again this same life, when a few particles of heat
have dispersed and air has been ejected out through the mouth,
it at once deserts the veins and leaves the bones.
Thus from this you can understand that not all particles
125   have the same functions nor do they equally sustain existence,
but rather that these, which are seeds of wind and hot
warmth, ensure that life remains in the limbs.
There are therefore heat and life-giving wind
present in the body which abandon our dying appendages.
130   Wherefore, since the nature of the mind and soul has been found
to be a part, so to speak, of a person, give up the name "harmony,"
conveyed to musicians from lofty Helicon — or maybe they
themselves in turn borrowed it from some other source and applied
it to a thing which then was lacking a name of its own — whatever
135   the case, let them have it: you pay attention to the rest of my words.
Now I maintain that the mind and soul are held joined together
with each other and make one nature from each other,
but that the rational principle which we call mind and intellect

---

12   The view that the soul is a type of harmony is discussed and rejected in
     Plato's *Phaedo*.

is the head, as it were,[13] and lords it over the whole body.
It is situated and stays in the middle region of the breast.   **140**
For here leaps panic and fear, around this location
feelings of pleasure radiate; here then is the intellect and mind.
The other part of the soul, spread through the entire body,
obeys and is moved at the direction and impulse of the mind.
The mind thinks alone for itself by itself, it rejoices for itself,   **145**
when nothing moves the soul or body at the same time.
And just as, when the head or eye is assailed by pain
and is troubled for us, we are not co-tortured[14] in our whole
body, so likewise the mind itself is sometimes troubled
or blooms in gladness, although the other part of the soul   **150**
is roused by no new sensation throughout the limbs and appendages.
But when the mind has been stirred by a more violent fear, we see
that the entire soul is equally affected throughout the limbs,
next sweat and pallor break out over the whole
body, the tongue stops working and the voice is aborted,   **155**
the eyes grow dark, the ears fill with noise, the limbs give way,
and indeed we often see people collapse because their minds are
so frightened. So from this anyone can easily recognize
that the soul is joined with the mind, and that when it is struck by the
      force
of the mind, it immediately strikes and pushes the body forward.   **160**
This same reasoning shows that the nature of the mind and soul
is corporeal. For when it is seen to push the limbs forward,
snatch the body from sleep, change facial expression,
and act as guide and turn the entire person —
and we see that none of these things can happen without touch, and
      again   **165**
that there is no touch without body — don't we have to admit
that mind and soul are made up of a corporeal nature?
Moreover you discern that our mind suffers commensurately
with the body and feels and is equally affected in the body.
If the shivering force of a spear does not smash out life   **170**
after it is driven within, separating the bones and sinews,
still faintness follows and a sweet swooning to the ground
and on the ground a churning of the mind which occurs,

---

[13] Lucretius writes, "head, as it were" because as becomes clear, Epicurus
taught that the mind was located in the chest, not in the head. Many
ancient philosophers, including Aristotle and the Stoics, believed the
same thing.

[14] "Co-tortured" translates *concruciamur*, a word Lucretius apparently
coined.

and now and then a wavering wish to rise.
175 Therefore the nature of the mind must be corporeal,
since it suffers trouble from corporeal weapons and blows.
What sort of body this soul has and from what things
it is composed I will now proceed to give an account with my words.
First, I assert that it is incredibly fine and is made up of
180 exceedingly small particles. That this is so you may,
if you pay attention, thoroughly grasp from the following.
Nothing is able to happen in such a rapid fashion
as what the mind proposes to itself to happen and itself commences.
Therefore the mind stirs itself more quickly than anything
185 whose nature is seen right in front of our eyes.   ·
But that which is so highly mobile must be made up of
exceedingly round particles and exceedingly tiny ones,
so that they are able to be moved when struck by a small impulse.
And so water is moved and ripples at the slightest impulse,
190 since it is composed of shapes small and ready to roll.
In contrast, honey by nature is harder to move,
its fluid lazier and its action less hurried.
For the whole mass of its matter sticks more
to itself, no doubt since it is not made up
·195 of particles so light, nor so fine and round.
For the merest breath of wind is able to cause a tall
pile of poppy seeds to lose its top before your eyes.
In contrast, in no way can it move a heap of rocks
or wheat spikes. Therefore the tinier and lighter
200 the particles are, the more mobility they enjoy.
In contrast, whatever things are found to have more
weight or are pricklier, the more stability they have.
Now then, since the nature of the mind has been discovered
to be incredibly mobile, it must consist
205 of exceedingly small, light, and round particles.
This thing, when known to you, dear reader,
in many things will be found useful and will be called opportune.
The following thing too shows the nature of the mind,
of what tenuous texture it is and in how small a place
210 it might be contained, if it could be gathered together:
that as soon as the untroubled quiet of death has taken hold
of a person and the nature of mind and soul has departed,
you cannot tell then that anything has been taken away
in appearance, anything in weight. Death preserves everything
215 except life-giving sensation and warm heat.
Therefore the whole soul must be made up of very small
particles and be interwoven through veins, flesh, and sinews.
Since, even when the whole soul has now left

4th Nature

the entire body, still the external configuration of the limbs
preserves itself unchanged and not a speck of weight is lost.   220
It is the same when the bouquet of Bacchus[15] fades or when
the sweet scent of perfume dissipates in the air
or when the flavor has now left some substance,
yet the thing itself appears not at all diminished to our eyes
because of it, nor does anything seem subtracted from its weight,   225
no doubt because many minute particles produce flavors
and smells in the whole substance of these things.
Wherefore again and again one can know that the nature
of the intellect and soul has been created from exceedingly small
particles, since when it escapes it takes away no weight.   230
Nor nevertheless should we think that this nature is single.
For a kind of tenuous breath leaves the dying,
mixed with heat, and heat then draws air with it.
Nor is there any heat at all which does not
also have air mixed in with it. For because its nature is attenuated,   235
many first beginnings of air must move within it.
Now therefore the nature of the mind has been found to be triple.[16]
Yet all these things are not enough to produce sensation,
since the mind will not admit that any of these can produce
motions that cause sensation and the thoughts the mind ponders.[17]   240
That is why a fourth kind of nature must also
be added to these. It is has no name at all.
Nothing exists which is more mobile or tenuous than it;
it is the first to distribute the motions that cause sensation throughout
    the limbs.   245
For it is the first to be roused, made up as it is of small shapes.
Next, heat and the invisible power of wind receive
the motions, and next air. Next everything is set in motion,
the blood is jostled, then the flesh begins to feel everything
throughout, last of all it is given over to the bones and marrow,   250
whether it be pleasure or its opposite stinging passion.[18]
Neither can pain penetrate so far[19] without effect, nor fierce

---

[15] Bacchus here = "wine."

[16] i.e., he has so far shown that there are three types of mind atoms: breath, heat, and air. He now argues that there must be a fourth, unnamed type of mind atom.

[17] The text of the last half of the line ("the thoughts the mind ponders") is uncertain.

[18] By pleasure's "opposite stinging passion" Lucretius probably means pain.

[19] i.e., as far as the bones and marrow.

injury permeate, without everything being thrown into such great turmoil
    that there is no place left for life and the soul's
255 parts disperse through every pore of the body.
    But more often it is very near the surface of the body that a stop is put
    to these motions. This is why we succeed in hanging on to life.
    Now while I yearn to give an account of how these things[20]
    are mixed with one another and in what ways they are arranged and function,
260 the poverty of our native speech holds me back unwillingly.
    But nonetheless I will treat the matter as best I can in brief.
    For the first bodies shoot back and forth among themselves
    with the motions of first beginnings, so that none[21] can be separated off
    by itself, nor can its power be separated off by space,
265 but they are the many powers, so to speak, of a single body.
    Just as in any flesh from living creatures commonly
    there is a certain smell, temperature, and taste, and yet from these
    taken altogether a single compilation of body is created,
    so heat and air and the invisible power of wind
270 mixed together produce a single nature together with that mobile
    force[22] which distributes from itself a beginning of motion to the others,
    from which source the motion that brings sensation first arises in the flesh.
    For deep down this nature lies hidden and concealed,[23]
    nor is there anything further below this in our body,
275 and further it is itself the "soul" of the whole soul.
    Just as in our limbs and whole body the force of the mind
    and power of the soul lie mixed and hidden,
    since it is composed of bodies small in size and number,
    so, you should know, this force without a name, composed of minute
280 bodies, lies hidden and further is itself the soul, so to speak,
    of the whole soul and lords it over the whole body.
    In a similar way it is necessary that wind and air
    and heat, mixed up together, function in the limbs,
    and one is situated further below or above the others
285 so that some single thing is seen to have been made from all,
    otherwise heat and wind separately and separately the power
    of air should if divided destroy and dissolve sensation.

---

[20] "These things" = the four parts of the soul.

[21] i.e., none of the four elements of the soul.

[22] "That mobile force" = the fourth unnamed type of mind atom.

[23] Lucretius here describes how the fourth unnamed element lies farthest from our senses.

Also present in the mind is that heat which it adopts when in anger
it boils up and fire flashes from fierce eyes.
There is also much cold breath, the companion of fear, 290
which stirs up trembling in the limbs and rouses parts of the body.
There is also too that state of peaceful air,
which occurs when the breast is calm and the face serene.
But there is more heat in those whose fierce hearts
and anger-prone minds readily boil over into anger. 295
First in this class is the violent violence of lions,
who often rupture their ribs roaring and growling
and are unable to contain the waves of anger in their breast.
But the chilly mind of the deer is more windy
and more quickly stirs up icy breezes in its flesh 300
which set up a trembling motion in the limbs.
But the nature of the cow gets its life more from peaceful air,
and the torch of anger never sparks and ignites it too much,
smoking and spreading its darkness of blinding black,
nor is it transfixed and immobilized by icy shafts of fear: 305
it is situated in between both deer and savage lions.
So it is with the human race. Although a standard education may
     make
some people fairly polished, it still leaves intact those
original traces of the nature of each person's mind.
You must not think that such evils can be pulled out by the roots, 310
so that one will not run off more quickly to sharp anger,
another be attacked a little more quickly by fear, or a
third put up with some things with more forbearance than is right.
And in many other respects too it is necessary that there be differences
     among
the various natures of people and their resulting behaviors. 315
I am unable now to explain the invisible causes of these
or to find enough names for all the shapes taken by
the first beginnings, from which this variety of affairs arises.
I see that I can assert this fact in these matters:
that the traces of our characters which reason cannot remove 320
from us are so small, that nothing prevents
us from living a life worthy of the gods.
This nature[24] then is protected by the whole body
and is itself the guardian of the body and the source of its life.
For they cling to each other with common roots 325
and obviously cannot be pulled apart without destruction.
Just as it is not easy to separate the scent from bits

---

[24] "This nature" = the soul.

of frankincense without its very nature also being destroyed,
so it is not easy to extract the nature of the mind
330 and soul from the whole body without all of them disintegrating.
With their first beginnings thus intertwined from the very start
with each other they come into being, endowed with co-partners for
     life.
And neither the power of the body nor the soul is seen to be able
to feel sensations separately for itself without the energy of the other,
335 but sensation is kindled and ignited throughout our flesh
by shared and interdependent movements from both sides.
Moreover the body is never created by itself
nor does it grow on its own nor is it seen to endure after death.
For never, just as the moisture of water often releases heat
340 which it has acquired, and it is itself not ripped apart for this reason,
but remains intact, never, I say, in this way can
the limbs left behind endure the dissolution of the soul,
but they are ripped apart and deeply destroyed, rotting away.
So from the moment life begins, the reciprocal union
345 of body and soul learns life-giving motions,
even when preserved in a mother's body and womb,
so that dissolution cannot happen without death and destruction.
Thus you can see, since the source of their life is conjoined,
so too does their nature stand conjoined.
350 What is more, if anyone denies that it is the body that senses
and believes that it is the soul which when mixed with the whole body
experiences this motion which we call sensation,
he wages an uphill battle against facts which are quite obvious and
     true.
For who will ever convey what it is for the body to sense,
355 if it is not what experience itself has demonstrated and taught us.
"But when the soul is dissolved the body is completely without
     sensation."
Yes — it loses what was not its own in life,
and it loses many things besides when it is driven out from life.
Further, to say that the eyes are unable to perceive anything,
360 but the mind gazes through them as if through open doors,
is difficult, since the feeling in the eyes leads us in the opposite direction.
For this feeling pulls and pushes us down to the eyes themselves,
especially since often we are unable to perceive shiny
things because our sight is hindered by bright sights.
365 This does not happen with doors. Nor indeed do doors, through which
we ourselves perceive, experience any distress when open.
In addition to that, if our eyes function as doors,
then the mind clearly ought to perceive things better
when the eyes are yanked out and the door posts completely removed.

In these matters you can in no way maintain   370
what the holy opinion of the great man Democritus asserts,
that the first beginnings of the body and mind, juxtaposed one
to another, are varied in alternation and fasten the limbs together.
For, as the particles of soul are much smaller
than those of which our body and flesh consist,   375
so too they are fewer in number and are sparsely scattered
throughout the limbs, so that at least you can assure this,
that however small the bodies are which first, when placed on us,
have the power to arouse sense-bearing motions in our body, so great
are the intervals which lie between the first beginnings of the soul.[25]   380
For sometimes we do not feel dust clinging
to the body, nor that chalk lies sprinkled on our limbs,
nor do we feel fog at night nor a spider's slender filaments
met straight on, when we are ennetted[26] as we go,
nor that its shriveled shroud has fallen on top of our heads,   385
nor birds' feathers or fibers floating from plants
which because of their incredible lightness usually fall with difficulty,
nor do we feel the movement of any and every crawling
creature, nor each and every single footstep
which gnats and other bugs take on our body.   390
So many particles must be stirred up in us
before the soul seeds which are mixed within our bodies throughout
     the limbs
begin to feel that the first beginnings have been struck,
and before they pound away at such great distances and are able
to rush at each other, meet, and leap apart in turn.   395
And the mind is better at keeping the doors of life locked
and a better master over life than the power of the soul is.
For without the intelligence and mind no part of the soul
can reside in the limbs for even a tiny part of time,
but follows easily as its companion and departs into the breezes,   400
and leaves the chilly limbs in the coolness of death.
But a person remains in life whose intelligence and mind remains.
However lacerated the trunk is, with its limbs cut off all around,
although the soul has been snatched off and removed from the limbs,
the person lives on and takes in life-sustaining ethereal breezes.   405
But if not the entire soul, but a great part of it, has been taken

---

[25] Lucretius means that we can tell how far apart the soul atoms are by
noting how big the smallest object is that we can feel when touched to
our skin. In the examples that follow, Lucretius also includes cases where
we fail to feel things because of their lightness, not just their small size.

[26] "Ennetted" translates *obretimur*, a word Lucretius apparently coined.

from a person, still he remains alive and hangs on.
It is just as when the eye has been lacerated all over: if the pupil remains
uninjured, the living power of sight stands firm,
410 provided only that you do not destroy the whole orb of the eye,
cutting around the pupil and leaving it all alone:
for this also could not occur without the destruction of both.[27]
But if this tiny middle part of the eye is eaten away,
its light immediately sets and darkness falls,
415 although the shining orb is not otherwise injured.
In such an arrangement the soul and mind are bound forever.
Now come, so that you might learn that the minds and light souls
of living creatures are born and subject to death,
I will proceed to set out my poem, sought for so long
and discovered with such sweet labor, so as to be worthy of your way
420   of life.
You, take care to link both of these[28] with one name,
and when I go on to mention, for example, the soul,
showing that it is mortal, understand that I also mean the mind,
inasmuch as it is a single unit and an interconnected entity.
425 First, since I have shown that the soul is tenuous and consists
of minute particles and is made out of first beginnings
much smaller than the limpid moisture of water
or fog or smoke — for it far surpasses them in speed
and is set in motion when struck by a weaker cause —
430 seeing that it is set in motion by images[29] of smoke and fog.
Just as when we are sleeping and in our dreams perceive
altars breathe out rising steam and send up smoke.
For no doubt these things are carried to us as likenesses[30] —
now therefore since when vessels are shattered you perceive
435 the moisture flowing in all directions and the liquid departing,
and since fog and smoke disperse outward into the air,
understand that the soul too is poured out and perishes much
more quickly and is dissolved more rapidly into its first bodies,
as soon as it is taken away from human limbs and departs.

---

[27] "Both" = the pupil and rest of the eye.

[28] "Both of these" = the mind and soul.

[29] "Images" = *imagines*; Lucretius uses the Latin words *imagines* and
simulacra as translations of the Greek *eidôla* ("images, likenesses")
Epicurus taught that *eidôla* are images given off by all objects and are
responsible for sensations and thoughts. Lucretius discusses them at
length in Book 4. 45-521, 722-857.

[30] "Likenesses" is a translation of *simulacra*, a likeness, image, or semblance.
See the previous note.

For indeed since the body, which constitutes its vessel, so to speak,   **440**
is unable to hold the soul together, when it is shaken by something
or made rare by a loss of blood from the veins, how
do you think the soul can be held together by any air,
which though more rarefied than our body still tries to hold it in?
Moreover, we see that the intellect is begotten along with the body,   **445**
and grows with it as one and becomes aged along with it.
For just as children totter around with a weak and delicate
body, so their mental capacity is correspondingly feeble.
Next when their age has grown up with hardy strength,
the rational faculty is stronger and mental power augmented.   **450**
Afterwards when the body is shaken by the sure strength of time
and the limbs fall slack, their strength beaten away,
thought limps, the tongue wanders, the mind totters,
everything gives out and fails at one time.
Thus it is fitting that the entire nature of the soul should also   **455**
be dissolved, like smoke, into the broad breezes of the beyond,
since we see that it is begotten along and grows along with the body
and, as I showed, fails and is exhausted at the same time.
In addition, we see that just as the body itself
suffers dire diseases and powerful pain,   **460**
so the mind suffers sharp cares, grief, and fear.
Therefore it is fitting that it too participates in death.
And furthermore, when the body is diseased the mind often wanders
aimlessly. For it loses its mind and says crazy things
and sometimes in an intense coma it is carried into deep   **465**
and continuous sleep, when the eyes and head fall slack,
whence it neither has the power to hear voices nor recognize
the faces of those who stand around and call it
back to life, bedewing their faces and cheeks with tears.
Wherefore it is necessary to admit that the mind too   **470**
is dissolved, since the contagion of disease penetrates into it.
For pain and disease are each architects of death,
which we have learned well from the departure of many before.[31]   **473**
Next why, when the sharp weight of wine penetrates a person   **476**
and the warm glow is distributed and departs into the veins,
does there follow a heaviness of limbs, why are the legs entangled
as he totters, why does the tongue slow, the mind grow soggy,
the eyes swim, shouting, sobbing, and arguing increase,   **480**
and soon the other things of this kind which follow,
why are these things, except because the wild working of wine

---

[31] Following other editors, I have omitted lines 474-475, which make no
sense in the context.

is constituted to confound the soul present in the body.
But whatever things can be thrown into confusion and impeded
485 show that if a slightly stronger cause had worked its way in,
it would have happened that they perished, deprived of future life.
And furthermore, often someone, suddenly struck by the power of an
    illness[32]
right before our eyes, as if by a bolt of lighting,
falls and spews foam, groans and shakes in the limbs,
490 raves, stiffens the muscles, twists about, breathes
irregularly, and wears out the limbs in tossing around.
No doubt because the power of the illness, scattered throughout the
    limbs,
drives the breath and rouses foam, just as on the salt
sea the waves are whipped by the wild will of the winds.
495 Further, a groan is elicited because the limbs are afflicted
with pain and in general since the voice particles are thrust out
and are carried heaped together outside the mouth
where they are, so to speak, accustomed and where a path has been
    prepared.
Raving occurs, because the force of the mind and soul
500 is confounded and, as I have shown, is torn apart
and scattered, ripped to pieces by that same poison.[33]
Then when the cause of the illness has at last reversed and the bitter
fluid of the infected body has returned to its hiding places,
then at first as if staggering the person gets up
505 and gradually returns to complete sensation and regains consciousness.
And so when these[34] are shaken by such great diseases while still
in the body, and are torn apart and suffer in unfortunate ways,
why do you believe that these same things can live
in the open air without a body in the company of warring winds?
510 And since we discern that the soul is cured like a body
which is sick, and we see that it is able to be changed by medicine,
this too foretells that the mind lives a mortal life.
For one must add parts or transpose the order
or take away some tiny bit from the total,
515 if someone is trying to alter the mind and gets started,
or seeks to change whatever other nature you wish.
But what is immortal does not allow its parts to be rearranged
nor anything to be added nor a tiny bit to flow away.

---

[32] The illness Lucretius describes here is epilepsy.

[33] The "same poison" refers to the "power of an illness" (epilepsy) that
Lucretius first mentioned in line 487.

[34] "These" = the mind and soul.

For whatever is changed and departs from its own limits,
this is immediately the death of that which it was before.[35]　　**520**
Therefore the mind when it is sick signals its mortality,
as I have shown, and when it is changed by medicine.
To such an extent then true fact is seen to oppose
false reasoning and to shut its escape route as it flees,
and to vanquish falsehood with double-edged refutation.　　**525**
Next, we often see a person die gradually
and limb by limb lose life-giving sensation:
first the toes and nails on the feet turn blue,
then the feet and legs die, and after this the tracks
of icy death gradually pass through the other limbs.　　**530**
Since this nature of the soul is sundered and passes away
and does not depart all at once, it must be thought mortal.[36]
But if by chance you think that on its own the soul can drag
itself inwards and contract its parts into one place,
and thus deduct sensation from all its limbs,　　**535**
yet still this place, where so great a supply of soul
is gathered together, should be seen to have greater sensitivity.
But since this place is nowhere, no doubt, as I said above,[37]
the soul is torn apart, dispersed abroad, and so perishes.
But even if one were now inclined to concede what is false　　**540**
and to grant that the soul can be massed together in the bodies of those
who leave the light by dying piece by piece,
still you would have to admit the soul is mortal,
nor does it matter whether it perishes dispersed through the air,
or is gathered together from its own parts and becomes dull,　　**545**
since ever more sensation deserts the entire person in every
part and in every part ever less of life remains.
And since the mind is one part of a person, which remains fixed
in a specific place, just like the ears and eyes are,
and the other sense organs which steer life,　　**550**
and just as hand and eye and nose if removed and
separated from us can neither have sensation nor exist,
but rather in little time are left to rot, so too
the mind is unable to exist by itself without body and the person.

---

[35]　3.519-520 = 1.670-671, 1.792-793, 2.753-754.

[36]　In this passage, Lucretius may be recalling Plato's description of Socrates'
physical symptoms after he drank the hemlock in *Phaedo* 117e-118a. In
the *Phaedo*, Socrates' physical symptoms seem to confirm his belief in
the immortality of the soul. Here Lucretius takes the same symptoms
as evidence of the soul's mortality.

[37]　3.531-532.

555 The body seems to be, so to speak, the mind's vase, or whatever
      other image you wish to invent more closely joined
      to it,[38] since the body clings to it with interconnections.
      Next, the living power of the body and mind
      thrive and enjoy life through their mutual conjoining.
560 For without the body, the nature of the mind is unable to perform
      alone by itself its life-giving motions, nor on the contrary
      devoid of the soul can the body endure and employ its senses.
      It is clear that just as the eye by itself, if torn from its roots,
      cannot perceive any object when it is separated from the entire body,
565 so the soul and the mind together clearly can do nothing on their own.
      Doubtless, because their first beginnings are held in by the whole body
      commingled through veins and flesh, through sinews and bones,
      and are unable to leap apart at great distances
      freely, thus enclosed they set in motion
570 sense-bearing motions, which the first beginnings, once driven outside
      the body after death into the breezes of the air, can in no way set in
            motion,
      because they are not held in by similar means.
      For air will be a body and indeed a living thing, if the soul
      can hold itself together and confine itself to those
575 motions which it used to make in the sinews and in the body itself.
      Wherefore again and again you must admit that once the whole
            covering
      of the body has been loosened and the life-giving breezes expelled
            outside,
      the mind's power of sensation, along with the soul, is dissolved,
      since the cause of life is linked together for both body and soul.
580 And next, since the body is unable to endure the soul's
      disintegration without wasting away with a withering odor,
      why do you doubt that, having risen from down deep within,
      the power of the soul flows out and is dispersed like smoke,
      and that, altered by so great a disaster, the body
585 collapses in catastrophe, since from deep within its foundations
      have shifted from their place, as the soul flows outside through the
            limbs
      and through all the winding paths which are in the body,
      and through its openings? Thus in many ways you can recognize that
            only after
      it was pulled apart did the nature of the soul exit through the limbs,
590 and that it was torn apart while still within the body,
      before it slipped out and started swimming on the currents of air.

---

[38] "It"= the mind.

Indeed, even while it is active within the limits of life,
often the soul yet appears, when shaken by some cause,
willing to depart and be released from the whole body,
and as if at the final hour the face begins to sag   **595**
and all the limbs, gone soft, fall from the bloodless body.
It is just like when it is said, "he slipped into unconsciousness,"
or "he lost consciousness," when at once there is panic and all present
desire to hold on to the final link of life.
For then the mind and all the powers of the soul   **600**
are shattered, and they collapse along with the body itself.
Thus a cause a little stronger would be able to dissolve them.
How then can you possibly doubt that the soul, once tossed outside
the body, weakened outdoors in the open, with its covering removed,
not only is not able to endure through all ages,   **605**
but cannot even last for the smallest amount of time?
Indeed it is clear that no one while dying feels
the soul going forth unharmed from his whole body,
nor first moving up into the lower or upper throat;
no, it gives out located in its fixed place,   **610**
just as he knows that each sense in its own place
is broken into its component parts. But if our mind were immortal,
it would not while dying so much complain that it was dissolving,
but would rather go forth and shed its garment, like a snake.
Next why do the intellect and rational faculty of the mind never   **615**
arise in the head[39] or feet or hands, but remain
in a single place and fixed region, unless
fixed places have been allotted to each thing for being born,
and where each thing is able to endure once created
and to exist with its limbs distributed in various ways,[40]   **620**
but so that the order of the limbs can never exist reversed?
To such an extent does one thing follow another, nor is flame
created from fluid rivers, nor is freezing forged in fire.
Moreover if the nature of the soul is immortal and is able
to have sensation when separated off from our body,   **625**
we must assume, I suppose, that it is equipped with five senses.
For in no other way can we possibly imagine for ourselves
souls wandering below the earth in Acheron.
Painters therefore and earlier generations of writers
have thus introduced souls equipped with senses.   **630**
But neither the eyes nor nose nor hand itself is able

---

[39] As Lucretius indicated earlier (3.136-160), Epicurus taught that the mind
     is located in the chest.

[40] "In various ways" probably means "in various ways in different species."

to exist for the soul when it is separated off, nor the tongue, nor ears.
Therefore not at all can souls have sensation and exist on their own.
And since we sense that there exists throughout all the body
635 life-giving sensation and we see the whole body is alive,
if suddenly some force chops it in two with a quick
blow so that it completely separates off each part,
doubtless too the force of the mind, divided
and detached, is divided in two along with the body.
640 But what splits and separates off into any parts
of course denies that it has an eternal nature.
They say that blade-bearing chariots hot
with indiscriminate slaughter often cut off limbs so suddenly
that the part which is sliced off and falls from the body is seen
645 to twitch on the ground, although the mind and force of the person
are unable to sense the pain because of the speed of the injury,
and also because the mind is consumed by its eagerness for battle.
With the body he has left he strives to reach the fighting and slaughter,
and often fails to grasp that his left arm has been lost with its
650 shield and dragged amidst the horses by the wheels and devouring
     blades;
another that his right arm is gone, as he climbs and presses on.
Then another attempts to rise with leg removed,
while nearby on the ground his dying foot wiggles its toes.
And a head, cut off from its warm and still-living trunk,
655 preserves even on the ground its living look and open eyes,
until it renders up every remnant of its soul.
And furthermore, if you were to decide for yourself to cut up
with a sword into many parts both halves of a snake
with its vibrating tongue, menacing tail, and extended body,
660 you would then see each part, cut up by its recent
wound, writhing and wetting the ground with gore,
and the part in front with its mouth seeking itself in the rear,
struck by the burning pain of the wound, so as to implant a bite.
Shall we then say that there are complete souls in all those
665 little parts? But with this reasoning it will follow
that one living creature had many souls in its body.
And so the soul which was one was divided off together with
the body. Therefore both body and soul must be thought mortal,
since each is equally split into many parts.
670 Moreover, if the nature of the soul is immortal, and works
its way into our body as we are being born,
why are we unable to remember our past life as well?
Why do we not hold on to any traces of things we have done?
For if the power of the mind is changed to so great an extent
675 that all recollection of things done before is lost,

Contra
Plato

that, I think, does not stray very far from death.
Therefore it is necessary to admit that what existed before
has perished and what exists now was created now.
Moreover if it were the case that the living power of the mind
is introduced to the body when it is already completely formed   680
at the time when we are born and when we cross the threshold of life,
it would not at all make sense that it be seen to grow
together with the body and with the limbs in the blood itself,
but it would make sense that it live alone by itself as if
in a cage, yet still so that the whole body overflows with sensation.   685
Wherefore again and again it must not be thought that souls are
without origin nor that they are exempt from the lethal laws of death.
For it must neither be thought that they can be fastened on so tightly
if they worked their way into our bodies from without — for the clear
      facts   690
show the whole thing happens in the opposite way.
For it is so connected throughout veins, flesh, sinews,
and bones, that even our teeth share in sensation,
as toothaches prove, and the twinge caused by ice-cold water,
and the biting down on a sharp rock if it is hidden in bread —
nor clearly, since souls are so interwoven with the body, can they exit 695
without harm and safely release themselves
from all the sinews, bones, and joints. But if by chance
you think that the soul, having worked its way in
from without, is the sort of thing that permeates our parts,
so much the more will it perish, fused with the body.   700
For what permeates is dissolved, and therefore passes away.
For just as food, when it has been distributed among all the pores of the
      body,
and when it is being divided up among the members and all the limbs,
is destroyed and from itself supplies another substance in its place,
so the soul and mind, even if they enter whole into the newborn   705
body, still are dissolved in the process of spreading out,
while, so to speak, through all the pores there are distributed into the
      limbs
particles out of which this nature of the mind is created,
which now is master in our body, born from that
which then perished, portioned into parts throughout the limbs.   710
Therefore the nature of the soul is seen neither
to lack a birthday, nor to be deprived of the experience of death.
Moreover, are or are not seeds of soul-life left
in the lifeless body? But if they are left and are present in it,
in no way will the soul deservedly be held to be immortal,   715
since it departs diminished with some of its parts lost.
But if it is carried off and flees with its members so intact

that it leaves no parts of itself in the body,
how do corpses, when their flesh is now rotting, wriggle with worms,
720 and how does such a great mass of living creatures,
boneless and bloodless, flow through the bloated limbs?
But if by chance you believe that souls work their way from the outside
into the worms and each are able to enter into their bodies,
and you do not think over why many thousands of souls
725 gather where one soul has departed, nevertheless there is this,
it seems, which must be sought after and brought to determination,
whether finally the souls go hunting for the appropriate seeds
of little worms and on their own construct for themselves places to live,
or whether, so to speak, they work their way into pre-formed bodies.
But it would not be easy to say either why they would do this on their
730   own
or why they would make the effort. For when they are without body,
they fly around untroubled by diseases, coldness, and hunger.
For the body is more liable to suffer from these disorders,
and the mind suffers many evils because of its contact with it.
735 But still, let it be as useful as you like for them to make a body
which they can enter. But there is clearly no way by which they could.
Not at all, therefore, do souls make bodies and limbs for themselves.
Nor, further, do they work their way into pre-formed
bodies. For neither would they be able to be so intimately
740 connected nor would the interconnections for shared sensation arise.
Next, why does fierce violence go with the stern breed
of lions, and craft with wolves, and why is fleeing passed on
to deer from their fathers and why does fatherly fear[41] rouse their limbs,
and why now do all other things of this sort
745 come into being in limbs and character from the beginning of life,
if not because a power of the mind, fixed by seed and breed,
grows in tandem with each and every body?
But if the soul were immortal and had the habit of changing
bodies, living creatures would have mixed-up manners.
750 A dog from Hyrcanian[42] seed would often flee the charge
of a horn-sporting stag, and the hawk would flee in terror
through the currents of the air at the coming of the dove, humans would
    lack
reason, and the wild races of wild beasts would be wise.
For this is put forward by false reasoning, when they say
755 that the immortal soul is altered with a change of body.

---

[41] By "fatherly fear", Lucretius means fear inherited from their fathers.

[42] The Hyrcani were people who lived by the Caspian Sea and were famous
for raising fierce dogs.

For what is changed is dissolved, and therefore passes away.
Indeed, parts are transposed and move from their order.
Therefore they must also be able to be dissolved throughout the limbs,
so that in the end they might all perish as one with the body.
But if they say that the souls of humans always go   **760**
into human bodies, still I will ask why from a wise soul
a stupid one can be produced, and why no child has practical wisdom,[43] **762**
and no foal of a mare is as well-trained as the powerful energy of a
    horse?   **764**
Naturally they will take refuge in the idea that the mind becomes
    juvenilized   **765**
in a juvenile body. But if this were to happen, it would be necessary to
    admit
that the soul is mortal, since if it is altered throughout the limbs
to so great an extent, it loses its life and former consciousness.
Or in what way will the force of the mind grow strong
together with each body and be able to attain the desired   **770**
flowering of youth, unless it is its co-partner from its first beginning?
Or what does it mean by going out from its aged limbs?
Can it be that it fears staying shut up in a rotting corpse,
lest its house, worn out by a long space of time,
crash in ruin? But no dangers threaten something immortal.   **775**
Next, that there are souls hanging around the marriage acts
of Venus and the births of wild beasts seems to be utterly absurd,
immortal souls awaiting mortal members,
innumerable in number, contesting in fierce frenzy with each other
over which will be first and foremost to work its way in.   **780**
Unless of course treaties have been drawn up among the souls
so that whichever flies and arrives first will work its way in
first and so they do not compete and struggle with each other at all.
Next, a tree is not able to live in the air,
nor clouds in the deep sea, nor fish in the fields,   **785**
nor blood in wood, nor can sap be present in stones.
It is fixed and laid down where each thing grows and is found.
Thus the nature of the mind is unable to arise without the body
on its own, nor can it be far from sinews and blood.
For if this were possible, far more easily would this force of the mind **790**
be able to exist in the head or shoulders or the bottom of the heels,
and be accustomed to be born in any part at all,
as long as it could remain in the same person and in the same container.
But since even in our body it is fixed and clearly laid down
where it is possible for the soul and mind to exist and grow   **795**
separately, so much more must it be denied

---

[43] Line 763 is identical to 746, and is omitted by editors.

Death is nothing to us

that they can survive and come into being totally outside the body.
Therefore, you must admit that when the body dies, the soul
also perishes, torn asunder throughout the entire body.
800 For indeed to join the mortal to the eternal and to think
they are affected as one and are able to mutually interact
is crazy. For what must be thought more different
or more disjointed and in disagreement with one another,
than that what is mortal should be joined to the immortal and everlasting
805 in a union and should put up with fierce buffetings?
Moreover, whatever endures eternally must do so
either by having a solid body and repelling blows
and not allowing anything to penetrate it which might be able
to dissociate its tightly-fastened parts within, just as the bodies
810 of matter are whose nature we have made known above,
or by being able to endure for all time for this reason,
that they are not subject to impacts, just as the void is,
which endures untouched and does not suffer from blows at all,
or also by having no supply of space around it,
815 into which things might be able, as it were, to disperse and be dissolved,
just as the universal universe is eternal, for neither is there outside of it
any place into which things may scatter nor are there bodies that
are able to encounter it and dissolve it with a forceful impact.
But if by chance the soul must be held to be immortal more because
of this,
820 that it is held together and protected by vital principles,
either because things foreign to its well-being never attack,
or because the things which attack for some reason withdraw
beaten back before we can feel how much harm they do,[44]

*   *   *   *   *   *   *   *   *   *   *   *   *

For besides the fact that it[45] grows ill with the diseases of the body,
825 there often comes to it that which torments it about things in the future
and vexes and terrifies it and wears it down with cares
and even when the misdeeds it has committed are past, its offenses
gnaw at it.
Add the madness peculiar to the mind and forgetfulness of things,
add that it is submerged in the dark waves of a coma.
830 Therefore death is nothing to us nor does it concern us at all,[46]
inasmuch as the nature of the mind has been shown to be mortal.

---

[44] One or more lines have been lost after line 823. The line(s) lost probably
stated that none of the conditions of immortality pertains to the soul.

[45] "It" = the mind.

[46] Lucretius here begins the third and final section of Book III with a Latin
translation of Epicurus' famous saying, "Death is nothing to us." See
Epicurus *Letter to Menoeceus* 124-127 and *Principal Doctrine* 2.

And just as in time gone by we felt no distress
at the Carthaginians rushing from all sides to attack[47]
when all things were shattered by the tremendous tumult of war,
shuddering and rocking beneath the lofty regions of the sky,　　**835**
and were in doubt as to which of the two[48] it must fall
to rule over all peoples on both land and sea,
so too, when we will no longer exist, when there will be a destruction
of the body and soul from which we have been joined together,
surely nothing at all will be able to happen to us,　　**840**
who will not exist then, nor move our senses,
not even if the earth be mixed with the sea, and the sea with the sky.
And even if the nature of the mind and power of the soul
have feeling after they have been dragged out of our body,
still this is nothing to us, who consist of the conjunction and connection **845**
of body and soul joined tightly together as one.
Nor, if passing time should collect our matter
after death and restore it again as it is now situated
and for a second time the light of life be given to us,
would it still matter at all to us even if this happened,　　**850**
when once the memory of ourselves has been broken apart.
And even now it makes no difference to us about who we were
before, nor does pain from those former selves affect us now.
For when you look back at the whole past extent
of boundless time , and then at how various are　　**855**
the motions of matter, you could easily come to believe this,
that these same seeds out of which we are now made
have been arranged before in the same order as they are now. **(865)**
Nor nevertheless can we recover this with our remembering mind, **(858)**
because a break in existence has been interposed and far
　　and wide　　**(859)** **860**
all the motions have wandered off all over from the senses.　　**(860)**
For if by chance someone is going to do badly and suffer　　**(861)**
in the future, the person who could do poorly must exist at that **(862)**
time too. Since death precludes this, and prevents　　**(863)**
the existence of him for whom these troubles could be assembled, **(864)** **865**
we may know that there is nothing for us to fear in death,
nor can a person who does not exist become miserable nor at all
does it matter whether he now will have been born at any time,
when immortal death takes away mortal life.

---

[47] Lucretius here describes Hannibal's invasion of Italy during the Second
Punic War (219-202 BC). He is apparently adapting a famous passage
from the Roman epic poet Ennius.

[48] i.e., to either the Romans or Carthaginians.

870 And so when you see a person getting angry that
after death it will happen that either he will rot once his body is buried,
or that he will be finished by flames or the jaws of fierce beasts,
you may know he does not ring true and that there exists beneath the surface
some invisible goad in his mind, however much he himself denies
875 that he believes that he will possess any sort of sensation in death.
For he does not, I think, grant what he professes nor its premises,[49]
nor does he root himself up and throw himself out of life,
but he makes something of himself survive without realizing it.
For when each person while still alive imagines what will happen
880 when birds and wild beasts tear his body apart in death,
he himself takes pity on himself— for he does not separate himself from it,[50]
nor does he sufficiently remove himself from the cast-out corpse and
he imagines that it is him and he infects it with his own feelings as he stands by.
This is why he gets angry that he has been made mortal
885 and he does not see that in real death there will be no other self
who will be alive and able to grieve for himself now bereft of himself,
and who standing can weep for himself lying there as he is mangled or burnt.
For if in death it is a disaster to be shredded by the jaws and teeth
of wild animals, I do not understand why it is not awful
890 to be placed on the fire and begin to burn over hot flames,
or to be placed in honey and be suffocated and to grow rigid
frigidly, resting on the smooth surface of ice-cold rock,
or to be flattened from above, ground down by the weight of the earth.
"Now, now never again will your joyful home or wonderful
895 wife receive you, nor will your sweet children
race to snatch kisses and touch your heart with silent sweetness.
Nor will you be able to provide protection for your flourishing affairs
and those close to you. Miserably for miserable you," they say,
"one awful day takes away all the many prizes of life."
900 On this topic they do not add this: "Nor does a desire
for these things then any longer weigh upon you."
If they kept this clearly in mind and followed it out in words,
they would free themselves from great mental anguish and fear.
"Yes you, just as you are now asleep in death, so you will
905 be for what remains of time, freed from all bitter sorrows.
But we nearby have wept inconsolably for you turned to

---

[49] "What he professes" = that he will not have sensation after death; "its premises" = that the soul perishes with the body.

[50] i.e., from his corpse.

ashes on the horrifying pyre, and no day will
come to remove eternal grief from our hearts."
Then we must inquire of this man the following: What
is so bitter, if it all comes down to sleep and repose,   **910**
that someone could waste away in eternal grief?
Thus, indeed, people often act when they recline at table
and hold their glasses and shade their brows with garlands,
as they say from their hearts, "Such enjoyment is fleeting for poor
    mortals.
Soon it will be over, and it will never be recoverable later."   **915**
As if in death this will be the foremost of their troubles,
that parching thirst should burn and scorch the miserable creatures,
or that longing for some other thing should settle on them.
For no one misses himself or his life,
when both his mind and body equally rest in sleep.   **920**
For all we care, sleep could be everlasting on these
terms, and no longing for ourselves affects us.
And yet those first bodies then do not stray
very far at all from the motions that bring sensation,
when a person is roused from sleep and pulls himself together.   **925**
Therefore we should think that death is much less to us,
if anything can be less than what we see is nothing.
For a greater turmoil and disruption of matter occurs
at death and no one wakes up and gets up
whom the cold break in existence has once overtaken.   **930**
And next suppose that the nature of things should suddenly raise
her voice and herself thus scold anyone of us about this:
"What is so troublesome to you, o mortal, that you indulge too much in
anxious lamentations? Why do you groan and bewail death?
For if your past and former life was pleasing to you   **935**
and all its blessings have not flowed out and perished
thanklessly, as if they were gathered in a vessel full of holes,
why do you not depart like a banqueter who is sated with life,
and embrace untroubled quiet with a calm mind, you fool?
But if those things which you enjoyed have been poured out and
    perished,   **940**
and life is hateful, why do you seek to add more,
which again will perish badly and pass away thanklessly?
Why not rather put an end to life and trouble?[51]
Moreover, there is nothing I can devise and invent for you

---

[51] Epicurus had taken a generally dim view of suicide, believing that the
    true Epicurean should almost always be able to find more pleasure in
    life than pain. He did allow suicide as an option, however, in extreme
    cases.

945 which will please you: all things are always the same.
Even if your body is not yet withered nor your limbs
worn and feeble, still all things remain the same,
even if you proceed to conquer all ages
by living, and even more, if you never are going to die."
950 What do we respond, except that nature is setting out
a just charge and with her words is pleading a true case?
But if now someone older and more advanced in years should
    complain   (955)
and wretchedly lament his death more than is right, would she
    not   (952)
call out even more deservedly and protest with a sharp voice? (953)
955 "Get your tears out of here, you ingrate, and cease your complaints. (954)
You have enjoyed all the prizes of life and are withering away.
But since you always want what is absent, and despise what is present,
your life has slipped away, incomplete and unsatisfying,
and death has unexpectedly taken his stand by your head
960 before you could depart satisfied and full of good things.
But now give up everything not suited to your age, and with a calm
mind yield to your years—come on!—it must happen."[52]
Justly she would plead, I think, and justly rebuke and reprove.
For old things, pushed out by new things, always
965 yield, and one thing must always be built up out of others.
Nothing is handed over to the underworld and black Tartarus.
Matter is needed so that later generations may grow, and yet they all,
once they have finished their life, will follow you, and so no less
than you have they passed away before now, and will pass away.
970 Thus one thing will never stop arising from another,
and life is a permanent possession of no one, but on loan to all.
Consider likewise how the vast expanse of time
gone by before we were born has been nothing to us.
Therefore nature holds this up for us as a mirror
975 of future time after our death finally comes.
Does anything appear frightening in this, does anything seem
distressing, isn't it more calming than any sleep?
And certainly these things which are said to exist
in the depths of Acheron are all present in this life of ours.
980 There is no wretched Tantalus who, as the story goes, is numbed
by empty terror and fears the boulder hanging in the air;
rather it is in this life that empty fear of the gods crushes
mortals, who fear the fall chance furnishes for each.
Neither is there a Tityos lying in Acheron whom birds
985 root around in nor at all are they able to keep finding
something in his huge chest to probe forever.

---

[52] There is a textual problem with this line.

However much he stretches out with the vast projection
of his body —say he not only covers nine acres
with his extended limbs, but the circle of the entire world —
still he will not be able to endure eternal pain, 990
nor provide food from his own body forever.
But Tityos is here among us, and winged creatures[53]
tear at him as he lies in love, and anxious anguish consumes him,
or cares carve him up with some other desire.
Sisyphus, too, is here in life before our eyes, 995
he who thirsts to seek the rods and awesome axes[54]
from the people and always goes away defeated and dejected.
For to seek power, which is empty and never really attained,
and always to undergo harsh labors in the process,
this is to struggle to push up the face of a mountain 1000
a stone which rolls still yet again from the highest summit
and rapidly seeks the level areas of the even plain.[55]
Next, always to feed the insatiable nature of the mind
and to fill it with good things and never satisfy it,
as the seasons of the year do for us, when they return 1005
round and bear their produce and various delights,
and yet we are never filled with the fruits of life,
this, I think, is what people recall: that girls,[56] in the flower
of their age, gather liquid into a vessel full of holes
which yet is unable to be filled in any way at all. 1010
Cerberus and the Furies, moreover, and the absence of light,
Tartarus belching forth terrifying heat,
these neither exist anywhere nor can they exist at all.
But in this life there exists remarkable fear of punishment
for remarkable misdeeds, and paying the price of crime, 1015
prison and a horrible casting down from the rock,[57]

---

[53] The Latin word translated "winged creature" (*volucres*) is the same word Lucretius uses in 984 to name the birds eating Tityos. The winged creatures that attack contemporary Tityoses here on earth are not birds, though, but the *Erotes*, or winged Cupids.

[54] The rods (*fasces*) and axes (*secures*) were symbols of power for Roman elected officials.

[55] Lucretius again plays on words: just as the rock seeks the level areas of the even plain (*campi*), so the unsuccessful candidate returns to the Campus Martius in Rome to try again for election.

[56] The girls are the Danaids, condemned to try to gather water in sieves forever.

[57] Lucretius refers to Roman forms of torture. With the word "prison" (*carcer*) Lucretius probably refers to the state prison located near the Roman Forum. The rock (*saxum*) refers to the Tarpeian Rock, a spot in Rome from which criminals were thrown.

whippings, executioners, the rack, pitch, hot-plates, torches.
And even if these are absent, still the mind, aware of its misdeeds,
fears in anticipation and goads and stings itself with whips,
1020 and fails to see meanwhile what the limit of its troubles
can be and what the end of its punishments will be at last,
and it fears that these same things will grow even greater in death.
The life of fools at last becomes hell here on earth.
This too you might tell yourself sometimes:
1025 "Even good Ancus left the light of day behind with his eyes,[58]
and he was much better in many ways than you, you reprobate.
Since then, many other kings and those who have power
over things have died, who governed great peoples.
And even that man himself, who once built a road
1030 across the great sea,[59] and let his legions go on a journey over the deep,
and taught his infantry to go over the salt waters,
and with his cavalry spurned and pranced upon waves' crashing,
        even he
saw the light slip away and poured out his soul from his dying body.
The descendant of the Scipios,[60] thunderbolt of war, terror of Carthage,
1035 gave his bones to the earth just as if he had been an ordinary household
slave. Add the discoverers of the sciences and the arts.
Add the companions of the daughters of Helicon,[61] over whom Homer
        had singular
supremacy, though even he went to sleep with the same repose as the
        others.
Next, after ripe old age warned Democritus
1040 that the motions of memory in his mind were slowing down,
he himself voluntarily directed his life in the direction of death.
Epicurus[62] himself died when the light of his life ran its course,
he who surpassed the human race in intellect and overwhelmed

---

58   In this line Lucretius is quoting the Roman poet Ennius. Ancus was the
     fourth king of Rome, regularly called "good."

59   Lucretius here describes the Persian King Xerxes' bridging of the
     Hellespont in 480 BC when he was leading an expedition against the
     Greeks.

60   "The descendant of the Scipios" is probably a reference to Scipio Africanus
     the Elder, who defeated the Carthaginian general Hannibal at Zama in
     202 BC during the Second Punic War. The phrase could also apply,
     however, to Scipio Aemilianus Africanus the Younger, who defeated
     Carthage decisively in 146 BC in the Third Punic War.

61   The daughters of Helicon are the Muses.

62   This is the only place in the poem where Lucretius mentions Epicurus by
     name.

everyone else, as the ethereal sun does the stars when it has risen.
Will you then really be hesitant and angry at dying? 1045
Life is even now almost dead to you while you are alive and alert,
you who waste the greater part of your years in sleep
and snore wide awake and never stop seeing dreams
and possess a mind plagued by empty fear, and who are unable
often to discover what the matter is with yourself, when in a drunken 1050
haze, you wretch, you are everywhere oppressed by many cares,
drifting and wandering with aimless missteps of the mind."
If people were able, just as they are seen to sense
that there is a weight on their minds because it wears them out by its
    heaviness,
to understand from what causes each thing happens 1055
and from what source such a mound of misery exists in their hearts,
not at all would they lead their lives as we now usually see them,
each not knowing what he wants for himself, and always seeking
to change location, as if he could put down his burden.
The man who is sick and tired of his home 1060
often leaves his mansion, and then suddenly returns,
since he feels things are not at all better outdoors.
Driving his imported ponies he races to his country villa
at top speed, as if rushing to bring help to a house on fire.
He immediately starts yawning when he touches the threshold of his
    villa, 1065
or goes off into a heavy sleep and just tries to forget,
or dashing off again he seeks to return to the city.
Thus each person flees himself, but he cannot, of course,
escape the one he flees, but clings to him unwillingly and hates him
because he is sick and does not understand the cause of his disease. 1070
If he understood this well, each would now drop other things
and be eager above all to understand the nature of things,
since what is at stake is the state of all time to come,
not just of one hour, the state in which mortals must
remain for the whole period which remains after death. 1075
Moreover, what destructive desire of life is so great
that it forces us to shake anxiously in times of doubt and danger?
Assuredly there is an unalterable limit of life for mortals,
and it is impossible for us to avoid death and not pass away.
Besides, we are involved and live always among the same things, 1080
and no new pleasure is ever hammered out by living.
But while what we desire is absent, it seems to surpass other things.
Afterwards, having attained this, we desire something else and the
    same
thirst for life holds us, our mouths always agape.
What fortune the years to come may bring us is uncertain, 1085

or what chance may bear us, or what end awaits us.
And by extending our life we will not subtract one jot at all
from the time we will be dead, nor can we take away anything
so that by chance we might be able to be dead for less long.
Accordingly, grant that you complete as many ages as you wish by

1090   living,
still no less at all will everlasting death await you,
nor will he who makes an end to his life from today's light
not exist from that moment any less than he,
who passed away many months and years before.

Handwritten notes at top:

"To free the mind from religion"

SENSES ← sight 94-105
sound 105-108
smell 108-110
dreams 112, 117-118

ON THE NATURE OF THINGS

BOOK IV

I am traversing the remote places of the Pierides,[1] untrodden by the
  sole
of anyone before. It is a joy to approach pure springs
and to drink from them, and it is a joy to pick new flowers
and to seek a preeminent crown for my head from that place
whence the Muses had wreathed the temples of no one before;[2]   5
first because I am teaching about great things and proceeding
to free the mind from the narrow bonds of religion,
next because I am writing so clear a poem about so obscure
a subject, touching everything with the charm of the Muses.
For this too seems to be not without reason.   10
For just as when physicians try to give loathsome wormwood
to children, they first touch the rim of the cup all
around with the sweet, golden liquid of honey,
so that the unsuspecting age of children may be tricked as far
as their lips, and so that meanwhile the child might drink down   15
the bitter wormwood juice and though deceived, be not deceased,
but rather by such means be restored and become well,
so I now, since this system seems for the most part to be
too bitter to those who have not tried it and
the common people shrink back from it, wanted to explain   20
our system to you in sweet-spoken Pierian[3] song
and touch it, so to speak, with the sweet honey of the Muses.
I have done so in the hope I might in this way be able to hold
your attention in our verses, until you perceive the whole
nature of things, and are fully aware of its usefulness.[4]   25

---

[1] Pierides = the daughters of Pierus, i.e., the Muses.

[2] Lucretius claims to be the first Roman to write a philosophic poem.

[3] i.e., sacred to the Muses.

[4] 4.1-25 = 1.926-950, with a few minor differences in lines 11, 24, and 25.

SIMULACRA

And since I have shown what the nature of the mind is
and from what things it thrives when joined with the body
and in what way, when separated, it returns to its first beginnings,
now I will begin to treat for you what closely relates
30 to these things: that there exist what we call images[5] of things,
which, like films ripped from the outer surface
of things, fly back and forth through the air.
These are the same things which strike our minds with terror
when they come to us awake, and in sleep, when often we behold
35 wondrous shapes and images of those who have left the light,
and which often wake us with a start when we are adrift in sleep,
lest by chance we think that souls make their escape
from Acheron or that shades fly about among the living,
or lest we think that something of us can remain after death,
40 when the body and the nature of the soul have been destroyed together
and have produced a parting, each into its own first beginnings.
I say, therefore, that semblances and fine shapes of things
are sent out from things, from their outer surface.
This can be understood, no matter how dull one's mind, from what
    follows.
45 [But since I have shown of what sort are the beginnings of all
things, and how, differing in their various shapes,
they fly around on their own, stirred up by eternal motion,
and how from them all things are able to be created,
now I will begin to treat for you what closely relates to
50 these things: that there exist what we call likenesses of things,[6]
which must be termed, so to speak, films or bark, because the image
bears an appearance and shape like that thing, whatever it is,
from the body of which it is said to be shed and wander forth.][7]
First of all, since in the case of visible things
55 many things give off bodies, in part scattered loosely,
as wood gives off smoke, and fire heat,
and in part more closely woven and compacted, just as at times
when cicadas shed their smoothly rounded clothing in summer,
and when calves while being born give off films[8]

---

[5] The word Lucretius uses for images (*simulacra*) is a Latin translation of
Epicurus' Greek term, *eidôlon*.

[6] 4.49-50 = 4. 29-30.

[7] Lines 45-53 are lines that Lucretius might have decided to remove in a
final revision of the poem. He probably wrote them originally when
Book 4 was meant to follow directly on Book 2, before he wrote Book 3.

[8] By films (*membranas*), Lucretius here refers to the amnion or caul that
surrounds the calf at birth.

from their outer surface, and likewise when a slippery serpent   **60**
sheds its covering on thorns (for we often see
bushes decorated with their fluttering body-armor).
Since those things happen, a thin image must also
be sent out from things, from their outer surface.
For why those should fall and recede from things   **65**
more than those which are thin, there is no possibility of uttering,
especially since there exist on the outer surface of things bodies
which are many and minute, which can be thrown off in the same
    order
which they had before and preserve the outline of the shape,
and much more quickly, being less able to be impeded   **70**
in as much as they are few and are located right up front.
For surely we see many things toss out and lavishly
give up bodies not only from deep within, as we said before,
but often from their surface, and even their very color.
And awnings commonly do this, yellow, red,   **75**
and purple, when they are stretched over large theaters
and flutter and wave above people on masts and beams.
For there they tint the crowd in their seats below, and the whole
spectacle of the stage, [the senators, and the mother of the gods],[9]
and make them flutter and flow with their own colors.   **80**
And the more the walls of the theater encircle and enclose,
the more all these things within are soaked
with splendor and laugh when the light of day is diminished.
Therefore since awnings emit color from their outer surfaces,
all things must also emit fine semblances,   **85**
since in both cases they are throwing off from their surfaces.
There are therefore then fixed outlines of shapes
which freely fly around endowed with subtle texture
and which are not able to be seen singly or separately.
Moreover, all odor, smoke, heat, and other things similar   **90**
pour out and stream away from things for this reason,
since as they are arising and coming out from deep within
they are split up on their winding journey, nor are there straight
passageways by which they can hasten to arise and depart together.
But in contrast when a fine film of surface color   **95**
is sent forth, there is nothing which can rip it apart,
since it is close by and located right up front.
Finally, whatever reflections are visible to us
in mirrors, on water, and on very shiny surfaces,
seeing that they are endowed with an appearance similar to the objects, **100**

---

[9] The text in brackets is uncertain.

101 must consist of images sent off from the objects.[10]
104 There are thus thin patterns of things and similar
105 semblances, which though singly no one is able to see,
     nevertheless by continuous and frequent repulsion they rebuff
     and return a visible image from the surface of mirrors.
     In no other way can they possibly insure
     that appearances so greatly resembling each thing are returned.
110 Now come: perceive how fine the nature of an image is.
     And first of all, since the first beginnings are so far
     below the reach of our senses and are so much smaller
     than the things which our eyes first begin to be unable to make out,
     now nevertheless so that I might convince you of this too,
115 perceive in brief how very fine are the beginnings of all things.
     First, there exist some living creatures so small that
     it is impossible to make out one-third of their body.
     What must we think a little portion of their intestines is like?
     What of the sphere of their heart or eyes? What of their limbs?
120 Appendages? How tiny are they? Even more, what about the
         individual first
     beginnings from which their soul and the nature of their mind must be
         composed?
     Don't you see how fine and how incredibly small they are?
     And next, whatever things breathe out from their body
     a strong odor — panaces, foul wormwood,
125 heavy-smelling southernwood, bitter centaury[11] —
     if by chance you <touch> any one of these lightly <between> two
         <fingers>[12] ...

         *   *   *   *   *   *   *   *   *   *   *   *   *

     but that you should realize that images of things wander about,
     many in a multitude of manners, with no power, unperceived.
     But lest by chance you think that the only things which wander
130 about are those images of things which depart from things,
     there are also those that are produced spontaneously and themselves
     are formed in this part of the sky that is called the air.
     These are formed in a multitude of manners and borne aloft,[13]   **(135)**
     just as we sometimes see that clouds easily gather   **(133)**
135 on high and spoil the serene beauty of the sky,   **(134)**

---

[10] Lines 102-103 are identical to lines 65-66, and make no sense here. They
     are omitted by editors.

[11] The Romans used all four plants for medicinal purposes.

[12] There is a lacuna in the text here, perhaps a leaf of a manuscript containing
     52 lines.

[13] I have followed editors who transpose line 135 so that it follows line 132.

caressing the air as they move. For often giants' faces
appear to be airborne and cast shadows far and wide,
sometimes majestic mountains and rocks ripped from
mountains seem to go ahead and pass before the sun,
then a monster seems to drag and pull in other clouds.   140
They never stop dissolving, changing their shapes,
and turning into the outlines of shapes of every kind.
Now how easily and quickly these images are created,
and how unceasingly they flow from things and slip off and depart...[14]

* * * * * * * * * * * * *

For something on the surface is always flowing from things   145
which they cast off. When it reaches some things
it passes through, especially glass. But when it reaches
rough rock or building timber, then at once
it is dispersed so it is not able to return the image.
But when things that stay shiny and solid have been interposed,   150
especially like a mirror, neither of these things occurs.
For neither can they pass through, as with glass, nor on the contrary
be dispersed. The smoothness remembers to preserve their safety.
Therefore it happens that the images flow back from it to us.
And however suddenly, at whatever time you place a mirror   155
in front of each thing, an image appears,
so that you may realize that constantly flowing from the outer surface
of things are thin textures and thin shapes.
Therefore many images are produced in a short time,
so that deservedly the birth of these things is said to be quick.   160
And just as the sun must send out much light
in a short time so that all things are constantly filled by it,
so likewise for a similar reason it is necessary that images
be carried off from things in a moment of time,
many in a multitude of manners, everywhere in all directions,   165
since wherever we turn the mirror towards the shapes of things,
objects answer back there with similar shape and color.
Moreover when the weather in the sky has just now been brilliantly
clear, all of a sudden it becomes stormy and foul,
so that you think that on all sides darkness has left Acheron   170
behind and fills up the vast caverns of the sky,
so greatly, when the bleak night of clouds has arisen,
do the faces of black fear hang over us from above.
How small a part of the clouds an image is there is no one
who can say nor render an account of it in words.   175
Now come, with how swift a motion the images are carried along,

---

[14] One or more lines are lost here. The sentence probably ended something
like, "...I will explain."

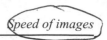
and what quickness has been granted them as they swim across the air
so that a brief hour is consumed in covering a great distance
in whatever direction each aims with different impulses,
180 I will set out with verses that are few but sweetly spoken.
Just so is the short song of the swan better than the cranes'
clamor scattered among the clouds of heaven on the south wind.
First, frequently we may see that things which are light
and made up of tiny particles are quick.
185 Now of this sort are the light of the sun and its heat,
because they are made up of tiny first bodies
which are hammered, so to speak, and do not stop traveling
through the intervening air since they are struck by blows from behind.
For light is immediately reinforced by more light
190 and, as if in succession, spark is goaded on by spark.
Therefore by similar reasoning images must
be able to traverse an inconceivably large distance
in an instant of time, first because there is a cause which,
though tiny, pushes and propels them at a distance from behind,
195 in addition because they are carried along with such rapid lightness,
next because they are sent off endowed with such a fine texture
that they can easily penetrate all sorts of things
and percolate through, so to speak, the intervening air.
Moreover, if those particles of things which are sent forth
200 from deep down within, like the light of the sun
and its heat, are seen in an instant of a day to flow
and diffuse themselves through the sky's whole space,
and to fly through sea and lands and drench the sky,
what then about those that are now ready right on the surface,
205 when they are shot off and nothing impedes their release?
Don't you see that they should travel more rapidly and farther
and cover many times the extent of space in the same
time in which the light of the sun spreads across the sky?
This also seems to be an exceptionally good demonstration of
210 with how swift a motion the images of things are carried along:
that as soon as the gleam of water is placed beneath the heavens
when the sky is star-strewn, immediately the peaceful
stars of the firmament answer back glimmering in the water.
Don't you see then how in an instant of time an image
215 falls from the shores of heaven to the shores of earth?
Wherefore again and again it must be admitted that with wondrous[15]

* * * * * * * * * * * *

---

[15] The text is uncertain. It seems that the conclusion of the section on the
speed of images and the beginning of the section on images and sensation
are lost.

bodies which strike the eyes and stir up sight.
And odors flow off continuously from certain things,
just like coolness from rivers, heat from the sun, and spray
from the waves of the sea, the gnawer of walls along the shore.   220
Nor do various voices ever forego flying through the air.
Lastly, a salty-tasting moisture often forms in our mouths
when we spend time near the sea, but when we see wormwood
being diluted and mixed, a bitter taste is experienced.
So from all things each thing in a flow is carried   225
away and is sent off everywhere in all directions;
neither delay nor any respite is given to the flowing,
since we continuously receive sensations, and it is always permitted
that we see all things, smell them, and sense their sound.
Moreover, since any shape which is felt by the hands   230
in darkness is recognized to be the same as that which
is seen in bright and brilliant light, it is necessary that
touch and sight are stimulated by a similar cause.
Now then if we handle a cube and it registers with us
in the dark, in the light what thing will be able   235
to strike our sight as a cube, if not the image of the object?
It is in images, therefore, that the source of perceiving is seen
to be, nor without them is anything able to be seen.
Now those which I am calling the images of things are carried along
everywhere and are tossed and scattered in all directions.   240
But since we are able to see with our eyes alone,
it therefore happens that wherever we turn our sight, all
things there strike it directly with their shape and color.
And how far each thing is distant from us, the image
makes us see and helps us distinguish.   245
For when it is emitted, immediately it thrusts forward and drives
whatever air lies between it and our eyes,
and thus the air all glides through our eyes and,
as it were, brushes through our pupils and thus goes by.
It therefore happens that we see how far off is   (251) 250
each thing. And the more air is set in motion   (250)
ahead of it and the longer the breeze brushes through our eyes,
the farther off each thing is seen to be.
Of course these things are carried out with amazing speed,
so that we see simultaneously what a thing is and how far away.   255
This in these matters must not be thought remarkable in the least:
why, although those images which strike the eyes cannot
be seen individually, the objects themselves are perceived.
For although the wind batters us little by little and although
cold flows fiercely, we are not used to feeling   (261) 260
each individual particle of this wind or cold,   (260)

but rather the whole all at once, and then we see blows
produced on our bodies just as if some thing
were battering us and providing a feeling of its body externally.
265 Additionally, when we tap on a rock with our finger, we touch
the very outer surface color of the rock,
and we do not feel the color by touch, but rather
we feel the very hardness of the rock deep within.
Now come, see why the image is seen beyond the mirror
270 (for it certainly is seen far off deep inside).
It is just as those things which are actually viewed outside,
when a door provides an open view through itself,
and enables many things to be seen outside the house.
This sight too is caused by twin streams of air.
275 For first then the air this side of the doors is discerned,
next the doors themselves to the right and left follow,
afterwards the outside light brushes through our eyes, and a second
air, and those things which are actually viewed outside.
So when an image of a mirror first projects itself forward,
280 while it is coming to our vision, it thrusts forward and drives
whatever air is located between it and our eyes,
and makes it so that we perceive all this air before
the mirror. But when we have perceived the mirror itself too,
immediately the image which is carried from us to it
285 reaches us after it has rebounded back and returned
and rolls along propelling another air before it
and makes it so that we see that before it,[16] and thus
it appears to be so far distant from the mirror.
Therefore again and again it is not at all right to wonder[17]

* * * * * * * * * * * * * *

290 for those things which return a vision from the surface of mirrors,
since the result in either case involves two airs.
Now it happens that the part of our limbs on the right side
appears to be on the left side in mirrors because
when the image reaches and strikes the flat surface of the mirror,
295 it is not reversed without change, but is driven straight back,
just as if someone, before a plaster mask has dried,
were to strike it hard against a column or a beam,
and if it immediately were to preserve its shape directly in front,[18]
and were itself to reproduce itself driven backwards.   (323)

---

[16] i.e., we see the second column of air before we see the reflected image of
ourselves in the mirror.

[17] One or more lines have been lost here.

[18] Lines 299-322 and 323-347 were transposed in the original manuscript.

So it will happen that what was the right eye before is itself   **(324) 300**
now the left, and from the left in turn comes the right.
It happens also that an image is passed from mirror to mirror,
so that even five or six reflections can often be produced.
For whatever things are hidden back within the interior of a house,
however distant along a twisting path deep within,   **(329) 305**
still all these can be extracted from within along bending
paths by many mirrors and be seen to be in the house.
Thus the image is reflected from mirror to mirror,
and when the left is transmitted, it comes about that it becomes the
    right,
but then again reverses and returns right to where it was.   **(334) 310**
Then again whenever curved sides of mirrors
possess a curvature like that of our own sides,[19]
they return correct reflections for these reasons,
either because the image is transported from a part of the mirror to
    another,
whence it is struck twice and flies to us, or perhaps because   **(339) 315**
the image is moved around when it has arrived, because
the curved surface of the mirror teaches it to rotate towards us.
Further, please suppose that our reflections proceed and plant
their steps along with us, and imitate our movements,
because whatever part of the mirror you vacate,   **(344) 320**
immediately reflections cannot be returned from there,
seeing that nature compels everything to return
and rebound from things, rendered back at equal angles.   **(347)**
The eyes also shun and avoid gazing at brilliant objects.   **(299)**
The sun even brings blindness, if you proceed to look straight at it, **(300) 325**
since its force is great and its images are born along
from on high through the pure air with significant effect,
striking the eyes and upsetting the way they are structured.
Besides, when a bright flash is sharp, it often burns
the eye because it contains many seeds of fire   **(305) 330**
which produce pain for the eyes by wending their way in.
So too all things jaundiced people see
turn pale yellow, because many seeds of pale
yellow flow from their body to meet the images of things,
and many seeds are also mixed in their eyes   **(310) 335**
which by their contagion dye everything with their paleness.
But while in darkness we view things which are in the light
because, when the black air of darkness which is closer
enters first and occupies the open eyes,

---

[19] i.e., possess a concave shape like that of the human flank.

340 bright brilliant air at once follows along   (315)
     and cleans them out, as it were, and disperses the black shadows
     of that former air. For the latter air is many times
     more mobile, many times smaller and more powerful.
     As soon as it fills the passages of the eyes with light
345 and opens those which the black air had blocked   (320)
     before, immediately there follow the images of things   (321)
     which are located in the light, and they stimulate us to see.   (322)
     But in contrast we are unable to see from light into darkness
     because the air of darkness enters second, and is much
350 thicker. It fills up every pore
     and blocks the passages of the eyes, so that none of the images
     of things can be projected on them and move them.
     When we see from afar the square towers of a city,
     it happens that they often appear rounded for this reason,
355 because every angle looks blunt at a distance,
     or rather it is not discerned and its blow perishes
     and its force does not slip all the way through to our vision,
     since, while the images are carried along through much air,
     the air forces it to grow dull through frequent collisions.
360 Thus when every angle similarly slips by our senses
     it happens that structures of stone are rounded as if on a lathe,
     still not like those which are truly round up close,
     but they appear somewhat similar in shadowy form.
     Likewise it appears to us that a shadow moves
365 in the sun and follows our footsteps and imitates our gestures,
     if you believe that air deprived of light can
     advance, following the motions and gestures of people.
     For that thing which we are accustomed to call a shadow
     is nothing other than air devoid of light.
370 Of course, because the earth is deprived successively in certain places
     of the light of the sun wherever we stroll along and block it,
     and likewise the portion of it we left is filled back up,
     it therefore happens that what used to be the shadow of the body
     seems ever to stay the same and follow us straight along.
375 For new rays of light are always pouring forth
     and old ones perish, like wool is spun into a fire.
     Therefore the earth is easily stripped of light
     and refilled again, washing off black shadows from itself.
     Nor yet do we admit that the eyes are at all deceived in this.
380 For it belongs to them to see at whatever point there is
     light and shadow. But whether the lights are the same or not,
     or whether it is the same shadow which was here and now moves over
         there,

or whether it rather happens as we said a little before,[20]
this the reasoning power of the mind alone should determine,
nor are the eyes able to know the nature of things. 385
Thus do not falsely attribute this fault of the mind to the eyes.
A ship on which we are riding moves, although it seems to be
    motionless;
the one which remains stationary is believed to be passing by.
And the hills and plains appear to flee astern
as we ride our ship past them and soar along on sails. 390
All the stars appear motionless, fixed in their heavenly
vaults, yet they are all in a state of continuous motion,
since they rise and return to their far away settings,
when they have measured out the sky with brilliant body.
Likewise the sun and moon appear to remain 395
stationary, although the facts themselves show they are in motion.
And mountains rising far distant from the middle of the deep
among which a wide and free passage lies open for ships — still
it appears a single island is formed from them all joined together.
That halls are spinning and columns running around 400
appear so certain to children when they themselves
have stopped twirling, that they scarcely can now believe
that all the walls are not threatening to crash down on top of them.
And further, when nature begins to lift up the light of dawn
red with flickering flames, and to raise it above the mountains, 405
the mountains above which the sun then appears to be
close by and touching and burning with its fire,
scarcely are they distant from us two thousand arrow shots,
scarcely often even five hundred javelin casts.
Between them and the sun lie huge expanses of sea 410
stretched out beneath vast shores of heaven,
and lying between are many thousands of lands
which different peoples and generations of wild beasts occupy.
But a puddle of water no deeper than a finger's breadth,
which lies between the stones on the pavement of the street, 415
provides a view beneath the earth as great in extent
as the lofty gap of heaven opens above the earth,
so that you seem to look down at clouds and see the sky and
bodies hidden wondrously in the sky beneath the earth.
Next, when a spirited horse of ours has halted in the middle 420
of a stream and we have looked down on the rapid waters of the river,

---

[20] Lucretius refers to his earlier explanation in 370-378 about why shadows
appear to move.

a force appears to carry the body of the horse sideways,
though it is standing still, and to thrust it rapidly against the current,
and wherever we cast our eyes everything appears to be carried
425 along and to flow in a manner similar to ourselves.
Next, although a colonnade has equal lines
and stands supported throughout on uniform columns,
still when its entire length is viewed from the end,
gradually it contracts into the apex of a narrow cone,
430 joining the roof to the ground and everything on the right to the left,
until the point of the cone contracts into obscurity.
To sailors at sea it happens that the sun appears to rise
from the waves and set and hide its light in the waves.
Of course, since they gaze at nothing else but water and sky.
435 Do not lightly assume that the senses are undermined from all sides.
But to those ignorant of the sea, ships in port seem deformed
and to be pressing down on the waves with shattered stern-posts.
For whatever part of the oars is raised above the salty dew
is straight, and rudders too are straight above.
440 Those parts which are submerged and penetrate the water, all appear
to be broken and twisted, and to be twisted back upwards again
and almost to be bent back and float on top of the water.
And when the winds carry along scattered clouds through the sky
at night time, then the sparkling celestial signs appear
445 to glide along against the clouds and travel high above
in a direction far different than they are carried on their true course.
But if by chance your hand is placed beneath one eye
and presses it, by a certain sensation it happens that all things
which we look at appear to be double even as we look,
450 double the light of lamps, flowering in flames,
double the furniture throughout the entire house is replicated,
and duplicated are the faces of people, their bodies double.
And next, when sleep overcomes the limbs with sweet slumber,
and the whole body lies in deep repose,
455 then nevertheless we seem to be awake and move
our limbs, and in the sordid gloom of night we think
we see the sun and light of day, and though
we are in an enclosed place, we seem to visit sky,
sea, rivers, mountains, and traverse plains on foot,
460 and to hear sounds, when the absolute silence of night
is everywhere, and to offer up words in our speechlessness.
We see an amazing number of other things of this type,
all of which seek to shatter one's trust, so to speak, in the senses,
but in vain, since by far the largest part of these deceive
465 because of the inferences of the mind, which we ourselves contribute,

so that things not seen by the senses are taken as things seen.[21]
For nothing is more difficult than to distinguish clear things
from doubtful ones which the mind adds immediately on its own.
Next, if anyone thinks that nothing is known, he also doesn't
know whether this can be known, since he admits he knows nothing. **470**
So I will cease pleading my case against such a person,
who on his own has stuck his head where his feet belong.
And yet even if I concede he knows this, still this very thing
I will ask: since he has never found any truth in things before,
from where does he know what it is to know and not know in turn, 　**475**
what thing created the concept of true and false,
and what thing has demonstrated that the doubtful differs from the
　　　sure.
You will find that the concept of truth is created first of all
from the senses, and that the senses cannot be refuted.
For greater trust ought to be granted to this, 　　　　　　　　**480**
which on its own is able to overcome false things with true.
What ought to be held in greater trust than the senses?
Or will reason, having arisen from false sensation, be strong enough
to speak against the senses, when it arose completely from the senses?
Unless they are true, reason too becomes completely false. 　　**485**
Or can the ears refute the eyes, or touch refute the ears?
Or further, will the mouth's sense of taste argue with this
touch, or will the nostrils refute it or the eyes defeat it?
I think not. For to each sense a function has been separately
assigned, each has its own power, and thus it is necessary 　　**490**
that you sense what is soft and what is cold or hot separately,
and sense separately the various colors of things,
and see whatever things are joined to colors.[22]
Separately too the mouth's sense of taste has its force, separately
smells arise, separately sounds. And so it is necessary 　　　**495**
that the senses cannot prove each other wrong.
And further, they cannot refute themselves,
since equal trust must always be granted them.
Accordingly, that which has appeared to the senses on each
occasion is true. And if reason is unable to unravel the cause, 　**500**
why those things which were square close-up, when far off

---

[21]　It was a tenet of Epicureanism that knowledge could be gained through
　　the senses, although one had to reason carefully because the mind often
　　made false inferences based on the sense data it received. See
　　Introduction pp. xvi-xviii.

[22]　By "whatever things are joined to color," Lucretius probably means
　　properties like shape and size.

seem round, still it is preferable, lacking reason,
to give a false account of the causes of each shape,
than to let fully evident things fall anywhere from our hands
505 and shatter our primary trust and shake all
the foundations on which our life and safety rely.
For not only would all reason be ruined, but life itself also
would cease at once, unless you dare to trust the senses
and shun dangerously high places and other things of this sort
510 which must be avoided, and seek out things just the opposite.
Therefore your supply of words is completely empty
which you have drawn up and positioned against the senses.
And next, as in construction, if the carpenter's rule is warped at the
    start,
and if the square deceptively deviates from straight lines,
515 and if the level is off at all in any part,
all the structures must turn out full of problems,
crooked, warped, bulging in front and back, and discordant,
so they seem to want to collapse at once, and they do collapse,
since they all were betrayed by false judgments at the start,
520 so too your reasoning about things must be
warped and false, when it has arisen from false senses.
Now to understand how each of the other senses senses
its own object requires no rocky road of reasoning.
First, every sound and voice is heard when they have worked their way
525 into the ears and struck the sense organ with their body.
For it must be admitted that the voice too is bodily,
and so also is sound, since they are able to strike upon the senses.
Moreover the voice often scrapes the throat, and shouting makes
the trachea rougher as it makes its way outside.
530 Naturally, when the first beginnings of voices are gathered
in a great throng and begin to go outside, doubtless
when the throat is full the door of the mouth is also scraped.
Therefore there is no doubt at all that voices and words are composed
of bodily first beginnings so that they can cause injury.
535 Nor likewise does it deceive you about how much body
a continuous speech removes, and what it takes out of
the physical power and strength of people, when it is stretched out
from the rising brilliance of dawn to the gloom of black night,
especially if it is delivered at the top of one's voice.
540 Therefore it must be that the voice is bodily,
since when someone speaks a lot he loses part of his body.
Furthermore, roughness of the voice comes from roughness of
    the first   (551)
beginnings and likewise smoothness is created by smoothness.[23] (552)

---

[23] Editors transpose lines 551-552 to follow line 541.

Nor do the first beginnings of the same shape penetrate   **(542)**
the ear when a trumpet rumbles deeply with a low roar   **(543)** 545
and quickly reverberates wildly back a raucous rumble,
and when <swans from the twisting valleys> of Mt. Helicon
lift their clear lament with saddened voice.[24]
And so when from deep within we squeeze out from our body
these voices and send them straight out through our mouth,   **(548)** 550
the agile tongue, artificer of words, divides them into parts,   **(549)**
and the shaping of the lips in turn forms them.   **(550)**
Thus when the space is not long from which each voice is launched
and arrives, it also must happen that the words themselves
are clearly heard and understood sound by sound.   555
For the voice preserves its shaping and preserves its forming.
But if the space in between is longer than is optimal,
the words must be jumbled about through a lot of air
and the voice mixed about, while it flies through the breezes.
And so it happens that you are able to sense sounds   560
and not distinguish what the meaning of the words is,
to such an extent the voice arrives confused and impeded.
Moreover a single word sent from a crier's mouth
often stirs the ears of everyone in a crowd.
Therefore in an instant one voice breaks up   565
into many voices, since it divides itself for individual ears,
affixing a shape and a clear sound to words.
But that part of the voices which does not fall on the ears
passes by and perishes uselessly scattered on the breezes.
Part, striking solid places and rebounding, return   570
the voice and at times delude us with the image of a word.
When you see this well, you indeed may be able to render a reason
both for yourself and others of how through remote locales
rocks send back matching shapes of words in order,
when we look for our scattered friends in the shadowy mountains   575
and summon them with a great shout when they are all spread out.
Even six or seven voices I have seen places return,
when you emit one. And so hills to hills spontaneously
were sending back and reiterating words taught to return.
Locals imagine that goat-footed satyrs and nymphs   580
inhabit these places, and say that there are fauns.[25]
It is by their night-wandering shriek and playful trickery,
they commonly say, that the still silence is broken

---

[24] Lines 543-548 contain some textual problems. I have translated one
possible emendation.

[25] Fauns were gods of the countryside, often regarded as the source of
strange voices.

and the sounds of strings arise and the sweet complaints
585 which the flute pours forth pressed by the fingers of the players.
In addition, they say, the country-dwelling sort commonly senses it
when Pan,[26] shaking the covering of pine on his half-civilized head,
often with his curving lip runs over the open reeds,
so that his pipes may not stop issuing their sylvan muse.
590 They tell of other odd creatures and portents of this sort,
so that they might not be thought perhaps to live in remote locales
deserted even by the gods. Thus with words
they boast of wonders or they are lead on by some other reason,
since the entire human race is too eager of ears.
595 As to what remains, we must not wonder how, through the
places the eyes are unable to see things openly,
through the same places voices arrive and stimulate the ears.
Often too we perceive a discussion though the doors are closed,
doubtless because the voice can make its way through the twisted
600 passageways of things intact, while visual images refuse.
For they[27] are ripped apart, unless they sail through straight
passageways likes those of glass, through which every image passes.
Moreover a voice is split up in all directions,
since some are produced from others, when one, once it has arisen,
605 has sprung apart into many, just as a fire's spark
is so often accustomed to spread itself out into fires.
Therefore places hidden far from sight are filled with voices
and they all boil over and are stirred up by sound.
But all visual images travel by direct paths
610 just as they are first sent off; thus no one can see
beyond walls, but can receive voices through them.
And yet even the voice itself, passing through closed-off rooms
in houses, is dulled and enters the ears in a confused state,
and we seem to hear mere sounds rather than distinct words.
615 Nor are the tongue and palate by which we sense flavor
any more difficult to understand or more difficult to explain.
First, we sense flavor in the mouth, when we squeeze it out
as we chew our food, as when someone by chance begins with his
     hand
to squeeze and remove the moisture from a sponge loaded with water.
620 Next what we squeeze out is distributed through all the pores
of the palate and the twisted passageways of the loose-knit tongue.
Therefore when the bodies of the dripping savory juices are smooth,

---

[26] Pan was worshipped as the Greek and Roman fertility god of flocks. He
     is represented as half human, half goat, with goat ears, horns, and legs.
[27] "They" = visual images.

sweetly they make contact and sweetly they touch entirely
the moist, salivating regions located around the tongue.
But in contrast bodies assail the senses and cause damage by their
    attack   **625**
to the extent that they each are more replete with sharp roughness.
Next, pleasure from flavors does not extend past the palate.
Indeed when it falls straight down through the jaws,
there is no pleasure, while it is all being distributed in the limbs.
Nor does it matter with what food the body is nourished,   **630**
so long as what you take in you are able to digest and distribute
among the limbs and safeguard the moist tenor of the stomach.
Now how a thing can be food for some creatures and poison for others,
I will explain, or why what is bitter and harsh to some
still nonetheless has the power to seem very sweet to others.   **635**
And so great is the distance and difference in these things,
that what is food to one creature is harsh poison to others.
Thus there is even a snake[28] that when touched by human saliva
perishes and commits suicide by gnawing away at itself.
Moreover the hellebore plant is toxic poison to us,   **640**
but it adds soft fat to goats and quails.
So that you might be able to understand how this happens,
it is first helpful to recall the things we said before,
that the seeds are found mixed in things in a variety of ways.[29]
Furthermore, all living creatures that ingest food,   **645**
just as they are dissimilar on the outside and the external configuration
of their limbs is determined each according to kind,
so also are they made up of seeds of varying shape.
Since, furthermore, their seeds vary, it is also necessary
that their intervals and paths, which we call passages, differ   **650**
throughout all the limbs, in the mouth and also in the palate itself.
Thus some passages must be smaller and some larger,
some living creatures must have triangular passages, others square;
many are round, others are multi-angled in many ways.
For just as the arrangement of shapes and the motions require,   **655**
in that way should the shapes of the passages differ,
and the paths vary in the way the structure compels them.
Therefore when what is sweet to some becomes bitter to others,
the one for whom it is sweet must have the smoothest bodies
slowly and caressingly enter the openings belonging to his palate,   **660**
while to those for whom the same things are bitter within

---

[28] For the belief that human saliva is noxious to snakes, see Aristotle *History of Animals* 607a30 and Pliny *Natural History* 7.2.15.

[29] 1.814-829; 1.895-896; 2.333-380.

doubtless rough and hooked things enter their openings.[30]
Now it is easy from these things to understand everything.
For indeed when someone contracts a fever and the bile rises
665 or in some other way a disease process is set off,
then the entire body is thrown into confusion and all
the arrangements of the first beginnings are then changed around;
the result is that bodies which before were suitable to sensation
now are not suitable, and others fit better,
670 which when they have entered are able to produce a bitter sensation.
Both sorts of seeds are mixed together in the flavor of honey.
This we have already often demonstrated to you before.[31]
Now come and I will explain how the impact of smell touches
the nostrils. First there must be many things
675 from which a diverse flood of smells flows and emanates,
and we must suppose that they flow, disperse, and scatter everywhere.
But different types of smells are more suited to different creatures
because of differing shapes.[32] And so through the gentle breezes
bees are attracted by the smell of honey no matter what the distance,
680 and vultures by dead bodies. Moreover, wherever the cloven
hoof of beasts has planted a step, the violence of dogs
unleashed pushes on, and the odor of men is sensed from afar
by the white goose, the savior of the citadel of Romulus' descendants.[33]
Thus different smells are given to different creatures and lead
685 each to its own food and forces it to recoil from bitter
poison, and in this way the generations of creatures are preserved.
Therefore this very smell that is able to activate the nose
is such that one smell can be spread further than another.
But still in no way can any of them be carried as far
690 as a sound, as a voice, not to mention as those things
which strike the pupils of the eyes and activate vision.
Smell goes wafting around slowly and soon perishes,
easily sundered little by little in the breezes of the air,
first because it is emitted with difficulty from deep within a thing.
695 That smells flow and depart from far within things
is shown by the fact that all things that are broken, that are crushed,

---

[30] By "openings" (*fauces*), Lucretius probably means openings of the pores in the palate.

[31] Lucretius had discussed honey in 2.398 and 3.191, and the mixture of smooth and rough first beginnings in things in 1.407ff.

[32] "Differing shapes" probably refer both to the shapes of the odor particles and the shapes of the openings within the nostrils of the animals.

[33] According to tradition (see Livy 5.47), geese warned the Romans of an attack on the Capitol in Rome by the Gauls shortly after 390 BC.

that are liquefied by fire seem to give off smells more strongly.
Second, it can be seen that smells are made of larger first
beginnings than voices, since they do not penetrate a stone wall,
through which voices and sounds commonly carry.   **700**
Therefore you will also see that it is not an easy thing
to track down in what area a smell is located.
For the impact grows cold as it tarries about in the breezes
nor do the messengers of things run hot to the senses.
Thus dogs often roam around and search for traces.   **705**
Nor is this[34] the case only for smells and the class of flavors,
but in similar fashion the appearances of things and shades of colors
are not all so suited to the senses of all living creatures
that certain things are not too piercing for the vision of some.
Yes even the cock, who drives the night away by beating its wings   **710**
and is wont to summon the dawn with its clear-pitched cry,
is such that enraged lions cannot take their stand before it
and gaze upon it, so mindful are they at once of fleeing,
doubtless because in the body of the cock there are certain
seeds which when let fly into the eyes of lions   **715**
enter and stab their pupils and give them piercing pain,
so that for all their ferociousness they simply cannot hold out against
    it.
Yet these things lack all power to harm our sight,
either because they do not penetrate or because when they penetrate
a free exit from our eyes is provided, so they will not by delaying   **720**
be able to damage any part of the apparatus of sight.
Now come, hear about the things that move the mind,[35] and briefly
learn from where comes that which comes into the mind.[36]
To begin I say this: many images of things move
about to and fro in many ways and in every direction.   **725**
They are very fine, and easily join together in the breezes
when they come into contact, like spider's web and gold leaf.
For indeed these images are much more fine in texture
than those which take hold of the eyes and strike the faculty of sight,
since these pass through the pores of the body and stir   **730**
the fine nature of the mind within and provoke sensation.

---

[34] "This" refers to what Lucretius argued in 684-686: that different smells affect different animals differently.

[35] Lucretius here begins to discuss the atomic images (*simulacra*) that are a necessary part of all thinking. He argues that these mental images are finer than the images involved in sight.

[36] It is important to remember that by mind (*mens*) Lucretius refers to the thinking faculty that Epicurus taught was located in the chest. See 3.136-142.

And so we gaze upon Centaurs and body parts of Scyllas
and Cerberus-like faces of dogs and images of those
who have met death and whose bones the earth embraces,
735   since images of every sort are carried along everywhere,
some which occur on their own accord in the air itself,
some which shoot back from things of various sorts
and which are jointly formed and created from the shapes of these.
For surely the image of a Centaur does not derive from a living creature,
740   since no nature of any such animal ever existed,
but when the image of a horse and man chance to come together,
they stick together easily and at once, as we said before,[37]
on account of their subtle nature and thin texture.
Other things of this type are created in the same manner.
745   Since these are carried along quickly with amazing lightness,
as I showed before,[38] any single subtle image
easily moves our minds by a single blow.
For the mind is itself thin and marvelously mobile.
That these things happen as I say, you can easily understand from this:
750   since the two are similar, what we see with the mind and what we see
with the eyes, it must be that they happen by a similar process.
Now therefore since I have shown that I see, for example, a lion
by means of images which strike my eyes,
one may realize that the mind is moved by a similar process,
755   by images of a lion and other things which it sees equally
no less than the eyes, except that it perceives much finer images.
Nor in any other way, when sleep drains our limbs,
is the rational part of our intellect awake, except because
these same images strike our minds as when we are awake
760   to such an extent that we seem certainly to see him
whom, once life has departed, death and earth now possess.
Nature compels this to happen thus, because all the senses
of the body are blocked off and lay quiet throughout the limbs,
nor can they refute what is false by true facts.
765   Moreover the memory lies helpless and languishes in sleep
and does not protest that the person whom the mind thinks it sees
alive was overcome by death and destruction long ago.
Moreover, it is not remarkable at all that the images[39] move
and shift their arms and other limbs in smooth succession.
770   For it happens that an image in sleep seems to do this,
since, when the first image perishes and another is then born

---

[37]   4.726-727.

[38]   4.176-229.

[39]   Lucretius is still discussing the images we see in dreams.

with a different position, the first seems to have changed its posture.
Of course this must be thought to occur in rapid fashion,
so great is the mobility, so great the plentiful supply of things,
so great the supply of particles in any one   775
noticeable moment of time, so that a ready source is available.
Many questions are raised about these things, and many
must be answered by us, if we desire to explain things clearly.
First it is asked why, whatever someone wants
to consider, immediately his mind thinks the very thing.   780
Do images really keep watch over our wills
and as soon as we wish an image hurries to meet us,
whether it is dear to our hearts to think of sea, earth, or sky?
Gatherings of people, a ceremonial procession, banquets, battles:
does nature create and make ready all of them at a word?   785
And that too although others in the same vicinity and location
have their minds thinking of all sorts of very different things.
What further, when we see images move forward in smooth
succession in sleep and shift supple limbs about,
when they stretch out supple arms in rapid alternation   790
and repeat for our eyes the gesture with the foot also in step?
The images are certainly steeped in art and circulate
highly trained so they can present their productions at nighttime.
Or rather will the following turn out to be true? Since in a single time
which we perceive, that is, when a single sound is emitted,   795
many times are concealed which reason discovers to exist,
because of this it happens that in whatever time you wish
appropriate images are present ready in each place.
So great is the mobility, so great the plentiful supply of things.
Thus when the first image perishes and another is born   800
from there with a different position, the first seems to have changed its
     posture.
And since they are thin, the mind cannot see sharply
any except those to which it attends. So all which exist
besides perish, except those for which the mind has prepared itself.
It prepares itself, moreover, and hopes that it actually happens   805
that it sees what follows upon each thing, and therefore it happens.
Don't you see that the eyes, too, when they begin
to discern things that are fine attend and prepare themselves,[40]   809
and that without this it is not possible that we see sharply?   810
And nevertheless in the visible realm too you are able to notice
that if you do not turn your mind to a thing, then it is as if

---

[40] Following modern editors, I have omitted line 808, identical to line 804
     and repeated by a scribal error.

it has been separated and far removed the whole time.
So why is it surprising if the mind lets other things go
815 except for those things to which it has given itself?
Moreover we base large conjectures on small evidence
and entangle ourselves in being deceived through self-deception.
It happens too that sometimes an image of the same kind
is not readily supplied, but what was a woman before
820 seems to be present close at hand changed into a man,
or one face or one age follows upon others.
Sleep and forgetfulness ensure we are not amazed by this.[41]   **(826)**
We avidly desire that you avoid this mistake in these   **(822)**
matters, and that you try to escape error by anticipating it anxiously, **(823)**
825 in order not to represent the clear vision of the eyes as created **(824)**
so that we can gaze ahead, or that, for us to be able to advance **(825)**
with long strides, therefore the tops of the calves and thighs,
resting on the foundation of the feet, have the ability to be bent and
       folded,
and further that the forearms are fitted to strong upper arms
830 and that hands have been given us as helpers on both sides,
so that we might be able to do what is necessary to support life.
Other things of this sort that people expound
are all backwards, the product of upside-down reasoning,
since nothing arises in the body so that we might make use of it,
835 but that which arises in the body creates its own use.
Neither did seeing exist before the light of the eyes arose
nor did beseeching with words exist before the tongue was created,
but rather the birth of the tongue came far sooner
than speech and the ears were created much earlier
840 than sound was heard, and in short all parts of the body
existed, I believe, before there existed a use for them.
Thus they were not able to evolve for the sake of using them.
But in contrast to make trial with one's hand at the contests of battle
and to tear apart limbs and to befoul body-parts with gore
845 were around long before gleaming missiles flew,
and nature forced people to watch out for wounds
before the left arm was trained to interpose a shield.
And of course to give over the exhausted body to sleep
is of much greater antiquity than the soft folds of a bed,
850 and to quench thirst came into existence earlier than cups.
These things therefore which were invented out of the needs of life
can be thought to have been discovered for the sake of using them.
But all those things are quite separate which

---

[41] Editors transpose line 826 to follow line 821.

themselves arose before conveying a concept of their own usefulness.
We see that first in this class are the senses and limbs.   855
Therefore again and again there is no way you can
believe that they could have been created for the purpose of utility.
This, likewise, is not to be wondered at: that on its own
the nature of the body of each animal seeks food.
For indeed I have demonstrated[42] that many bodies flow and exit   860
from things in many ways, but even more must flow
from living creatures. Since the bodies are driven out by motion,
and many, squeezed from deep within, are carried off by sweat,
many exhaled through the mouth, when they grow tired and pant,
by these things therefore the body grows thin   865
and its whole nature is undermined.[43] Pain ensues from this.
Therefore food is taken to prop up the limbs
and, placed in between, to restore strength and stop up
the gaping desire for eating throughout the limbs and veins.
Likewise moisture disperses into all the places which   870
have need of moisture. Many particles of heat
gather together and expose our stomachs to a destructive conflagration;
these the approaching liquid scatters and extinguishes like fire,
so that the arid heat cannot scorch our appendages any longer.
In this way, therefore, is the breathtaking thirst washed away   875
from our body, in this way is the hungry desire filled up.
Now how it happens that we are able to advance our steps forward
when we will it, and how it is given to move our limbs variously,
and what thing is accustomed to thrust forward the large
mass of our body, I will relate. You, hear what I say.   880
I say that first images of moving fall upon
our mind and strike the mind, as we have said before.[44]
Thence the will[45] happens; for no one begins to do
anything before the mind sees in advance what it wishes.
That which it sees in advance, an image of that thing is present.   885
Therefore when the mind so stirs itself that it wishes to go
and to move forward, it immediately strikes the power of the soul
which is spread out through the limbs and joints in the whole body.
And it is easy to do, since the soul is held in close connection with it.
Thence the soul in turn strikes the body, and thus   890

---

[42] 2.1128-1143.

[43] Lucretius uses the analogy of a building which is undermined at its base
and is then shored up to illustrate how food helps repair the body.

[44] 4.724-731.

[45] Lucretius here uses the word *voluntas*, which can be translated "will,"
"wish."

gradually the whole mass is thrust forward and moved.
In addition then the body also becomes rarefied
and air (as of course it must since it is always quick to move)
enters and penetrates through the opened passageways in abundance
895   and is dispersed all about to each and every tiny part
of the body. Here it then happens by two things[46] working together
that the body is carried along, like a ship by sails and wind.
Nor nevertheless is this to be wondered at in these things,
that such tiny little bodies can twist so great a body
900   about and change the direction of our entire weight.
For indeed a light wind with a body of fine texture
drives and pushes a massive ship with massive effort
and one hand controls it going at whatever speed,
and one steering-oar twists it about wherever you wish,
905   and by pulleys and wheels a machine is able to move and lift
many things of heavy weight with light effort.
Now in what ways this sleep[47] floods the limbs
with rest and releases the cares of the mind from the chest,[48]
I will relate in verses more sweetly spoken than they are many,
910   just as the brief song of the swan is better than that clamor
of cranes which is scattered on the ethereal clouds of the south wind.
You, give me discriminating ears and a discerning mind,
so you do not keep on denying that what I say is possible
and depart with your chest beating back my true words,
915   although you yourself are at fault and are not able to see it.
First, sleep occurs when the force of the soul has been scattered
throughout the limbs, when part is driven outside and withdraws,
and part is pushed back and withdraws more deeply within.
It is then at last that the limbs are loosened and go limp.
920   For there is no doubt that it is the soul's work that is responsible
for this consciousness in us; when sleep prevents it from occurring
then we must think that the soul has been thrown into turmoil
and has been driven outside, but not all of it, for then the body
would lie suffused with the everlasting chill of death.
925   For indeed when no part of the soul remains hidden
in the limbs, just as fire often hides covered by many ashes,
from what source could consciousness be rekindled suddenly
throughout our limbs, just as flames spring from hidden fire.
But from what things this new state occurs and from what

---

[46] i.e., the open pores of the body and the air.

[47] "This sleep" = "the sleep I mentioned before" (in 4. 757 and 788).

[48] The Epicureans believed that the mind was located in the chest. See 3.136-142.

source the soul can be thrown into confusion and the body droop,　　**930**
I will explain: see that I do not toss words to the wind.
First, it must be that the body's exterior surface,
since it is touched by the airy breezes that surround it,
is struck repeatedly and beaten by frequent blows of air,
and therefore almost all things are covered either by thick hide　　**935**
or also by seashell or hard skin or bark.
This same air also beats on the insides of animals
as they breathe, when it is brought in and exhaled back out.
Therefore since the body is buffeted differently on both sides,
and since the blows penetrate all the way through the small openings　**940**
of our bodies to the first parts and first elements,[49]
a gradual collapse, so to speak, occurs throughout our limbs.
For the arrangements of the first beginnings of body and soul are thrown
into confusion. It then happens that part of the soul
is driven out and part withdraws hidden within,　　　　　　　　**945**
and a part also is broken up throughout the limbs
and is unable to be joined together and execute motions as a group.
For nature cuts and blocks off its meetings and passageways.
Therefore consciousness departs deep within when the motions are
　　disturbed.
And since there is nothing which props up the limbs, so to speak,　　**950**
the body becomes feeble and all the limbs go slack,
arms and eyelids droop, and when you recline the knees
are often bent and let go their strength.
Next, sleep follows food, since what air does,
sleep does the same thing, when it is distributed throughout　　　**955**
all the veins. And that sleep is the deepest by far
which you take when you are full or exhausted, because then
numerous bodies are disturbed, weakened by their great struggle.
In the same way the withdrawal inward of part of the soul is
deeper and a larger part of it is sent outside,　　　　　　　　**960**
and it is more divided from itself and pulled apart within.
And usually to whatever pursuit a person is devoted and persistently
　　clings,
and in whatever things we have been engaged in before
and on which our mind has been more intent,
in dreams we often seem to engage in the same things.　　　　**965**
Lawyers seem to plead cases and draw up contracts,
commanding officers fight and engage in battle,
sailors carry on contracted war with the winds,
and I perform my task and seek the nature of things

---

[49]　i.e., all the way to the atoms that make us up.

970 constantly and, finding it, set it out in our native language.
So other pursuits and skills seem for the most part
to occupy the minds of humans deceptively in dreams.
Whenever anyone has devoted continuous attention to the games
for many days in a row, we often observe,
975 when they have now stopped apprehending these things with their
    senses,
that paths still have remained open in their minds,
by which the same images of things are able to enter.
And so for many days these same things are observed
before their eyes, so that even when they are awake they seem
980 to see people dancing and shifting supple limbs about,
and to hear with their ears the clear-voiced song of the lyre
and its speaking strings and to see the same crowd
along with the multicolored decorations of the stage shining bright.
Such a great difference eagerness and pleasure make,
985 and in what things not only human beings are accustomed
to be actively engaged, but indeed all animals.
Indeed you will see strong horses, when their limbs are reclining,
in their sleep still sweat and not stop panting,
and exert their greatest strength as if for the victory palm
990 or as if, with the starting gates open, [they wanted to fly],[50]
and hunters' dogs in soft sleep still frequently[51]   **(999)**
toss their legs about suddenly and all at once   **(991)**
make noise and often draw in air with their noses,
as if they were glued to the tracks of wild beasts they had discovered,
995 and, awakened from sleep, they often pursue the empty   **(994)**
images of stags, as though they saw them given over to flight,
until their delusions are dispelled and they come back to themselves.
But the agreeable breed of puppies domesticated at home are quick to
999 rouse their bodies and snatch them up from the ground[52]   **(998)**
1004 just as if they saw forms and faces they did not recognize.
1005 And to the extent that each breed of animals is wilder,
the more it is necessary for them to vent their rage in sleep.
But diverse creatures of the air take to flight and all at once with their
    wings
break the silence of the groves of the gods at nighttime,
if in their light sleep hawks seem to offer
1010 battles and fights as they fly and pursue them eagerly.
Further, the minds of people, which from mighty motions produce

---

[50] The text is uncertain here. I have translated Munro's suggestion.

[51] Editors transpose line 999 to follow line 990.

[52] Lines 1000-1003 = lines 992-995 above, and are omitted by editors.

mighty things, often make and act similarly in sleep:
kings lay siege, are captured, join in battle,
raise a shout, as if their throats are being slit on the spot.
Many enter the arena and emit groans in pain   **1015**
and, as if bitten by the bite of a panther or savage lion,
they fill up the whole area with great shouts.
Many speak about great affairs in the course of sleep,
and have very often been key witnesses to their own misdeeds.
Many have met death. Many, as though falling   **1020**
suddenly from high mountains to the earth with their whole body,
are terrified, and as if they had lost their minds they scarcely return
to themselves from sleep, completely disturbed by the seething of their
     body.
Likewise someone thirsty sits beside a stream
or beautiful spring and takes up almost an entire river with his jaws. **1025**
Often if innocents,[53] held fast by sleep, believe
that they are lifting their clothes beside a basin or shallow jar,
they let out a stream of filtered liquid from their whole body,
when they soak Babylonian coverlets in all their magnificent splendor.
Then to those, in the stormy crossing of youth, whose semen is first   **1030**
winding its way, when the very ripeness of time creates it
in the limbs, images arrive externally from some body,
messengers of a radiant face and beautiful skin color,
which rouse and stimulate spots swollen with much semen,
so that often, as if the whole act had occurred, they pour forth   **1035**
great waves of moisture and stain what they are wearing.
This semen is excited in us, as we said before,
as soon as the age of adulthood gives strength to our limbs.
For different objects move and arouse different things,
but only the power of a human rouses human seed from a human.   **1040**
As soon as it goes out, sent forth from its locations,
it departs through the limbs and joints through the entire body,
gathering in fixed places in the groin and stirs up
without delay the very genital parts of the body.
The places are excited and swell with seed and a wish[54] occurs   **1045**
to send it forth to where the awful desire strains,[55]

---

[53] The Latin manuscripts read *puri*, "undefiled," "innocent." The text may
      be corrupt, but if *puri* is correct, Lucretius probably is referring to young
      children.

[54] Lucretius again (see line 883 above) uses the word *voluntas*, which can be
      translated "will," "wish."

[55] Editors omit line 1047, which is nearly identical to line 1034, and is out of
      place here.

1048 and the body seeks that by which the mind is wounded with love.
1049 For generally all fall toward the wound and blood
1050 jets out in the direction from which we are struck by a stroke,
and if it is close, the red liquid stains the enemy.
So therefore he who receives wounds from the weapons of Venus,
whether a boy with womanly limbs strikes him
or a woman radiating love with her whole body,
1055 from where he is struck, there he tends and longs to have intercourse
and to send fluid drawn from his body into the other body.
For silent desire gives forewarning of future pleasure.
This is our Venus. From this too is the name of love,[56]
From this that drop of sweet Venus first trickled
1060 into our hearts and frigid care came after.
For if what you love is absent, still there are images available
of it, and its sweet name makes its way to your ears.
But it is fitting to flee the images[57] and to drive off from yourself
what nourishes love and to turn your mind elsewhere
1065 and to send your fluid, gathered together, into whatever body,
and not to retain it, once troubled by the love of one,
nor to cause care and certain pain to continue for yourself.
For the sore is kept alive and grows older by feeding
and daily the madness swells and the affliction grows worse,
1070 unless you overwhelm the first wounds with fresh blows
and, wandering to a widely-wandering Venus,[58] cure them while fresh
or are able to direct the motions of your mind in a different direction.
Nor does the one who shuns love lack the enjoyment
of Venus,[59] but rather receives the enjoyment without the penalty.
1075 For certainly the pleasure from this is more pure for the healthy
than the lovesick. For at the very moment of obtaining it
the passion of the lovers rises and falls in uncertain ways
and they are unsure what first to enjoy with their mouths and hands.
What they seek, they press closely and create pain
1080 in the body, and often drive their teeth hard into their lips
and crush mouths together, since the pleasure is not pure
and there are hidden goads which incite them to hurt the very thing,
whatever it is, from where these sprouts of madness arise.

---

[56] The "name of love" in Latin to which Lucretius refers is *cupido*, "Cupid,"
"love," "desire."

[57] i.e., images of the beloved.

[58] By a "widely-wandering Venus," Lucretius seems to mean a prostitute.

[59] Lucretius distinguishes between love (*amor*), which he says brings pain,
and simple physical pleasures (*Venus*), which he says do not.

But lightly Venus breaks the punishments in the midst of their love
and the alluring pleasure intermingled holds back their biting.   **1085**
For in this there is hope that, where the source of their passion is,
there too the flame can be extinguished from the same body.
Nature, though, objects that it happens completely otherwise.
And this is the one thing that the more we have of it,
so much the more our breast burns with awful desire.   **1090**
For food and drink are taken up within by the limbs.
Since they are able to take up their positions at fixed places,
thus the desire for liquid and bread is easily filled.
Yet from the face and beautiful color of a person
nothing is given to the body to enjoy except images,   **1095**
insubstantial. This pitiful hope is often snatched by the wind.
Just as when someone thirsty seeks to drink in his sleep
and water is not given which could extinguish the burning in his limbs,
but he seeks images of liquids and works hard in vain
and is thirsty even while drinking in the midst of a rushing stream,   **1100**
so in a love affair Venus teases the lovers with images
nor are they able to be satisfied by gazing at the bodies before them
nor with their hands can they rub off anything from the soft
limbs as they wander without direction over the whole body.
Finally, when with limbs intertwined they enjoy the flower   **1105**
of their age, now when the body looks forward to joys
and Venus is present there to sow the woman's fields,
they fasten bodies eagerly together and join the saliva
of their mouths and breathe heavily, pressing mouths to teeth,
in vain, since they cannot rub off anything from there   **1110**
nor penetrate nor depart into a body with their entire bodies.
For sometimes they seem to wish to do this and strive for it,
so passionately do they cling together in the binding-seams of Venus,
while their limbs liquefy, loosened by the power of pleasure.
At last when the desire built-up in the loins explodes,   **1115**
a small pause of the violent passion ensues for a moment.
Then the same insanity returns and this madness is back,
when they seek for themselves what they themselves desire to attain,
nor can they discover a device to overcome this evil,
so directionless are they as they waste away from the invisible wound. **1120**
Add that they squander away their strength and perish from the effort,
add that their life is led at the beck and call of another.
Meanwhile wealth slips away and becomes Babylonian coverlets,
official duties are forgotten and reputation sickens and wavers.
Lotions and beautiful Sicyonian sandals sparkle on her feet,   **1125**
of course, and huge emeralds glowing green with light
are set in gold and the sea-purple-dyed tunic is worn out
continuously and, overworked, it soaks up the sweat of Venus.

The hard-earned wealth of fathers becomes headbands and
    headscarves,
1130 sometimes turns into a cloak or things from Alinda and Ceos.[60]
Banquet feasts with exquisite tapestries and food, games,
countless drinks, lotions, wreaths, and garlands are prepared,
all in vain, since from the very middle of the fountain of delights
something bitter surfaces which causes distress even among the
    flowers,
1135 either when the mind chances to torment itself, realizing
that it is passing its life in idleness and is dying in debauched places,
or because she has tossed out an ambiguous word as she left
which, embedded in his passionate heart, lives like fire
or because he thinks she glances around too much or gazes
1140 at another, and he sees the traces of laughter in her face.
And these evils are found in a love that is secure and going
extremely well — but in an adverse and unfulfilled love they
are, as you are able to apprehend even with your eyes closed,
innumerable. Thus it is better to be on guard beforehand,
1145 in the way I have shown, and to beware lest you be led astray.
For to avoid being tossed into the hunting nets of love
is not as difficult as, once trapped, exiting
from the nets and bursting through the sturdy knots of Venus.
And yet, although entangled and hindered, you can still
1150 escape the snare, unless you get in your own way
yourself and from the start overlook all the mental and
physical faults of her whom you ardently seek and want.
For people very often do this, blinded by desire,
and ascribe to others qualities which in reality they do not possess.
1155 Therefore we see that those who are variously misshapen and ugly
are treated as sweethearts and flourish, held in the highest esteem.
For some people mock others and urge them to appease
Venus, since they are afflicted with a foul love, nor do the wretches
often perceive their own amazingly large problems.
1160 A dark woman is "honey-gold", one unwashed and filthy, "natural",
the light-eyed, "a little Pallas",[61] the skinny and lanky, "a gazelle",
the small and dwarfish, "one of the Graces", "all pure spice",
the huge and immense, "an astonishment" and "full of honor".
She is tongue-tied and can't speak, "she lisps", silent, "she is modest";

---

[60] There are textual difficulties with the two place names. Alinda was a
city in Caria (Southern Turkey), and Ceos is an island in the Cyclades
Islands between the Greek mainland and Turkey.

[61] Pallas Athena traditionally was given the Greek epithet "light-eyed"
(*glaukôpis*).

but the burning, tiresome gossip becomes "a little torch."   **1165**
She becomes a "slender little darling" when she can't survive
because she's so thin; "trim" when dead from a cough.
But the swollen with huge breasts, "Ceres herself from Iacchus",[62]
the snub-nosed, "Silenus- and satyr-like", the big-lipped, "all kiss".
It would be tiresome if I tried to mention others of this type.   **1170**
But nevertheless let her possess as beautiful a face as you want,
and have the power of Venus emanating from all her limbs:
Of course there are others too; of course we lived earlier without her.
Of course she does, and we know her to do, everything the same
as an ugly woman, and she fumigates her poor self with foul   **1175**
odors, while her maids flee far away and cackle in secret.
But the weeping lover, shut out, often covers the threshold
with flowers and garlands and anoints the proud door posts
with marjoram and, poor wretch, plants kisses on the doors.
If, once admitted, just a single whiff hits him   **1180**
as he is entering, he would try to find a plausible reason for leaving,
and his protest, carefully considered and deeply felt, would collapse,
and he would condemn himself on the spot for his stupidity, because
        he sees
he has attributed more to her than it is right to grant to a mortal.
Nor does this escape our Venuses. All the more do they themselves   **1185**
strive to conceal everything behind the scenes of life
from those whom they wish to ensnare and to be held fast in love,
all in vain, since with your mind you are able nonetheless to drag
everything into the light and to seek the reason for all the laughter
and, if she possesses an attractive mind and is not annoying,   **1190**
in return to overlook and concede something to her human weaknesses.
Nor does a woman always sigh with feigned passion
when, embracing a man, she joins body together with body
and holds him, moistening kisses with sucked lips.
For she often does this from the heart, and seeking shared   **1195**
joys she urges him to complete the circuit of love.
Nor in any other way would birds, cattle, wild beasts,
sheep, and mares be able to submit to males,
unless because their own nature, overflowing, is in heat and burns
and gladly draws in the love of the mounting mate.   **1200**
Don't you also see that those whom mutual pleasure
overcomes are quite often tortured in common chains?
For frequently dogs at the crossroads, desiring passionately to leave,

---

[62]   Ceres, the Roman goddess of growth and agriculture, was the mother of
       Iacchus, who (it is implied) made his mother Ceres' breasts large by
       nursing.

pull eagerly with all their strength in opposite directions,[63]   [1210]
1205 when meanwhile they cling together in the strong bindings of
        Venus.   [1204]
    This they would never do unless they experienced mutual   [1205]
    joys, which can trap them and hold them bound.   [1206]
    Wherefore again and again, I say, pleasure is shared.   [1207]
    And when, in the mixing of the seed,[64] by chance the woman
        subdues   [1208]
1210 the force of the male with sudden force and has mastered it,   [1209]
    then offspring are born similar to the mother from maternal seed,
    as they are similar to the father from paternal seed. But those whom
    you see are of both appearances, mixing together the looks of their
        parents,
    grow from both the father's body and the mother's blood,
1215 when the seeds, aroused throughout the limbs by the goads of Venus,
    are brought into direct collision by mutual, deep-breathing passion,
    and neither of the two of them conquers or is conquered in turn.
    It happens too that sometimes offspring can come into being
    similar to their grandparents and recall often features of great-
        grandparents
1220 because parents often conceal many first-beginnings
    mixed about in many ways in their own bodies,
    which, starting from the stock, fathers pass on to fathers.
    From this, Venus produces features by varied lot
    and calls to mind the looks, voices, and hair of ancestors,
1225 since indeed these things occur by fixed seed
    for us as much as our facial features, bodies, and limbs.
    And the female breed also arises from the father's seed,
    and males are born and come into being from the mother's seed.
    For an offspring is always the product of two-fold seed,
1230 and to whichever of the two parents what is created resembles more,
    of that it has more than an equal share. This you can see
    whether the offspring is one of the male sex or a female birth.
    Nor do divine powers take away generative
    sowing from anyone, so that he might never be called "father"
1235 by sweet children and live his days in sterile love,[65]
    as most people think and, grieving, shower altars
    with much blood and fire high altars with their gifts,
    in order that they make their wives pregnant with abundant seed.

---

[63] Editors transpose line 1210 to follow line 1203.

[64] Epicurus, following earlier Greek philosophers including Parmenides
      and Empedocles, taught that both males and females contributed "seed"
      in the process of conception.

[65] "In sterile love": Literally, "with Venus sterile."

In vain do they fatigue the power of the gods and sacred lots.
For some people are sterile because of excessively thick seed,   **1240**
and others because of seed which is runny and thin beyond what is
    right.
The thin seed, since it cannot attach and adhere to places,
runs off at once and withdraws backwards abortively.
Further since for others the seed is emitted too thick
or too congealed, either it flies forward with insufficient thrust,   **1245**
or is unable to penetrate places as well or, having penetrated,
the seed is mixed together poorly with the woman's seed.
For the couplings of Venus are seen to vary greatly.[66]
For some men impregnate some women more easily,
and some women take on weight by some men more easily   **1250**
and grow pregnant. Many women have been sterile before
in a series of marriages and later obtained a husband from whom
they could conceive toddlers and grow rich in sweet offspring.
And for men in whose house fertile wives often
before could not bear, a compatible nature has been found   **1255**
for them too, so they could fortify their old age with children.
Thus it is of very great importance that seeds be able
to mingle with seeds in a way well-suited for reproduction,
and that thick seeds unite with runny and runny with thick.
And it thus matters on what diet life is supported,   **1260**
for on some things the seeds grow thick in the limbs,
and on others again they grow very thin and melt away.
And in what ways the alluring pleasure itself is practiced,
this too makes a great difference. For wives are thought
for the most part to conceive better in the manner of beasts   **1265**
and similar to quadrupeds, for thus the proper places are able
to receive the seeds, with the breasts lowered and the loins raised.
Nor are soft movements necessary at all for wives.
For a woman stops herself from conceiving and fights against it,
if with her buttocks she gladly draws in the love of a man   **1270**
and, with her entire breast relaxed, produces undulating motions.
For she thrusts the furrow away from the straight direction and the
    path
of the plow and turns the force of the seed away from her places.
Prostitutes are accustomed to move in this way for themselves,
so that they not be impregnated frequently and lie around expecting, **1275**
and so the act of Venus itself be more refined and pleasurable for men.
It seems that our wives have no need of this at all.
Sometimes neither by divine agency nor by the shafts of Venus
it happens that a woman of lesser worth and beauty is loved.

---

[66] "Couplings of Venus" = reproductive compatibility.

1280 For sometimes a woman herself by her very own actions
and compliant ways and neatly groomed body makes it
so that she easily accustoms you to spend your life with her.
What is more, close familiarity brings love into existence.
For however lightly anything is struck by frequent blows,
1285 it is yet overcome in a long period of time and yields.
Don't you also see that drops of liquid falling
on rocks bore through the rocks in a long period of time?

a women wears you down... ?

ON THE NATURE OF THINGS

BOOK V

Who is able with strength of mind to compose a poem
worthy of matching the majesty of things and these discoveries?
Or who is so powerful with words that he is able to fashion praises
matching the merits of the one who left behind for us
such prizes, sought out and obtained by his mind?   **5**
There will be no one, I think, born of mortal body.
For if we must speak as the majesty of things now
known to us demands, he[1] was a god, a god, illustrious Memmius,
who was the first one to discover this system of life which
now is called wisdom and who by his scientific method   **10**
rescued life from such great waves and such great darkness
and situated it in such calm waters and such clear light.
For compare the ancient god-like discoveries of others.
For Ceres is said to have introduced grain to mortal humans,
and Liber[2] the flowing juice of the vine-grown liquid.   **15**
Yet it would have been possible to maintain life without these things,
as the report is that some peoples live even now.
But it was not possible to live well without an untroubled mind,
so that more deservedly he seems to be a god to us,
from whom even now sweet comforts for life   **20**
are spread throughout great peoples and soothe their spirits.
But if you think the deeds of Hercules[3] excel his,
you will be carried much too far from true reasoning.
For what harm to us are the huge open jaws
of that Nemean lion now, or the bristling Arcadian boar?   **25**
Next, what power does the bull of Crete have,

Epicurus is a god

---

[1] "He" = Epicurus.

[2] Liber is one of the Roman names for Bacchus (Dionysus).

[3] Lucretius may have chosen to discuss Hercules because the Stoics held
   him up as an example of a great hero who benefited humans by clearing
   the earth of monsters.

or the scourge of Lerna, the hydra, palisaded with poisonous snakes?
Or what of the three-breasted force of threefold Geryon?[4]

*   *   *   *   *   *   *   *   *   *   *   *   *

How great is the harm to us by <the birds> inhabiting Stymphalus **(30)**
30 or by the horses of Thracian Diomedes, breathing fire from their
        nostrils,[5]   **(29)**
close by the Bistonian regions[6] and Mount Ismara?[7]
And guarding the gleaming golden apples of Hesperus' daughters,
harsh, gazing sharply, the serpent with an immense body
wrapped around the trunk of the tree—what harm could he do
35 close to the Atlantic shore and the forbidding tracts of the sea,
where none of our people goes nor barbarian dares to approach?
And all the other monsters of this kind which were destroyed,
if they were not vanquished before, what harm could they do us if
        alive?
None, I think: so the earth even now teems to fullness
40 with wild beasts and is filled up with trembling terror
throughout groves and great mountains and deep forests.
Most of the time it is in our power to avoid these places.
But unless our mind is washed clean, then what battles
and dangers must we be involved with against our will?
45 How many sharp cares of desire carve up
a human being in distress, and equally how many fears?
Or what of pride, filthy avarice, and arrogance? How many
disasters do they bring about? What of soft living and idleness?
Therefore he who subdued all these things
50 and drove them from the mind with words, not arms—isn't it fitting
that this human be deemed worthy of being numbered among the gods?
Especially since he was accustomed to write many words
well and in a godlike way about the immortal gods themselves
and to lay open the whole nature of things with words.
55 I walk in his tracks while I follow out his reasonings
and show with my words how it is necessary that all things
remain unchanged in that pact by which they were created,
and lack the power to revoke the powerful laws of time:
first in this class, the nature of the mind has been found
60 first to have come into being and to consist of a body which was born,
nor is it able to remain intact for a long time,

---

[4] There are textual difficulties here, and editors think lines have dropped
     out or been transposed.

[5] Editors transpose lines 29 and 30.

[6] The Bistones were a tribe that lived in Thrace, in northern Greece.

[7] Mt. Ismara is located on the southern coast of Thrace.

but images are accustomed to play tricks on the mind in sleep,
when we seem to make out him whom life has left.
For what remains, now the order of my plan has carried me here,
I must render an account of how the world consists of a mortal　　　**65**
body, and how at the same time it has come into being,
and in what ways this coming-together of matter laid
the foundations of the earth, sky, sea, stars, sun,
and sphere of the moon, then which living creatures have arisen
from the earth, and which have come into being at no time,　　　**70**
or in what way the human race began to use
different utterances with one another by naming things,
and in what ways that fear of the gods insinuated itself
into their hearts, which throughout the world keeps holy
the shrines, lakes, groves, altars, and images of the gods.　　　**75**
In addition, I will explain by what force governing nature
directs the courses of the sun and movements of the moon on its path,
so we don't suppose that they light up their yearly paths
traveling freely of their own will between sky and earth,
obliged to foster crops and living creatures,　　　**80**
and so we don't think that they move by any divine plan.
For those who have learned well that the gods live a tranquil
life, if still at times they wonder in what way
things can take place, especially in those events
which are seen in the shores of heaven up above their heads,　　　**85**
are brought back again to ancient religious beliefs
and take on harsh masters, whom they believe
in their misery to be all-powerful, ignorant of what can be
and what cannot, in short, by what process each thing
has its power limited, and its deep-set boundary stone.　　　**90**
For what remains, so that I not delay you any longer with promises,
begin by taking a look at the seas and lands and sky.
Their triple nature, their three bodies, Memmius, their three
forms so different, three such textures,
a single day will give over to destruction, and the massive structure　　　**95**
of the world, sustained through many years, will come crashing down.
Nor does it escape my mind how novel and strange a thing
it is to contemplate, that sky and earth will be destroyed,
and how difficult this is for me to prove conclusively with words.
This happens when you convey to the ears something previously
　　unknown　　　**100**
and yet cannot set it beneath the eyes' gaze
nor place it within the hand, whereby the paved road of belief
leads quickest into the human heart and regions of the mind.
But nevertheless I will speak out. The thing itself perhaps
will lend belief to my words, and in a short time you will see everything　**105**

shaken hard when massive movements of the earth occur.
May governing nature keep this distant from us,
and may reason rather than the thing itself persuade us
that all things can be overcome and fall with a horrific crash.
110 Before I proceed to issue oracles about this thing
with more holiness and with much more certain reasoning than
the Pythia[8] who speaks out from the tripod and laurel of Apollo,
I will present many solaces to you with learned words,
lest held in check and bridled by religion you by chance suppose
115 that the earth and sun and sky, sea, stars, and moon,
must abide in place forever, endowed with divine body,
and therefore think it is right, just as in the case of the Giants,[9]
that all those should pay the penalty for their monstrous crime
who by their use of reason assail the walls of the world
120 and who wish to extinguish the brilliant sun shining in the sky,
shamefully branding immortal things with mortal speech.
These things are so distant from divine power
and are so unworthy to be counted among the number of the gods
that they are rather thought able to illustrate the concept
125 of things devoid of life-giving motions and sensation.
For indeed it is not the case that the nature of the mind and deliberation
can be thought to exist with any and every body.
Just as a tree is not able to exist in the sky, nor clouds
in the salty sea, nor fish live in fields,
130 nor a stream of blood exist in wood, nor sap in stones.
Where each thing grows and is present is certain and fixed.
Thus the nature of the mind cannot come into existence without the
      body
on its own, nor can it be far from sinews and blood.
For if this were possible, far sooner could this force of the mind
135 exist in the head or shoulders or the bottom of the heels,
and be accustomed to be born in any part at all,
as long as it could remain in the same person and in the same container.
But since even in the case of our body it is fixed and is seen to be clearly
laid down where it is possible for the soul and mind
140 to exist and grow separately, so much more must it be denied
they can survive outside the whole body and form of an animal
in rotting clods of earth or in the burning fire of the sun
or in water or the lofty shores of the sky. Not at all, therefore,

---

[8] The Pythia was the priestess of Apollo at Delphi in Greece, and the most famous oracle in the ancient world.

[9] The Giants were huge creatures who challenged the Olympian gods. Zeus and the Olympian gods defeated them with the help of Hercules, and buried them beneath the earth.

do these exist endowed with divine sensation,
since they are not able to be animated with the breath of life.   **145**
This likewise is not possible for you to believe:
that the holy dwellings of the gods are in any part of our world.
For the nature of the gods, rarefied and far removed from our senses,
is seen with great difficulty by the intellectual faculty of the mind.
And since it has always escaped the touch and stroke of the hands,   **150**
it ought not to touch anything which is able to be touched by us.
For what is not itself permitted to be touched is not able to touch.
Therefore too their dwelling places ought to be different
from our dwelling places, being rarefied in accord with their bodies.
I will prove these things to you later in a long discourse.[10]   **155**
To say further that for the sake of human beings the gods
wished to prepare the brilliant nature of the world and therefore
it is fitting to praise it as the praiseworthy work of the gods
and to think that it will be eternal and will not perish,
and that it is not right that what was firmly established by the ancient
    reasoning   **160**
of the gods with everlasting life for the races of human beings
ever be shaken from its resting place by any force,
nor be harassed by argument and overturned top to bottom,
and to pile up other falsehoods of this type, Memmius,
is to lack all reason. For what advantage could gratitude   **165**
on our part bestow on beings who are immortal and happy,
so that they attempt to do anything for our sakes?
Or what new thing could have enticed them, peaceful before,
to change so long afterwards their former way of life?
For it seems that the one who ought to rejoice in new things   **170**
is the one for whom the old are a nuisance. But to the one who had no
trouble before, when he was leading a wonderful life,
what could have ignited a love of something new in such a person?
What harm would there have been for us not to have been created?
Or was life, I suppose, lying prostrate in darkness and grief   **175**
until the generating beginning of things brought the break of day?
For whoever has been born must wish to remain in life
as long as alluring pleasure works to hold him there.
But for one who has never experienced the taste of the love of life
nor was numbered among the living, what harm is it never to have
    been created?   **180**
Further, from what source was there first implanted in the gods

---

[10] Most editors take this line as a promise by Lucretius to discuss the gods
at greater length, a promise which is not fulfilled in the poem as we have
it.

a model for creating things or even a conception[11] of humans,
so that they might know and see with their minds what they wished to
    make,
or in what way was the capacity of the first beginnings ever recognized,
185 and what they could do with each other with their order rearranged,
if nature herself did not provide a pattern for creating?
For so many first beginnings of things in so many ways,
propelled by blows from infinite time until the present day
and impelled by their own weight, have been accustomed to being
    borne along,
190 and to meet in all sorts of ways and to try all combinations,
whatever they are able to create when brought together among
    themselves,
that it is no wonder if they also fell into such arrangements
and settled into such movements, as these now by which
the sum of things continues on by renewing itself.
195 But even if I didn't know what the first beginnings of things
were, still this I would dare to affirm from the very workings
of the heavens and to declare from many other things as well,
that in no way has the nature of things been created for us
by divine forces, so great the faults with which it is endowed.
200 First, as much as the huge sweep of the sky covers,
the mountains and forests of wild beasts have taken a greedy
part, rocks and vast swamps hold it,
and the sea which keeps the shores of lands distant and apart.
Further, almost two-thirds of it the burning heat
205 and the continually falling frost steal away from mortals.
Of the arable land that remains, nature would envelop it
by its own effort with brambles unless human effort resisted,
accustomed to moan over a sturdy two-toothed mattock
for the sake of life and to split the earth with the force of plows.
210 For if by turning over the fertile clods with a plowshare
and working the soil of the earth we didn't stir them to birth,
they would not be able to spring into the clear air on their own;
And yet sometimes things attained by great labor,
when they are now leafing out over the earth and are all in bloom,
215 either are burned up by the sun in the sky with its excessive heat
or are destroyed by sudden rains and ice-cold frosts,

---

[11] The word Lucretius uses here, *notities*, is a Latin translation of Greek
term *prolêpsis*, a key term in Epicurean philosophy. A *prolêpsis* of an
object is a general conception or idea of a class of objects that living
creatures form from previous perceptions of individual objects of that
class. See Introduction p. xvii.

and are harried by blasts of wind with their violent whirling whippings.
Besides, why does nature feed and foster the horrifying
race of wild beasts, so hostile to humankind,
by land and sea? Why do the seasons of the year bring   220
illness? Why does untimely death wander around?
Then further a child, like a sailor tossed up by the harsh
waves, lies naked on the ground, speechless, in need of every
kind of life support, when first onto the shores of light
nature has poured it from its mother's womb with birth-pangs,   225
and it fills the place with sad wailing, as is right for one
for whom so much evil remains to pass through in life.
But different flocks and herds and wild beasts grow up
and have no need of infant rattles nor must sweet
and halting baby-talk be employed by a wet nurse   230
nor do they need different clothes to match the season,
and finally they need no weapons, no high city walls
with which to protect their own, since the earth herself and nature
the artificer of things provide everything in abundance for all.
To begin first,[12] since the body belonging to the earth and water   235
and the light breath of the airy breezes and hot heat,
from which this sum of things is seen to be put together,
all consist of a body which has been born and is mortal, the whole
nature of the world should be thought to consist of the same body.
For indeed those creatures whose parts and members we see   240
to be endowed with body that was born and exists with mortal shapes,
these same creatures we constantly see to be subject
likewise to birth and death. Therefore since I see the greatest
members and parts of the world destroyed and re-created,
I may know that likewise too sky and earth had some time   245
of first beginning and will meet total destruction in the future.
So that you don't think that I have asserted this without proof
for myself, because I have assumed that earth and fire are mortal
and I have not doubted that water and air perish,
and I said that these things are born and increase again,   250
first, some part of the earth, thoroughly roasted
by incessant sun, disturbed by the force of many feet,
breathes out a fog of dust and flying clouds
which the strong winds scatter all throughout the air.
Part, too, of the land is called back to flooding   255
by rains, and rivers scrape and gnaw away at their banks.
Moreover, whatever the earth nourishes and grows is returned

---

[12] Lucretius here resumes the argument, interrupted at line 109, intended
to show the world is mortal.

proportionally. And since undoubtedly the same parent of all[13]
is seen to be the universal tomb of things, therefore,
260 you see, the earth is diminished and grows and increases again.
Further, there is no need to express in words that the sea,
rivers, and fountains always overflow with new water
and moisture flows continuously: the great downrush of waters
everywhere declares it. But each drop of water in turn
265 is removed and it happens that water does not overflow in sum,
partly because the strong winds sweeping the seas and the heavenly
sun, unravelling the water with its rays, diminish it,
partly because it is dispersed underground throughout all the earth.
For the brine is filtered and the substance of the water drips back
270 and all assembles together at the sources of rivers, whence
it flows over the earth in a fresh-water column, on which path,
once cut, it carries its waves on liquid foot.[14]
And now I will discuss air, which changes
in its entire body innumerable times in a single hour.
275 For always, whatever flows off of things, all of it
is carried on a great ocean of air. Unless it gave
back bodies to things again and renewed them as they flowed,
all would by now have been dissolved and turned into air.
Not at all then does air stop coming from things and falling
280 back into things, since it is certain that everything is constantly in flux.
Likewise the large source of liquid light, the sun
in the aether, continually floods the heavens with fresh radiance
and light is reinforced without delay by new light.
For each particle of its brightness passes away in turn
285 wherever it falls. You may understand this from what follows:
as soon as the clouds first have begun to pass beneath
the sun and to break apart, so to speak, the rays of light,
at once the lower part of the rays all perishes,
and the earth is in shadows wherever the clouds are carried.
290 Thus you may know that things always need new
brilliance and each successive projection of light perishes
and in no other way can things be seen in the sun,
unless the very source of light itself should supply it perpetually.
And further, you notice lights at night on earth,
295 lamps hanging down from ceilings, and torches, bright
with gleaming flashes and thick with much black smoke
hasten quickly in like manner with the help of fire
to supply new light. They are urgent to flicker with fire,
urgent, nor is the light broken, so to speak, nor deserts the place.

---

[13] "The same parent of all" = the earth.

[14] 5.269-272 = 6.635-638, with two minor differences.

So quickly is the light's passing away kept hidden 300
by the swift birth process of flame from all of the fires.
So then we must think that the sun, moon, and stars
cast their light out from one new rising up[15] after another
and each successive flame always passes away,
lest by chance you believe that these thrive in indestructibility. 305
Next, don't you perceive that stones too are conquered
by time, that tall towers collapse and rocks crumble,
that shrines and statues of the gods grow tired and crack,
and that the holy presence can neither prolong the bounds of fate
nor put up a struggle against the laws of nature? 310
Again, do we not see that the monuments of men are in ruins
<and that they ask moreover whether you believe they grow old?>[16]
Don't we see crags torn from high mountains tumble,
unable to endure and suffer the powerful forces of even limited
time? For they would not fall or be torn off suddenly, 315
if for an infinite stretch of time they had held out against
all the batterings of age without breaking up.
Next, now gaze at that which is above and surrounds the whole
earth in its embrace. If it brings forth everything
from itself, as some relate, and takes them back when they perish, 320
then the entirety of it exists with a body that was born and will die.
For whatever makes other things grow and nourishes them from itself
must be diminished, and be restored when it receives things back.
Besides, if indeed there was no generating first beginning
of the earth and sky, and they have always been without beginning or 325
     end,
why haven't other poets also sung of other events
before the war at Thebes and the violent end of Troy?[17]
To where have so many deeds of men vanished so many times,
neither planted nor blossoming with everlasting monuments of fame?
But, I think, the sum of things is new, and the nature 330
of the world is recent and did not take its beginning long ago.
Therefore certain arts are even now being perfected,
even now expanding. Now many things have been added to ships,
and lately musicians have given birth to melodious sounds.
Next, this nature and account of things was discovered 335

---

[15] "Rising up" translates the Latin term (*subortus*) Lucretius invented to capture the idea of the rising up of a continually fresh supply of light.

[16] Editors consider Line 312 corrupt. I have translated the suggestion proposed by Munro.

[17] Lucretius here refers to the epic poems, including the *Iliad* and the lost epic the *Thebais* which related the stories of the Trojan War and the Seven Against Thebes.

recently, and now I myself have been found to be the very first[18]
to be able to turn it into the language of our native land.
But if by chance you believe that the same things existed
before, but that the ages of humans were destroyed by scorching fire,
340   or that cities came crashing down by a great upheavaling[19] of the world,
or that from continuous rains ravaging rivers went astray
all throughout the earth and covered over towns,
so much the more you must confess that you are defeated
and that there also will be a complete destruction of heaven and earth.
345   For when things were assailed with such great disorders and such
great dangers, if a more grievous cause had then been pressing,
they would have caused widespread devastation and great ruin.
Nor are we seen to be mortal for any other reason,
except that we grow sick one after another with the very
350   same diseases as those whom nature has removed from life.
Moreover, whatever endures eternally must do so
either by having a solid body and repelling blows
and not allowing anything to penetrate it which might be able
to dissociate its tightly-fastened parts within, just as the bodies
355   of matter are whose nature we have made known earlier,
or by being able to endure for all time for this reason,
that they are not subject to impacts, just as the void is,
which endures untouched and does not suffer from blows at all,
or also by having no supply of space around it,
360   into which things might be able, as it were, to disperse and be dissolved,
just as the universal universe is eternal, for neither is there outside of it
any place into which things may leap apart nor are there bodies
that could encounter it and dissolve it with a forceful impact.
But neither, as I have made clear, is the nature of the world composed
365   of solid body, since void is mixed in with things,
nor nevertheless is it like the void, nor indeed are there bodies lacking
that are able to gather together in infinite space by chance
and overthrow this present sum of things in a violent whirlwind
or bring in some other form of dangerous disaster,
370   nor further is the nature of place and the space of the abyss

---

[18] Lucretius' claim to be the first to present Epicurean philosophy in Latin
is hard to understand, because according to Cicero (*Tusculan Disputations*
4.6) a certain Amafinius was the first to do so. We know little about
Amafinius' work or dates, though, and it may be either that he and
Lucretius are contemporaries, or that Lucretius considered his poem to
be the first fully comprehensive treatment of the Epicurean system in
Latin.

[19] "Upheavaling" translates Lucretius' *vexamen*, a word he apparently
invented.

lacking into which the walls of the world are able to be scattered,
or they are able to be struck by some other force and perish.
Therefore the door of death is not shut for the heavens,
nor for the sun, earth, nor the towering waves of the ocean,
but it stands open and waits with its monstrous and vast chasm.   375
Wherefore too it must be confessed that these same
things had a birth, for things endowed with mortal body
would not have been able from infinite time until now
to stand in defiance of the powerful forces of immeasurable time.
Next, since the greatest members of the world[20] fight among themselves 380
so much, stirred up into an unholy war,
do you not see that some end of the long contest
can be given to them? Either when the sun and all heat,
with all moisture drained away, attain victory,
which they are struggling to do and have not yet executed their attempt, 385
just as much do rivers supply and threaten besides
to wash over everything from the swirling depths of the sea,
all in vain, since the winds sweeping the seas and the heavenly
sun, unraveling the water with its rays, diminish it,
and they trust confidently that they can dry up all things   390
before liquid is able fully to complete the end of its undertaking.
So great a war do they breathe out in their balanced contest
as they struggle among themselves to come to a decision about great
     things,
nevertheless fire once gained the superior position,
and once, as the story goes, water ruled in the fields.   395
For fire prevailed, licking and roasting many things,
when the fierce force of the sun's horses, off course,
forced Phaethon[21] through the whole sky and over every land.
But the omnipotent father[22] roused then by sharp anger
blasted great-hearted Phaethon from his horses to the earth   400
with a sudden bolt of thunder, and the Sun,[23] meeting him
as he fell, caught the eternal lamp of the world from beneath,
gathering the scattered horses and joining them trembling together,
and then guiding them on their appropriate path restored all things—
or so at least the ancient poets of the Greeks have sung.   405

---

[20] "Greatest members of the world" = earth, air, fire, and water.

[21] Phaethon was the son of Helios, the god of the sun, and drove his father's
sun-chariot on a disastrous course, nearly destroying the earth. The story
of Phaethon is told at greater length by Ovid in *Metamorphoses* 2. 1-328.

[22] Jupiter.

[23] The Sun = Helios, Phaethon's father.

But this is very far removed from true reasoning.
For fire is able to prevail when a great number
of bodies of its matter are brought together from infinite space,
and next its force wanes when it is conquered in turn by some
410 cause or things perish, consumed by its superheated blasts.
Moisture likewise once came together and began to prevail,
as the story goes,[24] when it overwhelmed many humans with waves.[25]
Thereupon when its force, whatever had been brought together from infinite
space, was turned aside by some cause and receded,
415 the rains ceased and rivers lessened their force.
But in what ways this gathering-together of matter laid
the foundations of the earth, sky, and the vast depths of the sea,
and the courses of the sun and moon, I will set out in order.
For certainly not by design did these first beginning of things
420 arrange themselves in their own order with knowing intelligence,
nor surely did they reach an agreement about what motions each would take.
But since many first beginnings of things in many ways,
propelled by blows from infinite time up to the present day
and impelled by their own weight, have been used to being borne along,
425 and to meet in all sorts of ways and to try all combinations,
whatever they are able to create when brought together among themselves,
therefore it happens that, circulating for a great quantity of time,
by trying out every type of meeting and motion,
at last these assemble which, when suddenly brought
430 together, often become the beginnings of great things:
of the world, sea, sky, and the race of living creatures.
Then in these circumstances neither the disc of the sun, flying high
with its vast light, could be observed, nor the stars of the great heavens
nor the sea nor sky nor indeed even the earth nor air
435 nor could any thing similar to our things be seen,
but some new storm, gathered together as a mass
out of first beginnings of every type whose spacings,[26]   **(440)**
paths, connections, weight, blows, meetings, and motions   **(441)**
strife, setting them in battle, was throwing into massive disorder, **(442)**

---

[24] Lucretius probably has in mind the story of Deucalion, Pyrrha, and the
Great Flood, which Ovid later included in his *Metamorphoses* (1.253-415).

[25] The text of this clause is somewhat uncertain. Translations of other
possible emendations include "...overwhelmed many cities of humans"
and "...overwhelmed the lives of humans with waves."

[26] For the next nine lines (437-445) I follow Reisacker's reordering, which
has been accepted by most modern editors.

because, on account of their dissimilar shapes and varying figures, **(443) 440**
not all things were able to remain thus linked together   **(444)**
nor to give and receive suitable motions among themselves.   **(445)**
Next the parts began to disperse and equal things   **(437)**
to join together with equals and to separate out the world   **(438)**
and to divide the members and lay out the major parts,   **(439) 445**
that is, to separate the lofty heavens from the earth,
and the sea by itself, so that it is open with its moisture set apart,
and likewise the fires of heaven by themselves, pure and set apart.
Indeed first each and every body of earth,
because in fact they were heavy and enmeshed, came together   **450**
in the middle and all took up the lowest positions,
and the more enmeshed they were among themselves as they came
      together,
the more they squeezed out the things which would produce the sea,
stars, sun, and moon, and the walls of the great world.
For all these are made up of lighter and rounder   **455**
seeds and possess much smaller elemental particles
than earth. Thus bursting forth from the parts of the earth
through passable passageways, first the fiery aether lifted
itself up and in its lightness lifted many fires with itself.
This is not very different at all from what we often see,   **460**
when first thing in the morning the golden light of the radiant
sun glows red through the grass glimmering with dew
and lakes and ever-flowing rivers breathe out mist,
as at times the earth itself is seen to give off vapor.
When all these join together in the sky above,   **465**
with congealed composition clouds weave beneath the sky.
So therefore at that time the light and expansive aether
with congealed composition bent itself around everywhere
and having expanded everywhere far and wide into all parts
thus fenced in all that remained in its greedy embrace.   **470**
Following upon this were the beginnings of the sun and moon,
whose spheres turn in the air midway in between.[27]
These neither the earth appropriated for itself nor did the great aether,
because they were neither so heavy that they sank down and settled,
nor so light that they could glide across the furthest shores,[28] **475**
and still they are thus midway in between so that they revolve
like living bodies[29] and exist as parts of the whole world,

---

[27] i.e., midway between the earth and aether.

[28] i.e., the furthest shores of the universe, where the aether is.

[29] They revolve like living bodies, but are not in fact alive. See lines 5.122-
     125 above.

just as also in us certain limbs are allowed
to remain at rest, while there are still those that move about.
480 And so when these things were withdrawn, the earth suddenly,
where now the great dark expanse of the sea extends,
subsided and suffused its hollows with salty swells.
And day by day the more the seething of the aether and the rays
of the sun constrained the earth on all sides
485 to be more compact by frequent beatings on its outer edges,
so that, propelled, it was condensed and came together at its own center,
the more did the salty sweat, squeezed out of its body,
increase the sea and the swimming plains by flowing out,
and so much more did those many bodies of heat
490 and air slip out and fly and cause the lofty,
gleaming regions of the sky to thicken far from the earth.
The plains settled, and the heights of lofty mountains
increased. For neither were rocks able to subside further
nor could all parts sink equally to the same extent.
495 So therefore the weight of the earth with its composition congealed
became fixed and all the heavy slime, so to speak,
of the world flowed to the bottom and settled below like dregs.
Then sea, then air, then the fire-bearing aether itself,
with their fluid bodies were all left in a pure state,
500 some lighter than others, and aether, the most fluid
and lightest of all, floats along above aerial breezes,
nor does it mix its fluid body with the turbulent breezes
of air. It allows all here below to be twisted by violent
disturbances, and allows them to be disturbed by uncertain storms,
505 while it glides along and carries its fires[30] on its certain path.
For that the aether can flow with a single speed and force
the Pontus[31] shows, a sea which flows with certain current
constantly preserving a single, uninterrupted course of gliding.
Now let us sing what is the cause of the motions of the heavenly bodies.
510 First, if the great sphere of the sky turns about,
we must say that the air presses on the pole at each
end and holds it from outside and encloses it at both ends,
and then that other air flows above and stretches in the same
direction in which the stars of the enduring world revolve and shine,
515 or that other air flows below, which conveys the sphere in the opposite
direction, as we see rivers turn water wheels and their scoops.
It is also the case that the whole sky might remain fixed

---

[30] "Its fires" = the heavenly bodies.

[31] Pontus = the Black Sea. Ancient writers believed that water flowed out
of Pontus into the Propontis (Sea of Marmara) with a steady current,
and that the water never flowed the other way.

in place while the luminous constellations yet are borne along,
whether because rapid currents of aether are shut within,[32]
and seeking an exit turn round and cause the night-　　　　　　　**520**
thundering regions of the sky to revolve this way and that,
or whether air, flowing in from places outside,
turns and drives the fires, or whether they themselves
can creep wherever their food calls and invites them as they go,
feeding their flaming bodies this way and that through the heavens.　**525**
For to assert as certain which of these is true in this world
is difficult, but what can and what does happen throughout the universe
in different worlds brought forth in different ways,
this I teach and am proceeding to set out the many causes
which are able to exist for the motions of the stars throughout the
　　　universe.　　　　　　　　　　　　　　　　　　　**530**
Yet one of these must be the cause also in our world
that imparts movement to the constellations; but which of these it is
is not at all to declare for one who is progressing step by step.
So that the earth remains at rest in the middle region of the world,
it is natural that its mass should grow thinner little by little and diminish　**535**
gradually, and possess a different nature down below
attached from its earliest existence and linked together as one
with the airy parts of the world in which it is implanted and lives.
Therefore it is not a burden nor does it weigh down the air,
just as one's own limbs are not a weight to each person　　　　　**540**
nor is the head a burden for the neck nor in short do we feel
the entire weight of the body resting on top of our feet.
Yet whatever weights come from without and are placed on us
cause pain, although often they are very much smaller.
So great a difference does it make what each thing can do.　　　**545**
So therefore the earth has not been brought in suddenly
like something alien and been tossed from elsewhere onto alien air,
but came into existence together from the first beginning of the world
and is a fixed part of it, as our limbs are seen to be for us.
Moreover, shaken suddenly by a great clap of thunder,　　　　**550**
the earth shakes all things that are above it with its motion.
In no way at all could it do this unless
it were tightly bound to the sky and airy parts of the world.
For they cling fast, one to the other, with common roots
attached from their earliest existence and linked together as one.　**555**
Don't you see, too, how the thinnest force of the soul
sustains the body for us despite its great weight
because it is so attached and linked together as one?
Again what is now able with a quick leap to lift

---

[32] i.e., shut within the sky (*mundus*).

560 the body, except the force of the soul which steers the limbs?
Now do you see what great power a thin nature
is able to possess when it is attached to a heavy body, as air
is attached to the earth and the force of our soul is to us?
Neither much greater nor less can the disc of the sun
565 and its brightness be than it appears to be to our senses.
For from whatever distances fires are able to cast
light and breathe out warm heat upon our limbs,
not at all do they take away by these intervals from the body
of flames, not at all is the fire any smaller in appearance.
570 Accordingly, since the warmth of the sun and the light it pours
     forth   **[573]**
reaches clear to our senses and places shine brightly,   **[570]**
so too the shape and size of the sun should be seen so truly   **[571]**
from the earth that you can add nothing more or less to it.[33] **[572]**
575 The moon, too, whether it moves illuminating places with bastard
light,[34] or releases its own light from its own body,
whatever the case may be, it moves with no greater size
than that which it is seen to have when we discern it with our eyes.
For all things which we gaze at far distant
580 through much air are seen to have a blurry appearance
before their size diminishes. Therefore the moon must,
since it presents a distinct appearance and a well-defined shape,
be seen up above by us from the earth as well-marked
on its outer edges and just the size that it really is.
585 Finally, whatever fires of heaven you see from earth—
since whatever fires we gaze upon here on the ground,
as long as their flickering is clear, as long as their brightness is observed,
are seen sometimes a very tiny bit to change
their size in one direction or another, the further they are away—
590 so we may know that they[35] can be smaller by only an exceedingly **[594]**
small amount, or larger by a small and trivial degree.   **[595]**
This likewise is not to be wondered at: how   **[590]**
the sun, though so small, is able to produce so much light,   **[591]**
so that it fills up the sea and all the lands and the sky   **[592]**
595 by soaking them and washes over everything with its warm heat.[36] **[593]**
597 For it is possible that from that place one wide-flowing[37] fountain

---

[33] There are textual difficulties in lines 570-575. Editors transpose line 573
to follow line 569. Line 574 is identical to (571), and is omitted by editors.

[34] "With bastard light" = "with light not its own".

[35] "They" = the heavenly bodies.

[36] Line 596 is identical to 584, and is omitted by editors.

[37] "Wide-flowing" translates Lucretius' *largifluum*, a word he apparently
coined himself.

of the whole world opens up, gushing and bubbling light,
since thus from the whole world particles of heat
come together from everywhere and thus their gathering together   600
flows out, so that here from a single source the heat flows forth.
Don't you also see how widely a small spring
of water sometimes soaks meadows and overflows in the fields?
It is also possible that from the sun's fire, though not great,
heat grabs hold of the air with feverish burnings,   605
if by chance the air is thus prone and suitable
so that it is capable of igniting when struck by small amounts of heat.
Just so we sometimes see widespread conflagrations
catch on crops and dry grass from a single spark.
Perhaps too the sun, shining with its rosy torch   610
on high, has around itself much fire with invisible
burnings, which is marked off by no radiant light,
so that, bringing heat, it greatly increases the blow of its rays.
Nor is there a single and straightforward explanation of the sun
      available,
in regards to how from its summer regions it draws near   615
its winter turning-point in Capricorn and how returning
from there it turns to the solstice goal-post in Cancer,
and how the moon is seen to traverse the space monthly,
in which the sun consumes a year's time on its course.
No single cause, I say, can be assigned to these things.   620
For perhaps first of all this seems able to occur,
what the holy opinion of the great man Democritus posits:
the closer individual heavenly bodies are to the earth,
the less they are able to be carried along with the whirl of heaven.
For the strong and rapid force of the whirl grows weaker   625
and diminishes down below, and for this reason the sun
is little by little left behind with the constellations that follow,
because it is much lower than the glowing constellations.
Even more than this the moon: to the extent that its lower path,
lies far from the sky, and is in closer proximity to the earth,   630
so it is less able to match its pace with the constellations.
To the extent, too, that it is carried along by a weaker whirl
and is lower than the sun, the more do all the constellations
circle and catch up to it as they are carried past.
Therefore it happens that the moon is seen to revert more quickly   635
to each constellation, since the constellations are coming back to it.
It happens too that from transverse regions of the world alternate
airs can flow alternately each at a fixed time,
one which can thrust the sun away from the constellations of summer
to the winter solstice turning point and its icy stiffness,   640
and one which drives it back from the icy shadows of cold

to the regions of hot weather and the constellations that bring heat.
We must also think in a similar way about the moon and the stars
which revolve around in great orbits for great years,

645 that they can travel from alternate regions on alternate airs.
And don't you see that because of different winds lower
clouds travel in different directions than clouds above them?
How should these stars be less able to be carried
by currents differing among themselves through great orbits of ether?

650 But night covers over the earth in great darkness,
either when the sun after its long journey has struck against
the limits of the sky and, weary, breathed out his fires
buffeted by the journey and rendered unsteady by much air,
or since the same force compels it to direct its course

655 beneath the earth as it conveys its orb above the earth.
Likewise at a fixed time Matuta[38] scatters rosy
dawn through the regions of ether and pours forth light,
either because the same sun, returning beneath the earth,
grabs the sky beforehand and tries to ignite it with its rays,

660 or because fires gather together and many seeds
of heat are accustomed to flow together at a fixed time,
which always make the new light of the sun come into being.[39]
Just so it is reported that from the high peaks of Mt. Ida[40]
scattered fires are observed just as the first light rises,

665 and next they assemble into a sort of single globe and produce an orb.
Nor still should this be a source of wonder in these things,
that these seeds of fire are able to flow together
at so fixed a time and create anew the brightness of the sun.
For we see much that happens at a fixed time

670 in all things. At a fixed time trees begin
to flower and at a fixed time they let their flowers fall.
Likewise our age orders teeth to fall out at a fixed
time, and a child to reach puberty with a soft covering[41]
and let the soft beard fall equally down his cheeks.

675 Finally lightning, snow, rain, clouds, and winds
usually happen at fairly fixed times of the year.
For since the first beginnings of causes were thus,

---

[38] Matuta was a Roman goddess of the dawn and childbirth. She had a temple in the Forum Boarium in Rome.

[39] i.e. , a new sun may be created every day by seeds of heat coming together.

[40] Mt. Ida was located in Phrygia (in modern Turkey), near Troy.

[41] By "soft covering," Lucretius refers to the growth of body hair at puberty.

and things have so chanced from the first origin of the world,
one after another they even now return in fixed order.
Likewise days may increase and nights wither away,   **680**
and light in turn diminish, when nights gain increase.
This may be because the same sun, running beneath
the earth and above it, divides the regions of ether into unequal
curved portions and splits its orbit into non-equal parts.
And what it has taken away from one of the parts, he replaces   **685**
so much the more to the opposite part as he is carried around,
until he arrives at that constellation of the sky,[42] where the node
of the year[43] makes the shades of nighttime equal the light.
For in the mid-course of the blast of the north and south winds
the sky keeps the turning-points apart by an equal amount   **690**
because of the position of the whole zodiac bearing the constellations,
in which the sun, creeping along, subdues the space of a year,
illuminating the earth and sky with its obliquely slanting light,
as the calculations of those people reveal who have marked down
all the areas of the sky adorned with the constellations in their proper
        places.   **695**
Or alternately because the air is thicker in certain regions,
and so the trembling radiance of its fire[44] is delayed beneath the earth
and has great trouble penetrating and breaking out for its rising.
Therefore nights in the wintertime are long and drag on,
until the day's visible sign arrives with its rays of light.   **700**
Or again, because in the same way at alternate times
of the year fires are accustomed to flow together more slowly
or quickly, which cause the sun to rise from a fixed place,
therefore it happens that those seem to speak the truth...[45]
The moon, struck by the rays of the sun, is able to shine   **705**
and day by day to rotate this light more towards our sight,
the more it moves away from the round shape of the sun,
until, opposite it,[46] it has shone with very full light
and, rising and lifted up on high, has seen its setting.
Then little by little it must likewise hide its light behind   **710**
its back, so to speak, the nearer it now glides toward the fire

---

[42] i.e. , either Aries at the spring equinox in March, or Libra at the autumn
        equinox in September.

[43] The "node of the year" refers to the two points when the path of the sun
        on the ecliptic crosses the equator at the spring and autumn equinox.

[44] i.e., the fire of the sun.

[45] There are textual difficulties here, and many editors think one or more
        lines have dropped out.

[46] i.e., opposite the sun.

of the sun from the opposite region through the circle of constellations,
as those maintain who imagine the moon to be similar to a spherical
object and to hold its course and path beneath the sun.

715 It is also possible there is a way it revolves around with its own
light and still displays various phases of brightness.
For perhaps there is another body which moves and glides along
with it, hindering and obstructing it in all sorts of ways,
and which cannot be seen, since it moves devoid of light.

720 It is possible, too, that it revolves around perhaps like the sphere
of a ball, tinged by shining light over half its surface,
and by turning its sphere gives rise to its different phases,
until that part, whichever it is that is provided with fires,
turns towards our sight and wide-open eyes.

725 Then little by little it rotates it behind and takes away
the light-bearing part of its sphere-shaped mass,
as the Babylonian teaching of the Chaldaeans,[47] arguing against the
       scientific
explanation of the astrologers, tries to prove in direct opposition,
just as if that for which each fights might not in fact be true,

730 or you had a reason to dare to endorse this less than that.
Finally, why it isn't possible for a new moon to be always
created with a fixed order of phases and fixed shapes,
and each day for the created moon to fade away
and then for another to be supplied anew in its place and location,

735 it is difficult to demonstrate by reasoning and convince with words,
since you see so many things created in a fixed order.
There come Spring and Venus, and Venus' winged harbinger[48]
walks on before them, and behind the steps of Zephyr
mother Flora, besprinkling the whole path for them,

740 covers it completely with amazing colors and scents.
Next in line follows dry Heat together with his comrade
dusty Ceres and the annual blasts of the North Wind.
Next comes Autumn, and along with him walks Euhius Euan.[49]
Next the other seasons and winds follow behind,

745 high-thundering Volturnus[50] and Auster,[51] powerful with his lightning.

---

[47] By the term "Chaldaeans," Lucretius probably has particularly in mind
the Chaldaean historian and astronomer Berosus, who lived in the late
4th and early 3rd centuries BC.

[48] Venus' winged harbinger is Cupid.

[49] "Euhius Euan" = Bacchus, named after the shouts ("Euoe") of his
followers.

[50] Volturnus is the southeast wind.

[51] Auster is the south wind.

772-1457

At last Bruma[52] brings snows and renews numbing
ice; Winter follows her, teeth chattering with cold.
The less wonder, then, if at a fixed time the moon
is born and again at a fixed time is wiped away,
since so many things can happen at a fixed time.   750
Likewise too you must suppose that eclipses of the sun and obscurings
of the moon are able to happen for a wide variety of reasons.
For why could the moon cut off the earth from the sun's
light and thrust its head in front of it[53] from the earth's perspective,
imposing its dark orb on the sun's blazing rays,   755
and at the same time another body which always glides
along without light not be thought able to do this?
And why too could the weary sun not put aside
its fires at a fixed time and revive its light again
when it has passed by places in the air hostile to its flames,   760
which make its fires be extinguished and pass away for a time?
And why would the earth in turn be able to deprive the moon
of light and itself up high hold the sun captive, while the moon
in her monthly course glides through the sharp conical shadow,[54]
and at the same time another body is unable to pass   765
beneath the moon or glide above the sun's orb,
to break in and interrupt its rays and abundant light?
And yet if the moon itself shines with its own light,
why would it not be able to be dim in a fixed part
of the heavens as it travels through places hostile to its own light?[55] 770
For what remains, since I have unraveled how everything   772
is able to happen in the blue expanses of the great heavens,
so that we might be able to understand what force and cause
stir the various paths of the sun and movements of the moon,   775
and how they are able to fade away with light obscured
and cover the unsuspecting earth with a deep shroud of darkness,
when they blink, so to speak, and once again with an open eye
gaze upon all places made brilliant by their clear light,
now I return to the beginning of the world and the soft fields   780
of the earth, and what first with new births they resolved
to lift onto the shores of light and to entrust to uncertain winds.

---

[52] Bruma is the shortest day of the year, the winter equinox.

[53] i.e., the moon thrust its head in front of the sun.

[54] Lucretius here imagines the moon moving behind the earth into the
conical shadow where the sun's rays cannot reach it.

[55] Line 771 is identical to 764, and is omitted by editors.

In the beginning the earth produced the class of grasses and bright-
growing greenery around the hills and over all the plains,
785 flowering fields shone with lush green color,
various trees thereafter engaged with free reins
in a great contest of growing high up into the air.
Just as feathers, hair, and bristles are created first
on the limbs of quadrupeds and on the bodies of creatures powerful-of-
wing,[56]
790 so then the new earth offered up grass and shoots
first, and next created the races of creatures that arose
in many types by many means and in various ways.
For animals could not have fallen down from the sky,
nor could terrestrial creatures have come from salt waters.
795 It remains that the earth well deserves the name of mother
it has obtained, since from the earth all things have been created.
And even now many animals spring from the earth,
congealed together by rains and the hot exhalation of the sun,
so it is less surprising if more and larger things arose
800 then, grown to fullness when the earth and air were new.
At first the class of fowls and different types of birds
hatched in spring time and ventured forth from eggs,
as now in the summer cicadas of their own accord leave
behind their smooth shells, seeking sustenance and life.
805 Then, you see, earth first produced animals.
For much heat and moisture were abundantly present in the fields.
Therefore wherever a suitable area of space was provided,
wombs would grow, clinging tightly to the earth by roots.
When the time was ripe and the age of the infants had opened
810 them,[57] fleeing the moisture and seeking out the air,
nature steered pores of the earth in their direction
and forced there to flow out from these open veins
a juice similar to milk, just as now each woman,
when she has given birth, is filled with sweet milk,
815 because all of this urge to nourishment is steered towards her breasts.
The earth provided food for her young, the warmth clothing,
the grass a bed rich in much soft foliage.
But the newness of the world stirred up neither harsh
frosts nor excessive heat nor extremely powerful winds.
820 For all things grow and attain their strength equally.
Wherefore again and again the earth has obtained and holds

---

[56] i.e., birds. "Powerful-of-wing" translates *pennipotentum*, a word Lucretius
apparently coined.

[57] Them = the wombs.

the name of mother deservedly, since she herself created
the human race and produced at an almost fixed time
every animal that rages here and there over the great
mountains, together with the birds of the air in their various forms.   825
But since she must have some end to her begetting,
she stopped, just like a woman exhausted by old age.
For time makes the nature of the whole world change,
and one stage has to receive everything from another,
and nothing remains similar to itself: everything shifts,   830
nature changes everything and forces them to veer.
For one thing rots and weakens enfeebled with age,
and then another grows up and emerges from scorned beginnings.
So therefore time makes the nature of the whole world
change, and one stage receives the earth from another,   835
so that what bore cannot, and what did not bear before, can.[58]
And then too the earth attempted to create many
aberrations which came into being with amazing appearance and limbs:
the man-woman, in between both but neither, different from each,
some deprived of feet, others in turn without hands,   840
others also speechless without a mouth, or found blind without sight,
some restricted by the adhesion of their limbs to their entire bodies,
so that they could not do anything nor move anywhere
nor run from evil nor obtain anything they needed.
She created other monsters and aberrations of this sort,   845
all to no avail, since nature forbade their growth,
and they could not attain the desired flowering of their age,
nor find food nor join together in the activities of Venus.
For we see that many things must come together for crea-[59]
tures to have the possibility of pounding out generations by
    propagating: 850
First there needs to be food, next a way for generating seeds
throughout the frame to pour forth from slackened limbs,
and, so that females be joined with males, they must
each have a way to exchange mutual joys with one another.
Then many races of animals must have died out   855
and lacked the possibility of pounding out progeny by propagating.

---

[58] i.e., the earth can no longer give birth, but animals now can. I here follow
the interpretation of D.A.West. A different translation of the line is also
possible: "so that she (the earth) is unable to bear what she bore, and is
able (to bear) what she did not bear before."

[59] As commentators point out, line 5. 849 is the only line in Lucretius which
is hypermetric, i.e. where the last syllable of the line must be elided (or
pronounced) with the first syllable of the next line. To indicate this, I
have split the word "creatures" between the two lines.

For whatever you see feeding on the life-giving breezes,
either craftiness or courage or at least quickness has guarded
and preserved this race from the time it first began.
860 And there are many that still survive now commended
to our protection by their usefulness and entrusted to our safekeeping.
First, the fierce race and savage stock of lions
were protected by courage, as foxes by craftiness and stags by flight.
But the lightsleeping[60] minds of dogs with their faithful heart,
865 and the whole race which is born from the seed of beasts of burden,
along with wool-bearing flocks and the stock of horned cattle,
all have been entrusted to the safekeeping of human beings, Memmius.
For they eagerly fled wild beasts, and sought peace
and abundant food provided with no exertion of their own,
870 which we give out as a reward for the sake of their usefulness.
But those on whom nature bestowed none of these things,
so that they could neither live on their own nor give us
any usefulness on account of which we might allow
their kind to feed under our protection and be safe,
875 these naturally lay around as booty and profit for others,
all of them hampered by the chains of their own fatal weaknesses,
until nature relegated the race to complete extinction.
But Centaurs never existed at all, nor at any time
can creatures with a double nature and two-fold body
880 exist composed of unlike sorts of limbs,
so that the power of this and that stock could be sufficiently equal.[61]
This can be understood no matter how dull one's mind from what
        follows.
First, the horse is at the peak of his energy when three years
have gone round, a boy not at all, for even then
885 he will seek the milky nipples of his mother's breasts in his sleep.
Later when in old age the solid strength and weary
limbs of horses give out as life flees,
only then in the flowering of childhood does early manhood
begin and provide the cheeks with a covering of soft down—
890 so you don't by chance believe that Centaurs can be put together
or made from a human and the seed of burden-bearing horses,
or that Scyllas exist with bodies that are semi-marine in nature,
girded with frenzied dogs, and other things of their type,
whose limbs we see are in complete disagreement with each other,
895 which do not reach their prime nor attain strength of body

---

[60] "Lightsleeping" translates Lucretius' *levisomna*, a word he apparently coined himself.

[61] The text of line 881 is uncertain.

at the same time nor let it fall away in old age,
nor do they burn with a similar love, nor are they in harmony
about individual habits, nor are the same things healthful
throughout their limbs: indeed you can often see bearded
flocks[62] fattening on hemlock, a bitter poison for humans.   **900**
And what is more, since fire is accustomed to char and burn
the tawny bodies of lions as much as every other
kind of flesh and blood that exists upon earth,
how can it happen that the Chimaera, one in its threefold body,
in front a lion, in back a snake, in the middle a goat,   **905**
could breath out of its mouth fierce flame from its body?
Likewise too he who imagines that when the earth was new
and the heavens recent that such creatures could have been born,
seeking support from this one, empty word, "new,"
can babble at the mouth in similar fashion about many things   **910**
and say that rivers of gold then commonly flowed
throughout the earth, and trees used to flower with jewels,
or that a human being was born with so great a stretch of limbs,
that he could place the stride of his feet across the deep sea
and with his hands rotate the whole sky around himself.   **915**
For although many seeds of things existed in the earth
at the time when the earth first produced living creatures,
there is still no proof that beasts of mixed type
could be created and limbs of animals joined together,
since those things that even now are abundant on the earth —   **920**
different kinds of grasses, fruits, and lush trees —
still are not able to be woven into existence together,
but each thing proceeds in its own manner, and all
by a fixed law of nature safeguard their individual differences.
And that original race of human beings was much hardier   **925**
in the fields, as was fitting, since the hard earth created it,
and its inner foundation was laid with larger and more solid
bones, secured with strong sinews throughout the flesh,
nor was it easily overcome by either heat or cold,
nor by a new food or any defect of the body.   **930**
During many revolutions of the sun orbiting through the sky
they passed their lives in the wide-roaming manner of wild beasts.
Nor did there exist any strong wielder of the curved plough,
nor did anyone know how to work the fields with iron,
nor to plant new shoots into the earth, nor   **935**
to cut old branches from tall trees with a blade.
What the sun and rain had provided them, what the earth had presented

---

[62] "Bearded flocks" = goats.

on its own, this gift pleased their hearts well enough.
They cared for their bodies amidst acorn-bearing oaks
940 for the most part, and the wild strawberries you now see
come to maturity with crimson color in the winter time
then the earth bore more, and even bigger than now.
Then, too, the flowering newness of the world bore many
things as rough food, but ample for poor humans.
945 But to slake their thirst, rivers and lakes summoned them,
as now the down rush of water from the high mountains
loudly summons from afar the thirsty races of beasts.
In addition they inhabited sylvan precincts of the nymphs, discovered
on their wanderings, from which they knew flowing streams of water
950 washed over the wet rocks with a great flood —
the wet rocks — dripping over the green moss from above,
and bubbling and gushing here and there on the level plain.
Not yet did they know how to treat things with fire
nor to use skins to clothe their bodies with the hides of beasts.
955 But they made their home in woods and mountain caves and forests,
and they kept their filthy bodies concealed among shrubs
when forced to flee the buffeting of winds and rainstorms.
Neither could they have regard for the common good, nor did they
    know
how to employ any customs or laws with each other.
960 Whatever prize fortune had offered to each, he took,
each taught to live and be strong for himself on his own.
And Venus[63] brought together the bodies of lovers in the forests.
For each woman was won over either by mutual longing,
or a man's frenzied force and excessive sexual desires,
965 or a prize, acorns and wild strawberries or choice pears.
And relying on the amazing strength of their hands and feet
they hunted down the races of wild animals in the forest
with stone projectiles and the great weight of clubs.[64]   **(975)**
They overcame many, and stayed away from a few by hiding. **(968)**
970 And like bristle-covered boars, they entrusted their bare, sylvan **(969)**
bodies to the ground when overtaken by nighttime,   **(970)**
wrapping themselves with leaves and foliage all around.   **(971)**
Nor with great wailing did they wander about in fear   **(972)**
through the fields in the dark of night seeking daylight and the sun, **(973)**
975 but they waited expectantly, silent and buried deep in sleep, **(974)**
until the sun with rosy torch would infuse the sky with light.
For since from their earliest childhood they were always accustomed to
    see

---

[63] Venus = passionate love.
[64] Editors transpose line 975 to follow line 967.

darkness and light come about at alternate times,
it was impossible that wonder should ever be able to arise,
or despair that everlasting darkness might hold the earth   980
and the sun's light be taken away for all time.
But it was of greater concern that the races of wild beasts
often made rest dangerous for wretched humans.
And, thrown out of their homes, they fled their rocky abodes
at the arrival of a foam-tinged boar or powerful lion,   985
and in the dead of night with great terror they yielded up
their beds strewn with foliage to their savage houseguests.
Nor then much more than now did the mortal races of men
leave behind the sweet light of the sun with lamentation.
For then more often some one of them would be caught   990
and provide living food for beasts, ripped by their teeth,
and fill the groves and mountains and forests with moaning,
watching his living flesh be entombed in a living grave.
But those whom flight had rescued with their bodies gnawed upon,
later holding out trembling hands over their horrible   995
sores, called upon Orcus[65] with frightening voices,
until the savagely intense pain took away their life:
no one helped, and they didn't know what their wounds required.
But one day did not consign many thousands
of men on active duty to their destruction, nor did the turbulent   1000
expanses of the sea make ships and men lide[66] with rocks.
Then senselessly, purposelessly, vainly the sea often rose
and raged and lightly put aside its empty threats,
nor was the deceptive allure of the serene sea able
to lure anyone to their doom with laughing waves: 1005
the evil art of sailing then lay undiscovered.
Then, too, a lack of food led enfeebled
bodies to death; now, in contrast, overabundance drowns them.
Once people often used to pour poison
for themselves unwittingly, now they give it to others more cleverly.   1010
Next, after they had obtained huts, pelts, and fire,
and women, joined to men, agreed into one...[67]

* * * * * * * * * * * *

...became known, and they saw offspring born from themselves,
then the human race first began to soften.

---

[65] Orcus was a Roman god of death and the underworld.

[66] "Lide" (shortened from "collide") translates Lucretius' *lidebant*, a word
he invented by shortening the Latin verb *allido*.

[67] There are textual difficulties here, and editors think a line may have
dropped out.

Social contract

1015   For fire ensured that their shivering bodies were not so
       able to endure cold beneath the cover of the sky,
       and Venus[68] lessened their strength, and children by their winning
       ways
       easily broke down the harsh characters of their parents.
       Then too neighbors began to form friendships
1020   among themselves desiring neither to injure or be harmed,
       and sought out protection for children and the race of women,
       and making it known by voices and gestures in stuttering speech

social contract

       that it was right for everyone to take pity on the weak.
       Nor nevertheless was harmony entirely able to be produced,
1025   but a good part, the majority, kept the agreements faithfully,
       or the human race even then would have all perished,
       nor could propagation have extended the generations until now.
       But nature forced them to utter the different sounds
       of the tongue, and practical advantage fashioned the names of things,
1030   in a way not far different than the tongue's very
       lack of speech leads children to employ gestures,
       when it makes them point with a finger at things that are present.
       For each creature senses how it can employ his own strengths:
       before horns erupt and extend from a calf's forehead,
1035   he attacks with them in anger and pushes out threateningly.
       But baby panther cubs and young tiger whelps
       still fight back with claws and paws and biting,
       even when their teeth and claws have scarcely started to grow.
       Further, we see the whole winged race place
1040   their trust in wings, and seek shaky assistance from their feathers.
       Likewise to think that one individual then distributed names
       to things and that humans learned the first words from him
       is absurd. For why would he be able to mark everything
       with utterances and emit different sounds of the tongue, and at the
            same
1045   time others not be thought capable of having done it?
       Besides, if others too had not used their voices
       with one another, from where was the notion[69] of utility implanted
       and from where was this power first granted to him,
       to know what he wanted to do and conceive it in his mind?
1050   Similarly, one person could not have prevailed and forced

---

[68]   "Venus" here means the passionate love and affection of a relationship.

[69]   Lucretius here employs the word *notities*, "notion, concept" to translate
       Epicurus' technical Greek term, *prolêpsis*. For Epicurus, a *prolêpsis* was a
       universal concept formed by the mind on the basis of encountering a
       number of individual examples of a thing. See Introduction p. xvii.

so many to want to learn the names of things so thoroughly,
nor is it easy in any way to teach and persuade
the uncomprehending about what it is necessary to do. For they neither
would have suffered or endured in any way the sounds of voices
unheard before to din further into their ears to no purpose. 1055
Finally, what is so absolutely amazing in this matter,
if the human race, which possesses a strong voice and tongue,
should mark things with various words for various feelings,
when the mute herds, when even the races of wild beasts
are accustomed to let out different and various voices 1060
when fear or pain is present, and then when they burst with joy.
Indeed it is possible to know this from obvious things.
When the huge soft mouths of Molossian hounds[70] first
start to growl in anger, baring their strong teeth,
they are drawn back furiously and threaten with a far different 1065
sound than when they bark and fill the whole area with noise.
But when they try to lick their puppies affectionately with their tongue,
or when they jostle them with their paws and, pursuing with a nip,
feign gentle swallowings with their teeth held back,
they tend to them with a whimpering voice far different than 1070
when they are left alone at home and howl, or when,
imploring, they lower their bodies and flee from blows.
Again, too, doesn't the whinnying seem different
when a young stallion at the peak of development runs wild
among the mares, struck by the spurs of winged Love, 1075
and lets go a snort with flaring nostrils for the skirmish,[71]
than when as sometimes happens he whinnies with shaking limbs?
Finally, the race of winged creatures and various birds,
hawks, birds of prey, and sea-birds, seeking
sustenance and life in the salt sea among the ocean waves, 1080
send out cries at other times far different
than when they compete for food and their prey fights back.
And some others change their squawking songs along
with the weather, as the ancient races of crows and flocks
of ravens, when they are said to cry out for water 1085
and rain, and at times to summon the winds and breezes.
Therefore, if various feelings cause living creatures,
although they are mute, to let out various calls,
how much more reasonable is it that humans
can indicate different things with one sound or another! 1090

---

[70] Molossian hounds, originally from Epirus in northwest Greece, were a
famous breed widely used for hunting and shepherding.

[71] i.e., for the skirmish of mating.

But in case you are now silently asking yourself about this,
it was lightning that first brought fire down to earth
for mortals, and from there the flash of fire has been spread about.
For we see many things, implanted with flames from the heavens,
1095 catch fire, when a blow from the heavens bestows its heat.
Yet again, when a branching tree bends and sways,
beaten by the wind, as it presses on the branches of another tree,
fire is squeezed and rubbed forth with great force,
occasionally a hot flash of flame blazes out,
1100 while the branches and stems are rubbed together with each other.
Either of these things could have given fire to mortals.
Next, the sun taught them how to cook food
and soften it with the heat of flame, since they saw many things
ripen in the fields, overcome by the blows and heat of its rays.
1105 Gradually more and more those who excelled in intelligence
and had strong minds showed how to change their sustenance
and former way of life for new practices and fire.
Kings began to found cities and set up
citadels to serve as a means of defense and refuge for themselves,
1110 and to divide up flocks and fields and distribute them
on the basis of the appearance of each and their strength and
     intelligence.
For appearance was highly valued and strength had great importance.
Then afterwards property was invented and gold discovered,
which easily took away honor from the strong and the beautiful.
1115 For most follow the party of the wealthier, no matter
how strong or beautiful they have been born.
Yet if anyone would govern his life with true reason,
great wealth for a human being is to live modestly
with a calm mind, for never is there want of a little.[72]
1120 Still, human beings wanted to be famous and powerful
so that their good fortune would stand fast on a firm foundation
and they with their wealth would be able to lead a smooth life —
all in vain, since struggling to advance to the height of honor
they saw to it that the path of their life was filled with danger,
1125 and yet envy, like a thunderbolt, sometimes strikes and hurls
them down with great scorn into bitter Tartarus,   **(1131)**
since envy, like a thunderbolt, usually sets ablaze   **(1132)**
the heights and whatever rises up higher than the rest.[73]   **(1127)**

---

[72] Lines 1118-1119 contain one of the most important principles of
     Epicureanism: to be happy, a person should live simply and calmly,
     knowing that life's needs are easy to meet.

[73] Editors transpose lines 1131-1132 to follow line 1126.

Thus it is much better to obey quietly   **(1128)**
than to desire supreme command over things and to rule
    kingdoms.   **(1129) 1130**
Therefore let them get exhausted and sweat blood in vain,   **(1130)**
struggling with difficulty along the narrow path of ambition,
since their wisdom comes from another's mouth and they are seeking
things more from hearsay than from their own feelings,
nor does it work better now or in the future than it did in the past.   **1135**
Therefore kings were killed,[74] and the ancient majesty of thrones
and proud scepters were toppled and lay sprawled on the ground,
and the famous symbol of the king's head,[75] now stained with blood
beneath the feet of the crowd, grieved for its great honor.
For what was excessively feared before is gladly trampled on.   **1140**
And so things reverted to the utmost dregs and disorder,[76]
when each sought power and the highest station for himself.
Then some showed them how to create magistracies
and establish statutes, so that they would want to follow laws.
For the human race, tired of passing its time in violence,   **1145**
lay exhausted from feuds, so that more easily it fell
of its own accord under the rule of law and strict statutes.
Because each man was prepared out of anger to avenge
himself more fiercely than now is granted by just laws,
therefore humans were sick of passing their time in violence.   **1150**
Hence the fear of punishment taints the prizes of life.
For violence and harm circle around to net a person,
and usually turn back on him who originated them,
nor is it easy to lead a quiet and peaceful life
for the one whose actions break the common bonds of peace.   **1155**
For even if he deceives the race of gods and humans,
still he must be unsure that it will be secret forever,
seeing that many are often said to have betrayed themselves
by speaking while dreaming or in a disease-induced delirium
and to have brought deeply[77] concealed misdeeds out into the open.   **1160**
Now what cause made the divinity of the gods known
throughout great nations and filled cities with altars
and saw to it that established rites were undertaken,
which rites now flourish in great states and places,

---

[74] In the following lines (1136–1160), Lucretius describes how monarchies
were overthrown and city-states or republics were instituted. His account
roughly follows the outline of early Roman history.

[75] The "famous symbol of the king's head" is probably a crown.

[76] An alternate translation of the line is also possible: "And so the
government (*res*) reverted to the dregs (of society) and mob rule."

[77] I translate M.F. Smith's suggested emendation of *alte* ("deeply").

1165 from which even now there is implanted in mortals a shuddering fear
which causes new shrines of the gods to rise all around
the world, and compels them to assemble on festival days,
it is not very difficult to give an account in words.
Indeed even at that time the races of mortals
1170 used to see with waking minds the amazing appearances of the gods
and, even more in sleep, the wondrous size of their bodies.
Therefore they attributed sensation to them, because of the fact
that they seemed to move their limbs and send out haughty
voices as befitted their outstanding appearance and impressive
    strength.
1175 And they attributed eternal life to them, since their appearance
was always being reinforced and their shape remained constant,
and yet above all because they thought that those possessed
of such strength could not readily be defeated by any force.
And for this reason they thought they far excelled in happiness,
1180 because the fear of death troubled none of them,
and since at the same time in sleep they saw them do
many amazing things and have no problem doing so.
Moreover they observed that the workings of the sky and the varying
    seasons
of the year come around again in fixed order,
1185 nor were they able to understand by what causes it happened.
Therefore they sought refuge for themselves in attributing everything
to the gods and maintained that all things are directed by their will.
And they located the dwelling places and haunts of the gods in the sky,
since the night and the moon are observed to circle around through the
    sky,
1190 the moon, day, and night, and the stern constellations of the night,
and the night-wandering torch and the flying flames of the sky,[78]
clouds, sun, rain, snow, winds, lightning,
hail, the rapid roar and the great menacing murmuring.[79]
O unhappy human race, to have attributed
1195 such activities and assigned fierce anger to the gods!
What groans did they then beget for themselves, what
great harm for us, what tears for our descendants!
Piety is not to be seen often with head covered[80]
turning towards a stone and approaching every altar,
1200 nor to lie prostrate on the ground with open palms
before the shrines of the gods, nor to sprinkle altars

---

[78] i.e., shooting stars and meteors.

[79] i.e., thunder.

[80] It was the Roman custom to perform religious rites with their heads
covered, unlike the Greeks, who did not cover their heads.

contemplation of stars

with a profusion of the blood of beasts, nor to join vow to vow.
It is rather to be able to look upon everything with a tranquil mind.
For when we gaze up at the heavenly regions of the great
universe and the ether above set with shining stars,   1205
and thoughts of the paths of the sun and the moon enter our minds,
then into our hearts oppressed by other evils this
care too begins to raise its awakened head,
that by chance we are faced with the immense power
of the gods, which rotates the bright stars with their varying motions.   1210

NB

For lack of a rational explanation assails our uncertain mind
about whether there was any first creation of the world,
and likewise whether there is an end, until which
the walls of the world can endure this work of restless motion,
or whether, forever granted protection by the gods' will,   1215
they are able to glide through an eternal tract of time
and stand in defiance of the powerful forces of immeasurable time.
Moreover, whose mind does not shrink in fear
of the gods, whose limbs do not creep with fright,
when the scorched earth shakes with a terrifying blast of a thunderbolt 1220
and murmuring rumblings race across the great sky?
Don't peoples and nations tremble, and haughty kings
draw back their limbs, struck by fear of the gods,
lest on account of some horrible crime or haughty remark
the heavy time of paying retribution is forced upon them?   1225
Again, too, when the massive force of a violent wind
sweeps the commanding officer of a naval force across
the ocean along with his mighty legions and elephants,[81]
doesn't he solicit the peace of the gods and seek with prayers
in a state of terror the peace of the winds and favorable breezes?   1230
In vain, since often nonetheless he is swept away
by a violent whirlwind and carried along to the shoals of death.
To such an extent does some hidden force[82] crush
human affairs, and is seen to trample upon the beautiful
rods and fearsome axes[83] and make a mockery of them.   1235
Finally, when the whole earth sways beneath our feet

---

[81] The Romans first met elephants in battle when they fought the forces of the Greek king Pyrrhus at Heraclea in southern Italy in 280 BC.

[82] By the phrase "some hidden force" (*vis abdita quaedam*), Lucretius seems to be referring to the atomic nature of the universe, which randomly works things out with no care for human wishes. Only by learning how the world works in atomic terms, and adopting the Epicurean view of things, can humans attain true happiness.

[83] The rods (*fasces*) and axes (*secures*) were symbols of power for Roman elected officials.

Earthquake

and cities shake and fall or totter as they threaten to collapse,
what wonder if the human race despises itself
and leaves room in world affairs for the great power
1240 and wondrous strength of the gods, which governs all things.
For what remains, copper and gold and iron were discovered,
along with weighty silver and lead with all its power,
when fire had incinerated vast forests with glowing heat
on great mountains, whether by lightning descending from heaven,
1245 or because people, waging a war in the forest against
each other, had introduced fire to scare their enemies,
or because, attracted by the excellence of the soil, they wished
to clear the fertile fields and make the land pasturable,
or to kill wild beasts and grow rich with booty.
1250 For hunting with pit and fire came about before
fencing in a grove with nets and flushing game with dogs.
However it is, by whatever cause flaming heat
had eaten up the forests with horrible noise down
to their deep roots and had thoroughly cooked the earth with fire,
1255 there flowed out in molten veins and collected together
into hollow pockets of the earth a stream of silver and gold,
and likewise of copper and lead. When they saw these afterwards
congealed together and shining on the ground in vivid colors,
they lifted them up, captivated by their smooth and shiny charm,
1260 and saw that they had been formed with a shape similar to
the imprints of the hollow pockets each had possessed before.
Then it hit them that these things that were liquefied
by heat could assume any form or shape of things,
even right up to being able to be shaped and pounded
1265 into amazingly thin and sharply pointed tips,
so they could produce weapons for themselves, and be able to cut
forests, and hew timber, and plane beams smooth,
and also bore and punch holes and open passageways.
Nor at first did they try to fashion things any less
1270 with silver and gold than the violent strength of sturdy copper—
in vain, since their[84] power was defeated and gave way,
nor were they able equally to withstand hard labor.
At that time copper was worth more, and gold
was devalued because it was useless, blunted with a dull edge.
1275 Now copper is devalued, and gold has gained the highest honor.
So revolving time changes the seasons of things.
What was once held to have worth later has no honor;
then another thing succeeds and arises from contemptible
beginnings, and daily is more sought after, and when

---

[84] "Their" = gold's and silver's.

discovered flourishes with praise and is honored amazingly among
    mortals.   **1280**
Now in what way the nature of iron was discovered
is easy for you yourself to understand on your own, Memmius.
Weapons of old consisted of hands, fingernails, and teeth,
and rocks and branches too, fragments of trees,
and flames and fires, after they first came to be known.   **1285**
At a later time the force of iron and bronze was discovered.
The use of bronze was known before that of iron,
since its nature is easier to work and there is a greater supply.
With bronze they worked the soil of the earth, with bronze they
stirred the waves of war and sowed wasting wounds,   **1290**
and snatched away flocks and fields. For all that were
bare and unarmed easily yielded to them with their arms.
Then little by little the iron sword made its appearance,
and the sight of a bronze sickle became a thing of scorn,
and with iron they began to cleave the surface of the earth's soil,   **1295**
and the contests of doubtful war were made equals.
And jumping up armed onto a horse's back
and guiding it with reins, and flourishing with the right hand, came
before trying the dangers of war in a two-horsed chariot.
And yoking two horses came before yoking four,   **1300**
and before an armed man mounted a scythed chariot.
Then the Carthaginians taught Lucanian cows,[85] with towers
on their bodies, fearsome beasts, snake-handed, to endure
war wounds and confuse the great throngs of Mars.
So sad discord begot one thing from another,   **1305**
to cause fear in battle for the races of human beings,
and day by day caused the terrors of war to increase.
They also tried to use bulls in the service of war,
and attempted to send savage boars against their enemies. ·
And some sent mighty lions ahead of them,   **1310**
accompanied by armed animal trainers and savage teachers
who would be able to control them and hold them in chains,
in vain, since hot with indiscriminate slaughter they savagely
threw the squadrons of cavalry into complete and utter turmoil,
shaking the terrifying crests of hair on their heads all around,   **1315**
nor was the cavalry able to soothe the hearts of the horses,
terrified by the roaring, and turn them against the enemy with their
    reins.
The lionesses hurled their enraged bodies around with a leap

---

[85] "Lucanian cows" = elephants, so called because the Romans first met
elephants in battle when they fought the forces of the Greek king Pyrrhus
at Heraclea in Lucania in southern Italy in 280 BC.

in different worlds (handwritten)

everywhere, and aimed for the faces of those coming at them,
1320 and dragged down troops all unawares from behind,
grasping them and tossing them wasted by wounds to the ground,
affixed to them by their strong bite and hooked claws.
And the bulls threw their own people and crushed them underfoot,
and gored the flanks and abdomens of horses from beneath
1325 with their horns and tore up the earth with threatening intent.
And with strong tusks boars cut down their allies
savagely staining broken-off weapons with their own blood
[savagely staining with their own blood weapons broken off in
themselves,][86]
and caused indiscriminate ruin for cavalry and foot soldiers.
1330 For, sideways, steeds tried to avoid the fierce thrusts
of their tusks and, rearing up, sought the breezes with their hoofs—
all in vain, since you would have seen them fall down
hamstrung and be strewn upon the earth in their heavy fall.
If they thought before that any had been successfully subdued at home,
1335 they saw them explode with fury as they did their work amid
wounds, battle din, retreat, terror, tumult,
nor were they able to call back any part of them.
For all the different kinds of wild animals scattered,
as often today Lucanian cows,[87] wasted by weapons,
1340 scatter, when they have dealt many deadly deeds to their people.
If in fact they did it.[88] But I can scarcely believe that
before this atrocious evil happened to them all, they could   **(1343)**
not foresee and imagine with their minds that this would
happen,[89]   **(1342)**
and you can hold more reasonably that this happened somewhere in
the universe
1345 in different worlds brought forth in different ways,
rather than in any one particular world you might choose.
But they wanted to do this not from a hope of winning
as much as to make their enemies moan, and themselves perish,
since they lacked faith in their numbers and were without arms.
1350 Plaited clothing came before loom-woven garments.[90]

---

[86] Most editors delete line 1328, taking it as a nearly word-for-word gloss
on 1327, explaining that the weapons were broken off in the boars.
Other editors see lines 1327 and 1328 as alternate versions that Lucretius
wrote himself.

[87] "Lucanian cows" = elephants. See footnote on line 1302 above.

[88] With this phrase, Lucretius raises doubts about whether wild animals in
fact were ever trained to fight in battles.

[89] I follow editors who transpose lines 1342 and 1343.

[90] Lucretius here begins a new section on the evolution of clothing and the
art of weaving.

Weaving comes after iron, since loom-making requires iron,
nor in any other way can treadles, spindles, shuttles,
and loud-sounding leash-rods be made so smooth.[91]
And nature compelled men to make wool before
the female sex — for as a general rule the male sex   1355
far excels in skill and is much more clever—
until grim farmers found fault with the activity,
so that they wished to give over the work to women's hands
and they themselves equally to withstand hard labor
and in hard labor to make hard their limbs and hands.[92]   1360
But the visible model of planting and the original source of grafting
in the very beginning was nature herself, the creator of things,
seeing that berries and nuts fell down from trees
and produced swarms of seedlings in season beneath them.
And thus too it was pleasing to graft stems onto branches   1365
and to plant new shoots into the earth throughout the fields.
Then they tried successive methods of cultivating their dear little
plots and saw wild fruits grow milder in the earth
by being tenderly looked after and lovingly cultivated.
And day by day they made the forests retreat further   1370
up the mountain and give the space below to cultivation,
so that on hillsides and plains they might have meadows,
lakes, streams, crops, and glad vineyards, and a bluish
dividing strip of olive trees might run between,
spreading out over knolls and glens and plains: 1375
just as you now see the entire landscape laid out
with delightful variety, which they adorn here and there
with sweet orchards and encircle with fruitful rows of shrubs.
But humans imitated the clear-toned voices of birds
with their mouths long before they could bring fame to   1380
smooth songs by singing and grant pleasure to the ears.
And the breeze whistling through the hollows of reeds first taught
country people to blow on hollow hemlock stalks.
Then little by little they learned sweet love laments
which the flute pours forth pressed by the fingers of the players, 1385
the flute invented in the pathless groves and forests and glades,
in the lonely haunts of shepherds and their bright-sky leisure.
[Thus time gradually draws each and every thing

---

[91] Lucretius' technical vocabulary for parts of the loom is difficult, and
scholars are unsure about how to translate the terms rendered as treadles
(*insilia*) and leash-rods (*scapi*).

[92] Many editors think that lines 1359 and 1360 are alternative versions of
the same line and that Lucretius would have eliminated 1359 in a final
revision of the poem.

into the open and reason lifts it up into the shores of light.][93]
1390 These songs soothed their minds and gave delight
when they had eaten sufficiently:[94] for then all things are pleasing.
And so often, reclining beside one another in the soft grass
beside a stream of water beneath the branches of a tall tree,
and at not great expense they delightfully cared for their bodies,
1395 especially when the weather smiled down and the seasons of the year
painted colorful flowers on the green-growing grass.[95]
Then joking around, then conversation, then sweet laughter often
occurred. For then the sylvan muse was alive and thriving,
then pleasing playfulness taught them to encircle their heads
1400 and shoulders with festive crowns woven from leaves and flowers,
and to step forward without rhythm, moving their limbs
clumsily and with clumsy foot pounding mother earth.
From this smiles and sweet laughter arose, since all
these things then thrived, new and wondrous.
1405 And to those awake there were these consolations for lost sleep:
holding tones in varied ways and modulating tunes
and running over reed pipes with a curving lip.
Whence watchman even now preserve these traditions
and have learned to keep different kinds of rhythms, nor
1410 meanwhile do they obtain any more enjoyment of sweetness
than the woodland race of earth-born people obtained.
For that which is present and available, unless what we knew before
was sweeter, is particularly pleasing and promises to exert influence,
and the better thing discovered later usually destroys
1415 the former things and changes our feelings towards anything old.
This is how distaste for acorns began, this how beds
strewn with grass and piled up with leaves were abandoned.
The garment of wild-animal skin also fell from favor.
I imagine it was then such an object of envy when discovered
1420 that he who first wore it was ambushed and put to death,
and yet it was torn apart among them with much blood
and destroyed, nor was it able to be put to good use.
Once it was skins, today gold and purple, that exercise

---

[93] Lines 5.1388-1389 = 5.1454-1455. They are slightly out of place here, and
seem to fit the context of 1454-1455 better.

[94] Lucretius probably refers to the Epicurean view that once pain (here
hunger) has been removed, pleasure cannot be increased, but can be
varied (here by music). In *Principal Doctrine* 18, Epicurus writes, "Pleasure
cannot be increased, as soon as pain caused by want has been removed,
but only varied."

[95] Lines 1392-1396 repeat almost word for word lines 2. 29-33.

the life of men with worry and wear them out with war.
In this the greater fault belongs, I think, to us. 1425
For cold was torture to the naked earth-born people
without skins, but we suffer no harm lacking
purple clothing embroidered with gold and elaborate designs,
as long as we have an ordinary plebeian garment to protect us.
Therefore the human race toils purposelessly and in vain 1430
forever and consumes its lifetime in empty cares,
doubtless since it does not know what the limit of possessing things is,
and in general how far true pleasure increases.[96] *decades*
This gradually has led life into the abyss
and set in motion from below the great tides of war. ~~1435~~
But the watchmen of the world, the sun and moon, traveling around
and illuminating with their light the great revolving space of the sky
demonstrated to humans that the seasons of the year cycle around
and that this happens with a fixed plan and in a fixed order.
Then they passed their lives surrounded by strong fortifications 1440
and the earth was divided up, partitioned off, and cultivated.
Next the high sea flowered with sail-sped ships,[97]
now they had reinforcements and allies once treaties were drawn up,
when poets began to hand down mighty deeds
in songs, nor had letters been discovered much before. 1445
Therefore our age is unable to determine what happened
before, except if reason somehow reveals traces.
Sailing vessels and the cultivation of fields, walls, laws,
arms, roads, clothing, and others of this kind,
the prizes and in addition all the many luxuries of life, 1450
songs, paintings, and skillfully worked polished statues:
these were gradually revealed by practice along with the inventiveness
of a quick mind to humans progressing step-by-step. *progress*
So time gradually brings everything into sight
and reason lifts them onto the shores of light. 1455
For they saw one thing after another become clear in their minds
until they reached the highest pinnacle of the arts.

---

[96] Lucretius here alludes to two important Epicurean ethical doctrines. First, Lucretius thinks our desire for fancy clothing indicating wealth, high office, or high status portrays our ignorance about the value of different kinds of desires. Second, Lucretius again reminds us that once pain (here suffering caused by cold) has been removed, pleasure cannot be increased, but only varied.

[97] There are textual difficulties with this line, and I have followed Merrill's suggested emendation. In the original manuscripts the line reads, "Then the sea flowered with sail-sped (things) on account of spices."

Athens / "divine discoveries"

→ on end of world

ON THE NATURE OF THINGS

BOOK 6

The first place to distribute cereal-producing crops
to mortals long ago was gloriously famous Athens. ←
Athens, too, reshaped lives and enacted laws,
and was first to give the sweet source of comfort for life,
when she bore a man[1] found to possess such intelligence,   5
who once spoke everything from his truth-revealing mouth.
Even after his death, because of his divine discoveries, his glory,
announced long ago, is now raised to the sky.
For when he saw that nearly all things that need
demands for living were ready close at hand for mortals,   10
and that, to the extent they could, their life abides secure,
that powerful people overflowed with wealth, honor,
praise, and excelled others in the fine reputation of their children,
and that still nonetheless at home their hearts were anxious,
and, despite their thoughts, caused trouble for their lives without   15
any pause and were compelled to rage with furious complaints,
he realized then that the vessel[2] was the cause of its own defect,
and all things within it were corrupted by its defect, all
that are brought together and come from outside, even good things;
partly because he saw it was leaky and full of holes,   20
so that in no way could it ever be filled up,
partly because he perceived that it completely polluted, so to speak,
everything which it had taken in with a noxious taste.
And so he removed impurities from our hearts with his truth-revealing
words and placed a fixed limit on desire and fear.   25
He set out what the highest good[3] is towards which

---

[1] Epicurus.

[2] Lucretius here describes the human mind or spirit as a vessel or vase.

[3] The highest good = pleasure. Epicurus taught that the highest good was
    pleasure in the sense of "freedom from pain." For more on Epicurus'
    conception of pleasure, see Introduction pp. xv-xvi.

we all strive and showed the way by which, on a little
footpath, we might struggle towards it in a straight line.
He showed what evil existed everywhere in human
30 affairs, which arises and flies around variously, whether
by natural chance or force, because nature has so determined,
and from which gates it was best to confront each evil.
And he proved that for the most part the human race in vain
rolled sad waves of cares in their hearts.
35 For just like children who tremble and fear everything
in the dark night, so we are afraid in the light sometimes
of things that ought to be no more feared than
the things that children tremble at and imagine will happen.
Therefore this fear and darkness of the mind must be shattered
40 apart not by the rays of the sun and the clear shafts
of the day but by the external appearance and inner law of nature.[4]
Therefore I will proceed further to weave my theme in words.
And since I have shown that the regions of the heavens are sure to
     perish
and that the sky is made up of a body which has been born,
45 and since I have unraveled almost everything that happens in it
and must happen, take notice of what still remains.
Since once to climb up on the glorious chariot…[5]

     *   *   *   *   *   *   *   *   *   *   *   *   *

…of winds arise, they are calmed, how all things
that were raging are calmed, turned aside from their fierce anger,
50 and other things that mortals see occur on land
and sea, when often they hang in suspense with terrifying thoughts,
and which make their minds grovel with fear of the gods
and press them deep down to the ground because
their ignorance of causes forces them to attribute things
55 to the supreme command of gods and give way to their rule
[the causes of whose activities they can in no way understand,
and they imagine they take place through divine power.][6]
For those who have learned well that the gods live a tranquil
life, if still at times they wonder in what way
60 things can take place, especially in those events
which are seen in the shores of heaven above their heads,
are brought back again to ancient religious beliefs

---

[4] 6.35-41 = 2.55-61, 3.87-93; 6.39-41 = 1.146-148.

[5] There is a lacuna after line 47, and possible textual corruption in lines
48-49.

[6] These lines, which are identical to 1.153-154 (and lines 90-91 below), seem
out of place here and are bracketed by most editors.

pp 169-180 = meterology

and take on harsh masters, whom they believe
in their misery to be all-powerful, ignorant of what can be
and what cannot, in short, by what process each thing   65
has its power limited, and its deep-set boundary stone,[7]
so that all the more they are led astray by blind reasoning.
Unless you spit such things from your mind and completely
abandon thoughts unworthy of the gods and foreign to their peace,
the holy divinity of the gods, diminished by you, will often   70
harm you: not that the great power of the gods
can be disturbed, so that it thirsts in anger to exact harsh punishment,
but since you yourself will suppose that they, though calm in placid
peace, set rolling great waves of anger,
neither will you approach the gods' shrines with placid heart   75
nor have strength enough to receive with tranquil peace
of mind these images that travel from their holy bodies
announcing the outward appearance of the gods to human minds.
You can see the sort of life that now follows from this.
And indeed so that the truest reasoning might drive such a life   80
far from us, although I have set forth many words,[8]
still many remain and must be adorned in polished verses:
the outward appearance and inner workings of the sky must be
    grasped,[9]
stormy weather and flashing thunderbolts must be celebrated in song,
how they act and by what cause they are borne along,   85
so you do not divide the regions of the sky and frantically worry
from where flying fire has come or to which of the two
parts[10] it then turns, how it wends its way through walled
places, and how, lord of all, it makes its exit.
[the causes of whose activities they can in no way understand,   90
and they imagine they take place through divine power.][11]
And you, Calliope,[12] point out for me as I run

---

[7] 6. 58-66 = 5. 82-90.

[8] In Books 1-5.

[9] There are textual difficulties with this line. An alternate reading is, "the inner workings of the earth and sky must be grasped."

[10] By "which of the two parts" Lucretius apparently means the right- and left-hand sides of the sky.

[11] These lines, which are identical to 1.153-154 (and lines 56-57 above), seem out of place here and are bracketed by most editors.

[12] Calliope was one of the nine Muses and was the Muse of epic poetry. The Greek poet and philosopher Empedocles had also invoked Calliope in his philosophical epic. Lucretius' invocation of Calliope was traditional, but as an Epicurean he would not have believed that a Muse was really inspiring him.

my course the white chalk finish line, skilled
Muse that you are, repose of humans and pleasure of gods,
95 so that with you leading I might win the crown with glorious praise.
First, the blue expanse of the sky is shaken by thunder
because clouds aloft flying along on high
clash together as winds fight one other.
For noise does not arise from a clear part of the sky,
100 but wherever clouds are arranged in denser formation, the more often
there arises from them roaring with great rumbling.
Besides, clouds can neither have so dense a structure
as stones and wood do, nor in turn are they as insubstantial
as mists and smoke, quick to fly away. For then
105 they must either fall, weighed down by sheer weight
like rocks, or, like smoke, fail to hold together
and be unable to contain icy snow and showers of hail.
They also produce sound above the surface of the spreading heavens,
just as the awning creaks at times when it is stretched over
110 great theaters and is tossed about among the poles and beams,
and sometimes it flutters wildly, split by unruly winds,
and calls to mind the crackling sound of papyrus sheets—
for this type too you can recognize in thunder—
or when drying clothes or flying papyrus sheets
115 are beaten by breezes' blows and whipped up by the wind.
For it sometimes happens too that clouds cannot clash
head on as much as pass by at an angle
with differing movements, slowly scraping their bodies together.
Then that harsh sound rubs against the ears and continues
120 for a long time, until they have left their narrow confines.
In the following way, too, everything often seems
to be struck by heavy thunder and rattle, and the massive walls
of the capacious world to have been rent suddenly and leapt apart,
when a gathered blast of a strong wind has suddenly twisted
125 itself into the clouds and, enclosed within, spinning
and whirling more and more on all sides, forces
the cloud to become hollow, its body thick all around.
Next, when its force and fierce impulse weaken it,
then with a terrifying crackle it splits open and roars.
130 Nor is it surprising, when a small little bladder full of air
so often makes a small noise when it suddenly bursts.[13]
There is also a reason, when winds flow through clouds,
that they make noise. For we often see clouds traveling
along, rough-hewn and branching in many ways,

---

[13] "Small noise" is the reading of the manuscripts, but some editors favor
emending the noise from "small" (*parvum*) to "large" (*magnum*).

just as, of course, when the blasts of the Northwest wind flow   135
through a dense forest, the foliage sounds and the branches creak.
It also happens that sometimes the rushing force of a strong
wind cuts and bursts head on through a cloud.
For what a blast of wind can do on high is readily apparent
here on earth where it is gentler, since it still overturns   140
tall trees, sucking them up by their deepest roots.
There are also waves among the clouds, which, so to speak, roar
loudly when they break. This likewise happens in deep
rivers and on the great sea, when the surging current breaks.
It also occurs, when the burning force of a thunderbolt passes   145
from cloud to cloud. If the cloud that has received the fire by chance
is extremely moist, it extinguishes it at once with a loud noise.
So iron white-hot from heated furnaces often
hisses, when we have doused it quickly in ice-cold water.
Further, if a drier cloud receives the lightning fire,   150
it ignites at once and begins to burn with a great sound,
as if flames are forced to wander laurel-coifed mountains
by a whirl of wind, incinerating them with a massive assault.
Nor is anything so consumed by crackling flame with a more
terrible sound than the Delphic laurel leaves of Phoebus.[14]   155
Next, a great shattering of ice and deluge of hail
often produce noise in the great clouds on high.
For when the wind packs them tightly together, mountains of clouds,
congealed into a narrow space and mixed with hail, are shattered.
Lightning, likewise, occurs when clouds collide and expel   160
many seeds of fire, just as if stone or iron
strikes hard against stone, for then too light
leaps out and fire scatters bright sparks.
But it happens that we take in thunder with our ears later
than our eyes see lightning because things always   165
arrive more slowly to our ears than things that move the eyes.
One can also recognize it from this: if you see from afar
someone cutting the bulk of a tree with a double axe,
it happens that you perceive the striking before the blow sends
sound to the ears. So we also perceive the lightning   170
before we receive the thunder that is sent out simultaneously
with the fire from a similar cause, born from the same collision.
In the following way also clouds brush places
with flying light and a storm flashes with quivering assault.
When the wind has invaded a cloud, twisting around inside,   175

---

[14]   Phoebus is one of the names of Apollo, god of music and prophesy, whose
       most famous oracle was located at Delphi in Greece.

and has made, as I have shown before,[15] the hollow cloud thicken,
it grows hot by its own speed, just as you see
everything become hot and glow by motion—why, a lead
projectile even melts as it spins on its long trajectory!
180 And so when this burning wind has ruptured the black cloud,
as if by force it suddenly squeezes out and scatters
seeds of heat which produce flickering flashes of flame.
Next noise follows which strikes our ears more slowly
than those things which reach the vision of our eyes.
185 Of course this happens with clouds that are dense and also heaped
high on top of one another in wondrous array,
lest you be deceived because we see from below their width
better than to what height they are heaped up and stand.
For be sure to gaze closely when the winds transport
190 clouds resembling mountains across the air above,
or when you see them stacked on massive mountains
on top of one another and pressing down from above,
stationary, when the wind has died down on all sides.
Then you will be able to understand their great masses
195 and to observe their caverns built up as if from hanging
rocks, which when a storm arises and the winds fill
them out, closed in by the clouds they show their anger
with great rumblings and threaten like wild animals in their cages.
Now here, now there they emit growls
200 in the clouds, and seeking an exit they turn around and roll
the seeds of fire together from the clouds and so assemble
many and spin the fire within the hollow furnaces,
until the cloud is ripped apart and they gleam and flash with lightning.
It happens too from the following cause that this quick, golden
205 hue of liquid fire swoops down on the earth:
because clouds themselves must possess many, many
seeds of fire. For when they are without any moisture,
their color for the most part is a brilliant flame-red.
For indeed they must receive many things from the light
210 of the sun, so understandably they redden and pour forth fire.
And so when the driving wind thrusts them together, assembling
and compressing them into one place, they squeeze and pour out
seeds that make the colors of flame flash forth.
There is lightning likewise too when the clouds of the sky thin out.
215 For when the wind lightly undoes the clouds as they pass along
and dissolves them, these seeds that produce lightning
must fall reluctantly. Then lightning occurs

---

[15] 6.124-129.

without horrible fear and sound, and with no turmoil.
As to the rest, with what nature thunderbolts are endowed
is revealed by their strikes and branded-in signs   **220**
of heat and marks exhaling thick fumes of sulfur.
For these fires are not the signs of wind or rain.
Moreover often too they ignite the roofs of houses
and with quick flames they completely dominate even the interiors.
Nature, you know, made this fire the subtlest of fires,   **225**
and constructed it with very tiny, quick-moving bodies.
Nothing is able to block it in any way.
For the powerful thunderbolt passes through the walls of houses
as do shouts and voices, it passes through rocks and bronze,
and turns bronze and gold to liquid in a moment of time.   **230**
Likewise it makes wine instantly disappear, leaving the vessels
untouched, since, no doubt, its heat as it travels easily
loosens everything around it and makes the clay sides
of the vessel porous, and, wending its way inside,
it quickly dissolves and scatters the first beginnings of the wine.   **235**
This the heat of the sun is seen not to be able
to accomplish in a lifetime, even though it is strong in its shimmering
        heat,
so much more rapidly moving and dominant is this power of the
        thunderbolt.
Now how these things are created and with what great
force they are made so they can split apart towers with their blows,   **240**
demolish houses, snatch away beams and rafters,
dislodge and move the monuments of men around,
kill humans, lay livestock low everywhere,
and by what force they can do other things of this type,
I will explain, nor will I delay you any further with promises.   **245**
Thunderbolts must be conceived to arise from clouds that are thick
and stacked high, for none are ever sent when the sky
is clear, nor when clouds are only slightly dense.
Things clearly show beyond a doubt that this happens,
because then clouds grow thick throughout all the air,   **250**
so that we think that on all sides darkness has left Acheron[16]
behind and fills up the vast caverns of the sky,
so greatly, when the bleak night of clouds has arisen,
do the faces of black fear hang over us from above,[17]
when a storm begins to set its thunderbolts in motion.   **255**

---

[16] Acheron was the name of one of the rivers of the underworld.

[17] 6. 251-254 = 4. 170-173, except that Lucretius has "you think" rather than
      "we think" in the earlier passage.

Moreover very often, too, a black cloud over the sea,
like a river of pitch sent down from the sky, packed with darkness
from afar, falls thus into the waves and drags along
a black storm heavy with thunderbolts and violent blasts,
260   itself stuffed as much as can be with fires and winds,
so that on land also people shudder and seek cover.
Thus therefore we must think that the storm extends high
above our heads. Nor would they cover over the lands
with such darkness, unless many clouds were built
265   up on many others and blotted out the sun.
Nor could they arrive and press down with such rains
that they make rivers swell and plains swim
unless the heavens had clouds piled up high.
So, therefore, everything is filled with winds and fires,
270   and thus on all sides growling and lightning come into existence.
Indeed I have shown above[18] that hollow clouds have very
many seeds of heat and must take in
many from the rays of the sun and the burning heat they possess.
Thus when the same wind that drives them together
275   into a chance place has squeezed out many seeds
of heat and simultaneously mixes itself with this fire,
a vortex enters there and twists in the narrow space
and sharpens the thunderbolt to a point in the hot furnaces within.
For it catches fire for two reasons: it grows hot
280   itself by its own speed, and by its contact with fire.
Next when the power of the wind has been super-heated and the
        overpowering
rush of fire has entered, then the thunderbolt, ripe, so to speak,
suddenly splits the cloud apart, and the excited blaze
travels illuminating all places with its shimmering light.
This is followed by an overpowering sound so that the regions of the
285   sky
above seem suddenly to explode and overwhelm the earth.
Next shaking overpowers and tests the earth and murmuring
rumblings race across the sky, for then almost the whole
storm is shocked and trembles, and growling sounds are produced.
290   From this shock follows heavy, plentiful rain,
so that the whole upper air seems to have turned to rain
and to fall so quickly that it is calling all back to the flood,[19]

---

[18]   6.206-210.

[19]   See 5.380-415. The flood Lucretius probably has in mind is from the
myth of Deucalion, Pyrrha, and the Great Flood. See Ovid *Metamorphoses*
1.253-415 for a fuller version of the myth.

so great a shower is emitted by the splitting of clouds and blast of
wind, when the sound flies forth with its flaming blow.
It occurs also when a force of wind from outside races   **295**
and falls upon a cloud pregnant[20] with a ripe thunderbolt.
When it splits the cloud, at once that fiery vortex falls
which in our native language we call a thunderbolt. This same thing
happens in other directions, wherever the force has traveled.
It also happens that sometimes a force of wind, though sent without
     fire,   **300**
nevertheless catches fire during the interval of its long travels,
losing as it goes on its course certain large bodies
that are not able to pass through the air with equal ease,
and it sweeps up and conveys from the air itself other
small bodies that when mixed create fire as they fly.   **305**
This is not much different from how a lead projectile
heats up on its trajectory, when it has shed many bodies
of icy coldness and caught on fire in the air.
It also happens that the force of the very blow rouses fire,
when the frigid force of the wind, sent without fire, has struck,   **310**
doubtless because, when it has hit hard with a forceful strike,
particles of heat can stream together from the wind itself
and simultaneously from that thing which then receives the blow,
just as fire flies out when we strike a stone with iron,
nor, because the force of the iron is frigid, do the seeds of hot   **315**
flashing hurry together at its blow any more slowly.
Therefore so too ought a thing to be kindled by a thunderbolt
if by chance it was well-situated and suited for flames.
Nor easily can that force of the wind be completely and absolutely
frigid, which has been sent forth on high with such force.   **320**
Rather, even if it is not kindled first with fire on its trajectory,
yet still it will arrive warmed and mixed with heat.
But the quick speed of the thunderbolt and its overwhelming strike
     happen,
and thunderbolts usually zip along with such swift gliding,
because the force itself is completely roused and gathered together   **325**
beforehand, and acquires a great power of movement.
Then, when the cloud is unable to contain the increasing impulse,
the force is squeezed out and thus flies with wondrous impulse,
like missiles travel that are launched from powerful siege-engines.
Add to this that it is composed of small, light particles,   **330**
nor is it easy for anything to offer resistance to such a substance.

---

[20] The text is uncertain here. I have translated Bentley's suggestion of
"pregnant" (*gravidam*), but other editors read Bernays' "hot" (*calidam*).

For it runs in between and penetrates empty passages,
and thus is not impeded and delayed by many collisions,
and for this reason it glides and flies with quick impulse.

335 Next, add that all weights by nature always
incline downwards, but when a blow has been added on, too,
the speed is doubled and this impulse becomes more forceful,
so that it scatters by blows more violently and more quickly
whatever blocks its way, and proceeds along its path.

340 Next, because it travels with long-lasting impulse, it ought
to add greater and greater speed that increases as it goes
and augments its sturdy strength and makes the blow harder.
For it brings it about that whatever seeds the thunderbolt has
travel together straight into one place, so to speak,

345 casting them all as they spin into the same course.
Perhaps as it goes it carries along from the air itself
certain bodies that incite great speed by their blows.
It passes harmlessly through things and keeps many
whole, because the liquid fire passes through their pores.

350 And it pierces many things, when the very particles of the thunderbolt
have happened upon the particles of things where they are held
    interwoven.
Further, it easily dissolves bronze and makes gold
fuse instantly, since its force is made up in miniature
scale of small bodies and of particles light in weight,

355 which wends its way easily, and, having wended, instantly
dissolves all the connections and opens up the bonds.
In autumn the heavenly abode, adorned with gleaming stars.
is shaken more often everywhere, as is the whole earth,
and also when the flowering season of spring unfurls itself.

360 For fires are absent from the cold, and in heat winds die
down and clouds do not possess so dense a composition. [21]
And so when the seasons of the sky lie in between the two,
then all the varying causes of the thunderbolt come together.
For the fluctuating periods of the year mingle cold and hot,

365 both of which a cloud needs to build thunderbolts,
so that there be discord among things and the air with great
tumult is tossed about in turmoil by fire and wind.
For the first part of heat is the last of rigid cold,
that is springtime. Therefore dissimilar things must

370 fight among themselves and cause turmoil when mixed.
And when the last heat mixed with the first cold rolls
around, a time which is referred to by the name of autumn,

---

[21] i.e., in the cold of winter and heat of summer.

then also sharp winters conflict with summers.
Therefore these should be named the "transition points"[22] of the year,
nor is it surprising if during this time many thunderbolts   **375**
arise and a turbulent tempest is roused in the sky,
since disturbance occurs with doubtful war on both sides,
here with flames, there with winds and moisture combined.
This is to investigate the true nature of the fiery thunderbolt
and to see by what force it does each thing,   **380**
not by unrolling the Etruscan divination books[23] in vain
to seek out signs of the hidden intention of the gods,
from where flying fire has come or to which of the two
parts[24] it then turns, how it wends its way through walled
places, and how, lord of all, it makes its exit,[25]   **385**
or what harm a blow of a thunderbolt from the sky can do.
But if Jupiter and the other divinities make the gleaming regions
of the sky shake violently with terrifying noise
and toss fire wherever each one wills,
why don't they make those who failed to guard against   **390**
loathsome crime be struck and breathe out flames
of lightning from their pierced breast, a pointed lesson for mortals?
Why rather is one who feels no guilt about anything
engulfed and caught up in flames, although innocent,
suddenly swept away by a fiery heavenly whirlwind.   **395**
And why do they aim at deserted places and labor in vain?
Or are they exercising their forearms and toning up their biceps?
Why do they allow their father's weapon to be blunted by the earth?
Why does he himself allow it and not save them for his enemies?
Again why does Jupiter never toss lightning at the earth   **400**
and pour forth thunder when the sky is clear all round?
Or as soon as the clouds form does he himself then descend
into them to direct the blow of his weapon from close in?
For what purpose, further, does he launch them at the sea? With what
does he accuse the waves, the massive waters and swimming plains? **405**
Besides, if he wants us to look out for the strike of a thunderbolt,
why does he refrain from letting us see it being launched?
If, however, he wants to catch us by surprise with fire,
why does he thunder from there, so we can avoid it,

---

[22] Lucretius uses the word *fretus*, literally "channels" or "straits."

[23] By "Etruscan divination books" (*Tyrrhenna carmina*) Lucretius refers to divination practices the Romans borrowed from the Etruscans.

[24] By "which of the two parts" Lucretius apparently means the right or left hand sides of the sky.

[25] 6.383-385 = 6.87-89.

410 why gather darkness, deep rumbling and roaring beforehand?
And how can you believe that he launches his thunderbolts at the
    same time
in many directions? Or do you dare to maintain that it has never
    happened
that many strikes have taken place at one time?
But it has very frequently happened and must necessarily happen,
415 just as it rains and showers fall in many regions,
so many lightning bolts occur at one time.
Finally, why does he shatter the sacred shrines of the gods
and his own renowned sanctuaries with a savage thunderbolt,
and split apart beautifully-wrought statues of the gods,
420 and subtract dignity from his own images with a wanton wound?
And why often does he aim at lofty places, and why
do we notice most traces of his fire on mountain tops?
As to the rest, it is easy to understand from the following things
how what the Greeks call presters[26] because of their nature
425 are sent down from on high into the sea.
For it sometimes happens that what looks like a column drops down
and descends from sky to the sea. The water boils furiously
around it, stirred up by blasts of wind,
and whatever ships are then caught up in this tumult
430 are pummeled over and over and undergo the greatest danger.
This happens at times when the force of the wind is roused
and tries in vain to burst a cloud, instead depressing it
so that what looks like a column drops down from sky to sea,
little by little, as if something is pushed out from above
435 by a fist and the thrust of an arm and stretches out to the waves.
When it splits the cloud, the force of the wind bursts forth from it
into the sea and causes an astounding seething among the waves.
For a revolving whirlwind descends and leads down
at the same time that cloud endowed with supple body.
440 And as soon as it thrusts the cloud down on the expanse of the sea,
it immediately injects itself whole and stirs up
the entire sea, forcing it to seethe with tremendous noise.
It happens too[27] that a vortex of wind on its own entangles
itself in clouds, scrapes together seeds of cloud
445 from the air, and imitates a sort of prester descending from the sky.

---

[26] A prester is a waterspout or whirlwind. The Greek word *prêstêr* is related
to the Greek verbs *prêthô* (to blow) and *pimprêmi* (to burn). Lucretius
does not discuss fire in connection with the prester. For the Epicurean
view of the *prêstêr*, see Epicurus' *Letter to Pythocles* 104-5.

[27] Lucretius here seems to relate another way presters or waterspouts can
form.

When it has let itself down on the earth and has dissolved,
it spews forth a huge force of whirlwind and storm.
But since this happens altogether rarely and mountains must
offer an obstacle on earth, the same thing appears
more frequently in the great prospect of the sea and in the open sky.   **450**
Clouds are formed when many bodies, rougher ones,
come together suddenly as they fly in this space of sky
above. The bodies, though but tenuously entangled, are able
to hold together packed closely one with another.
These at first cause little clouds to form,   **455**
which then catch hold of each other and flock together
and by joining together grow larger and are carried by the winds
until the point at which a fierce storm breaks out.
It happens too that mountain tops, the nearer they are
to the sky, the more at that exalted height they smoke[28]   **460**
continuously with the dark mist of a dust-yellow cloud.
This occurs because, when clouds first form,
so thin the eyes cannot see them yet, the winds
carry and force them to highest mountain-tops.
Here at last it happens that gathered and packed together   **465**
in a great throng they are able to become visible, and they seem
to rise as one from the top of the mountain into the upper air.
For that high places are exposed and windy, the facts
themselves and our senses reveal when we climb high mountains.
Moreover, too, clothes hung on the shore reveal   **470**
that nature takes a very great number of bodies
from the whole sea, when they receive a coating of moisture:
so it seems more likely that many bodies are also able
to rise from the salty motion of the sea to increase the clouds.
For the whole nature of the moistures is deeply related.[29]   **475**
Moreover, we see rising up from every river and the earth
itself, too, cloudy mist and hot vapor,
which like an exhalation are forced out from those places
and are carried upwards and suffuse the sky with their darkness, little
by little constructing clouds on high by coming together.   **480**
For the heat of the starry ether above also presses down,
and by condensing weaves clouds together beneath the blue sky.
It happens too that those bodies which create clouds
and flying storm-clouds enter into our atmosphere from outside.
For I have demonstrated that their number is beyond numbering and
the extent   **485**

---

[28] The mountain-tops appear to "smoke" because they are covered in clouds.

[29] Lucretius means that moisture in the sea and in clouds are related.

of the heavenly depths is infinite, and I have set out with what
speed these bodies fly and how in an instant
they are accustomed to travel across an indescribably large space.
It is not therefore amazing if often in a short amount
490 of time a storm and darkness tower above and cover
over land and sea with great storm-clouds,[30]
seeing that on all sides through all the pores of the ether
and round about through all the breathing-holes, as it were,
of the great world exits and entrances are provided for the elements.
495 Now come, I will explain how raindrops
are formed in lofty storm-clouds, and are sent down
and fall onto the earth as showers. First then I will succeed
in proving that many seeds of water rise up
with the clouds themselves from all things and both grow
500 equally, both clouds and whatever water exists in clouds,
just as our own bodies grow equally with our blood,
and sweat too and in short whatever moisture is in the limbs.
So too they often take in much
moisture from the sea, like hanging fleeces of wool,
505 when winds carry clouds along above the great sea.
Similarly, moisture is lifted up from all the rivers
into the clouds. There, when many seeds of water
have assembled in many ways, increased from every side,
the densely-packed clouds strive to release moisture
510 in two ways: for the force of the wind thrusts and the very
abundance of clouds, gathered together in a greater throng,
pushes and presses from above and makes showers pour out.
Moreover when the clouds are thinned out by the wind, too,
or dissolved, struck hard from above by the sun's heat,
515 they let loose and drip raindrops, like wax
over a hot fire melts away and flows freely.
But violent showers occur when clouds are violently squeezed
by both forces: their own accumulation and the wind's assault.
But rains are accustomed to last awhile and linger a long
520 time, when many seeds of water are stirred up
and clouds one on top of the other and dripping storm-
clouds are carried far and wide in every direction,
and when the entire earth steams and breathes back the moisture.
Then when the sun with its rays gleams amid the dark storm
525 with the spray of the storm-clouds set directly opposite,
then the colors of the rainbow stand out amid the black clouds.

---

[30] The text is uncertain here. I have translated Lachmann's suggestion of
nimbis ("storm-clouds") in place of the manuscript reading *montis*
("mountain").

Other things that grow above and are created above,
and that grow in thickness in the clouds, all of them, absolutely all:
snow, winds, hail, and ice-cold frosts,
and the great power of ice, the great hardener of waters   **530**
and delayer which everywhere reins in eager rivers,
it is still very easy to discover all these things
and to perceive with the mind how they happen and why they are
     created,
when you understand well what qualities the elements possess.[31]
Now come and see what explanation exists   **535**
for earthquakes. And first, be sure to think that the earth below,
as it is above, is filled in every place with windy
caves, and holds in its hollow places many lakes
and many pools and steep cliffs and precipitous rocks.
And it must be thought that many rivers beneath the earth's surface   **540**
cause waves and submerged rocks to roll violently.
For the facts themselves require it to be everywhere similar to itself.
Therefore with these things subjoined and employed as substructure,
the earth trembles above when it is shaken by a great collapse,
when time eats away from beneath huge caves below.   **545**
Indeed, entire mountains fall and suddenly there is a great
shock and tremors scurry out far and wide from there.
And with good reason, since houses next to a road, shaken
throughout by wagons of no great weight, tremble,
no less than wagons jump whenever a road-pebble[32]   **550**
jolts the ironclad circles of the wheels on both sides.
It happens, too, when a huge mass is toppled by age
from the earth into great and vast pools of water,
that the earth also sways and is shaken by the water's undulations,
just as at times a container is unable to be still unless   **555**
the liquid within stops being rocked in unsteady undulations.
Moreover, when the wind, gathered throughout the hollowed-out places
of the earth, pushes forward from one part and thrusts and
slams against lofty caves with great force,
the earth leans to where the headlong force of the wind presses.   **560**
Then towering homes constructed on the surface of the earth,
the more each one of them is built up towards the sky,
the more they sway and threaten, projecting in the same direction,
and the beams are pushed forward and suspended, ready to move.
And yet they are afraid to believe that some time of complete   **565**

---

[31] In lines 528-531 Lucretius skips over meteorological phenomena that
      Epicurus treats at greater length in his *Letter to Pythocles* 109-110.

[32] The text of line 550 is corrupt. I have translated Bailey's suggestion.

destruction and dissolution awaits the nature of the great world,
when they see so great a mass of earth leaning over!
If the winds did not pause for breath, no force could restrain
things nor be able to hold them back from destruction as they go.

570 But since they pause for breath and increase their force in turn,
and, as it were, regroup, rally, are repulsed, and retreat,
for this reason the earth more often threatens ruin
than accomplishes it. For it leans ahead and sways back again
and slipping forward returns the mass to its own location.

575 So thus do all buildings sway: the top more than the middle,
the middle more than the bottom, the bottom a teeny bit.[33]
This too is a cause of that same great shaking:
when wind and some huge force of air suddenly,
coming together from outside or inside the earth itself,

580 has hurled itself into the hollow places of the earth and there
first roars tumultuously within great caves and travels
and twists all around, and after, when the force is aroused
and stirred up, it bursts out and at the same time
deeply splits the earth and creates a great chasm.

585 This happened at Sidon in Syria and occurred at Aegium
in the Peloponnese,[34] both cities that this out-blast of air
and the resulting movement of the earth threw into great turmoil.
Moreover, many city walls have collapsed because of great
movements in the earth and many cities have sunk down

590 to destruction at the bottom of the sea along with their own citizens.
But even if it doesn't burst forth, still the very impulse of the air
and fierce force of the wind is distributed throughout the numerous
passageways of the earth like a shiver and thus instills trembling,
as when a chill works its way deep into our joints

595 and strikes them, forcing them to tremble and shake unwillingly.
So humans live in their cities in double fear:
they fear the buildings above, and dread the hollows below,
lest the nature of the earth dissolve them suddenly into pieces,
or lest torn asunder it spreads wide its jaws

600 and in its disorder wishes to fill them with its own ruins.
Accordingly let them believe as they wish that the heavens and earth
will continue to be imperishable, their case entrusted to eternal safety,
yet still at times a clear and present force of danger
also applies this goad of fear from somewhere or other,

---

[33] "Teeny bit" translates Lucretius' *perhilum*, a word he apparently coined.

[34] According to Strabo (1.3.16) and Seneca (*Nat. Quaest.* 6.24.6) a great
earthquake occurred at Sidon, probably in the 5th century BC. The
earthquake at Aegium occurred in 372 BC.

that the earth may be suddenly snatched from beneath our feet and
    carried   605
into the abyss and that the whole sum of things may completely
collapse and follow and that a jumbled wreck of a world may result.
First of all[35] some wonder that nature does not increase
the sea, into which there is such a great downrush of water,
into which all rivers come from every direction.   610
Add the passing rains and storms that fly by,
which sprinkle and soak all seas and lands,
add the sea's own fountains. Still, compared to the sum
of the sea, all these will be an adaugmentation[36] of scarcely a drop.
So it is less wondrous that the great sea is not augmented.   615
Moreover, the sun subtracts a great part by its heat.
For indeed we see that clothes soaked through by moisture
are dried out by the hot glowing rays of the sun,
and yet we see that there are many seas, spread out widely.
Accordingly let the sun sip away as small amount   620
of liquid as you wish out of every place from the sea, yet
in so great a space it subtracts substantially from the waves.
Furthermore, the winds too are able to take away
a great portion of liquid by sweeping the seas, since
we very often see that in one night roads   625
dry out and soft layers of mud grow hard.
Moreover I have shown[37] that clouds too take away
much moisture gathered from the great surface of the deep
and scatter it here and there among the whole circle of lands,
when it rains on earth and winds transport the clouds along.   630
Finally, seeing that the earth is endowed with a porous body,
and is closely joined to the sea, everywhere girding its shores,
the moisture of water, just as it goes from earth to sea,
ought likewise to spread onto land from the salt sea.
For the brine is filtered and the substance of the water drips back   635
and all flows together at the sources of rivers, whence
it returns over the earth in a fresh-water current, on which path,
once cut, it carries its waves on liquid foot.[38]
Now I will explain the reason why fires sometimes are exhaled

---

[35] A new topic, the constant size of the sea, is introduced here rather abruptly.

[36] "Adaugmentation" translates Lucretius' *adaugmen*, a word he apparently coined.

[37] 6.470-475, 503-505.

[38] 6.635-638 = 5.269-272, with two minor differences.

VOLCANO

640 through the jaws of Mount Etna with so great a swirling blast.[39]
For the fiery storm broke out with no small
disaster and played the tyrant throughout the fields of the Sicilians,
turning the eyes of neighboring nations upon itself,
when they saw every region of the sky smoke and send
645 out sparks, and filled their breasts with anxious care
about what new disturbance nature was setting in motion.
You must look broadly and deeply at these matters
and look carefully about at a distance in all directions,
so that you might recall to mind that the sum of things is vast
650 and see how tiny a part one heaven is
of the whole sum of things, how infinitesimal it is, not
so great a part, as one person is of the whole earth.
If you clearly gaze at and clearly see this that is well
set out, you would cease wondering at many things.
655 For none of us wonders, do we, if someone has caught
a fever arising together with burning heat in his limbs,
or some other pain in his members caused by disease?
For the foot suddenly begins to swell, a sharp pain
often assails the teeth and even invades the eyes,
660 sacred fire[40] develops and creeps through the body, burning
whatever part it has assailed, and crawls along through the limbs,
doubtless because seeds of many things exist,
and this earth and sky bear enough evil disease
from which the power of immeasurable disease can grow up.
665 In this way, then, we must suppose that all things
are well supplied from the infinite to the whole sky and earth,
so that the earth is able to be shaken around suddenly and moved,
and a fast-moving whirlwind to tear through sea and land,
the fires of Etna to overflow, and the sky to start to blaze.
670 For this also happens and the regions of the sky ignite,
and rainstorms appear in heavier assemblage, when
by chance the seeds of water have thus collected themselves.
"No—the wild heat of the conflagration is too huge."[41]

---

[39] Mt. Etna was one of the most famous active volcanoes in antiquity. In the lines that follow, Lucretius may be describing the eruption that occurred in 122 BC, about thirty years before he was born. Lucretius does not mention Mt. Vesuvius because its great eruption did not occur until 79 AD, over 100 years after Lucretius wrote.

[40] "Sacred fire" (*sacer ignis*) was the Latin term for erysipelas, an acute inflammatory skin condition.

[41] Lucretius here presents the thought of an imaginary objector, and then refutes it in the lines that follow.

Of course—so too a river, which seems the largest to him
who has never before seen a larger one, and a tree   675
and person seem huge, and all very large things
of every kind which someone sees, these he imagines
are huge, when all, even with the sky and earth and sea,
are nothing compared to the whole sum of the entire universe.
Nevertheless I will now explain how that flame, suddenly   680
roused, breathes forth out of the vast furnaces
of Etna. First, the whole mountain is by nature hollow
underneath, supported for the most part by basalt caverns.
Further, there is wind and air present in all the caves.
For air becomes wind when it has been stirred up and agitated.   685
When the wind has grown very hot and, raging, has heated all
the rocks and earth around where it touches them, and from them
has struck out fire hot with swift flames,
it rises and so drives itself high from its straight jaws.
And so it carries its heat far, far it spreads   690
its ashes and rolls out smoke with dense darkness
and at the same time expels rocks of amazing weight.
Do not doubt that this is the wild power of the wind.
Moreover, in large part the sea crashes its waves
against the roots of the mountain and swallows its surge again.   695
From this sea, caves stretch beneath right
to the lofty jaws of the mountain. By this path we must[42]
confess <that wind mixed with water> travels, and the situation
     compels
it < often to rise> and to penetrate deeply from the open sea
and to breathe out and thus lift up the flame
and to throw up rocks and raise clouds of sand.   700
For on the highest peak are craters, as they[43] call them,
which we for our part call jaws or mouths.
There are also a number of things for which it is insufficient to give
one cause, but many, only one of which nevertheless is true,
just as if you yourself were to see lying at a distance   705
a lifeless body of a person, it would be fitting to name all
causes of death so as to name the one true cause of his death.
For you would not be able to prove that he died by sword or from cold,
or from disease, or by poison, as might be the case,
but we know that it was something of this very sort that fell   710
upon him. Likewise we can say the same in many cases.

---

[42] There is a textual problem in lines 697-698. I translate Diels' suggested
      restoration.

[43] They = the Sicilians, who spoke Greek. *Kratêr* (crater) is a Greek word
      meaning "mixing bowl."

The Nile, river of all Egypt, alone on earth
increases its size in the summer and spreads over the plains.
It normally irrigates Egypt in the middle of blazing heat,
715 either because[44] in summer the north winds are against its mouths,
at the time of year when these winds are called "Etesian,"[45]
and blowing against the river, they delay it, and forcing
the waves back they cause it to swell and force it to wait.
For beyond a doubt these gusts, which are driven out
720 from the icy stars of the pole, move against the river.
The river comes from the south out of the heat-bearing places,
arising from deep within the midday region[46]
among the black races of men with their well-baked color.
It is also possible[47] that a great heap of sand
725 piles up against the river mouths, opposing its streams,
when the sea, agitated by the winds, drives the sand inward.
In this way it happens that the outlet of the river is less free
and likewise forward movement becomes less easy for its waves.
It happens too, perhaps, that it rains more at its source
730 at that time, when the Etesian gusts of the north winds
drive all the clouds then into those places.
It is evident that when they are driven to the midday region
and come together, there the clouds at last, crammed
against high mountains, are condensed and compressed by force.
735 Perhaps from deep among the high mountains of the Ethiopians
it grows, when the sun, illuminating everything with its withering
    rays,
drives the white snow to go down into the plains.
Now come, I will explain to you with what nature
whatever places and lakes considered Avernian are endowed.[48]
740 First, that they are called by the name "Avernian"[49] is imposed

---

[44] "Either because...": There is no corresponding "or because..." in the
sentences that follow.

[45] The "Etesian" ("annual") winds blow for about forty days every summer
after the rising of Sirius, the Dog Star, on July 23.

[46] "Midday region" = the south.

[47] This second possible explanation for the Nile's flooding is only found in
Lucretius.

[48] Lake Avernus near Cumae in the bay of Naples was famous in antiquity
because it was reported that birds that flew over it died. It was also
identified as a gate to the underworld, and was the place where the hero
Aeneas descended to the underworld in Book VI of Virgil's *Aeneid*.

[49] Lucretius derives the Latin word "Avernus" from the Greek *"aornos"*
("birdless").

on them because of the reality that they are injurious to all birds,
since when they have flown straight and reached these regions,
forgetting how to row their wings, they lower their sails,
droop with slackened neck, and plummet headlong
to the earth, if it chances that is the nature of the locale, or into   745
the water, if it chances the Lake of Avernus stretches below.
This spot is near Cumae, where mountains filled with acrid
sulfur smoke and are well supplied with hot springs.
There is also a spot within the walls of Athens, at the very top
of the citadel, near the temple of lifegiving Pallas Tritonis,[50]   750
where harsh-sounding crows never navigate their bodies
with wings, not even when altars smoke with offerings.
Thus they do not flee the sharp wrath of Pallas
because of their keeping watch,[51] as the Greek poets sing,
but the nature of the place accomplishes the job all on its own.   755
In Syria also they say that likewise a spot can be seen
where as soon as four-footed beasts first trod,
the very force of the place makes them collapse completely,
as if they have been suddenly offered as a sacrifice to the shades below.
All these things happen by natural processes,   760
and from which causes they come, the origin is evident,
so that it not be believed that there is a door of Orcus[52] in these regions,
nor next should we think that the gods of the dead below happen
to lead souls from here to the riverbanks of Acheron,
as wing-footed stags are often thought to use their nostrils   765
to draw the races of creeping creatures from their hiding-places.[53]
See how far removed this is from true
reasoning. For I am now attempting to speak about the real facts.
First I say what I have often also said before:[54]
there are shapes of every kind of thing in the earth,   770
many that are good for food and life-giving, and many
that are able to induce diseases and hasten death along.

---

[50] "The temple of Pallas Tritonis" = the Parthenon, the famous temple of
Athena (= Pallas Tritonis) on the acropolis in Athens.

[51] Lucretius here alludes to the myth of Erichthonius. According to the
story (see Ovid *Metamorphoses* 2.552-565 for a fuller version), Athena
gave the infant Erichthonius in a box to the daughters of Cecrops, and
told them not to open it. They peeked inside, and a passing crow told
Athena. Athena took part of her anger out on the tattle-tale crow, and
banished all crows from the Acropolis.

[52] "The door of Orcus" = door to the underworld.

[53] For the strange story of deer who entice serpents out of their holes by
breathing on them, see Pliny *Natural History* 28.42.149.

[54] 1.809-822, 2.398-477, 4.633-672.

And we have shown before[55] that different things are more
adapted to different living creatures for the purpose of life
775 on account of different natures, textures, and primary shapes
differing among themselves, the one from the other.
Many hostile things pass through the ears, many,
harmful and harsh to the touch, wander in through the nostrils
        themselves,
and there are not a few things which must be avoided by touch,
780 not a few things that must be shunned by sight, or are bitter in taste.
Next we may see how many things there are
that are disgusting and noxious, having violently harmful sensations
        for people.
First, the shade of certain trees[56] is said to be
so noxious that they often bring about headaches,
785 if anyone lies beneath them spread out on the grass.
There exists also in the lofty mountains of Helicon a tree
accustomed to kill people with the horrible smell of its flower.
Of course all these things arise from the earth
because the earth bears many seeds of things, much mixed
790 in many ways, and passes them on sorted individually.
And when a light recently extinguished at night offends the nose
with acrid fumes, it at once puts to sleep a person
who is prone by disease[57] to fall down and foam at the mouth.
And a woman falls back, put to sleep by noxious castor,[58]
795 and the elegant work slips out of her delicate hands,
if she has smelled it at the time when she has her menstrual flow.
And many other things besides make the drooping limbs
slacken throughout the frame and shake the soul in its seat.
Next, if you ever linger in a hot bathtub
800 and are too full, how easily it happens that you fall down
as you sit on a bath-seat in the middle of the steaming water!
And how easily the noxious force and smell of charcoal wends
its way into the brain, unless we have taken water beforehand!
But when a fiery fever has taken hold of the limbs of a person,
805 then the smell of wine has a force equivalent to a sacrificial blow.

---

[55] 4.633-72.

[56] Ancient sources (Virgil, *Eclogues* 10.76 and Pliny, *Natural History* 16.16.70
and 17.29.89) attribute harmful properties to juniper, box, and walnut
trees.

[57] Epilepsy, a condition which Lucretius has described earlier at greater
length (3.487-505).

[58] Castor was a pungent-smelling secretion obtained from the glands of a
beaver. It was used for medical purposes.

Don't you see also that sulfur too is formed in the earth
itself and that pitch hardens into a mass with a foul smell?
And when men pursue veins of silver and gold, probing
deep within the hidden recesses of the earth with their tools,
what smells Scaptensula[59] breathes out from below?   810
And what great evils gold mines may exhale!
What they make people look like, what colors!
Have you not seen or heard about how they usually die
in a short time, how the supply of life is wanting for those
whom the great force of necessity holds bound to such work?   815
Therefore the earth exhales all these exhalations
and breathes them forth out into the open expanses of the sky.
Thus too Avernian locales must emit a discharge
deadly to birds that rises from the earth into the air
so as to poison an area of the sky in one particular region.   820
As soon as a bird is carried on its wings to that place,
it is there held back and overpowered by the invisible poison
so that it falls straight down where the exhalation directs it.
When it falls down there, the same force of this exhalation
takes away what is left of life from all of the limbs.   825
For indeed at first it provokes a certain kind of disturbance.[60]
It later happens that, once they have fallen into the very source
of the poison, there too they must spew out their life
because there is a great supply of noxiousness around them.
It happens too that sometimes this force and exhalation of Avernus   830
strikes and disperses the air that is located between the bird
and the earth so that this place is left nearly empty.
When they have come flying straight over this place,
the flapping of their wings immediately is futile and falls short,
and every effort of their wings on either side is for naught.   835
When they are unable to support themselves and rely on their wings
          there,
of course they plummet to earth because of their weight, forced
by nature, and, now lying there, through this almost empty
air they disperse their souls through all the pores of the body.
Further,[61] moisture in wells becomes colder in summer,   840
because the earth grows porous from the heat, and whatever seeds

---

[59] Scaptensula was a mining town in Thrace, in northern Greece.

[60] The word that Lucretius uses for dizziness is *aestus*, the same Latin word
      he uses in 823 and 824 in the sense of "exhalation." The exhalation
      (*aestus*) of Avernus causes the mental "disturbance" (*aestus*) of the birds.

[61] The abrupt transition between 839 and 840 has caused many scholars to
      believe there may have been lines lost.

of warmth it happens to have on its own, it releases into the air.
Therefore the more the earth is exhausted and delivered of its heat,
845   the colder also the moisture concealed in the earth becomes.
Further, when all the earth is oppressed by cold and contracts,
and, so to speak, congeals, it of course happens that by coalescing
it squeezes out into wells any heat it has in itself.
It is said that near the shrine of Ammon[62] there exists a fountain
that is cold in the light of day and hot at night time.
850   People marvel at this fountain overmuch and think
in part that it is heated by the fierce sun beneath the earth
when night has covered the earth with its dreadful dark shroud.
This is exceedingly far removed from true reasoning.
For when the sun, caressing the naked body of the water,
855   could not cause it to warm on its upper side,
although its light in the upper air is blessed with such great heat,
how could it cook the moisture thoroughly from below the earth,
so dense in body, and revive it with warming heat?
Especially when it is scarcely able to work its own heat
860   in through the walls of houses by means of its burning rays.
What then is the reason? Undoubtedly because the soil
around the fountain stays more porous than the rest of the earth,
and there are many seeds of fire near the body of water.
Thus when night submerges the earth in dew-bearing waves,
865   the earth cools at once deep within and contracts together.
For this reason it happens that, as if it were squeezed by hand,
it squeezes out into the fountain the seeds of fire it has,
which make the touch and warmth of the liquid hot.
Then when the rising sun has loosened the earth with its rays
870   and opened its pores by mixing in warm heat,
the elements of fire again return to their former places
and all the heat in the water goes back into the earth.
Because of this the fountain grows cold in the light of day.
Besides, the water's moisture is tossed by the rays of the sun
875   and it is made thinner by the quivering heat as the light increases.
Therefore it happens that whatever seeds of fire it has
it releases, just as it often lets go of the frost
it contains in itself, and dissolves the ice and relaxes its bonds.
There is also a frigid fountain,[63] above which, if flax be held,

---

[62]   The shrine of Ammon, the Egyptian sky-god, was located in Libya in
North Africa. Its springs were famous, and described by the Greek
historian Herodotus (4.181).

[63]   The fountain Lucretius now discusses was located at Dodona, a sanctuary
of Jupiter (Zeus) in Epirus in Northern Greece.

it often catches fire at once and projects a flame,   880
and in similar manner a torch kindled among its waves
shines bright, wherever it floats and is driven by the breezes:
doubtless because there are very many seeds of heat in the water
and, from the earth itself deep below, bodies
of fire must rise up through the whole fountain   885
and at the same time are breathed forth and escape into the air,
but not so many that the fountain can become hot.
Moreover a force compels them to erupt dispersed
suddenly through the water and to assemble again above it.
Of like kind is the spring of Aradus[64] in the sea, which gushes   890
fresh water and parts the salt waves around it.
In many other locations too the sea's surface
provides well-timed assistance to thirsty sailors,
because it throws up fresh water among the salt waves.
So therefore those seeds[65] can burst forth   895
through this fountain and gush out, which seeds,
when they gather together on the flax or adhere to the body of the torch,
easily are ignited at once, since the flax and torches also
have and contain many seeds of fire within them.
Do you not also see that when you move a recently extinguished   900
wick towards a night lamp it catches fire before
it actually touches the flame, and similarly so does a torch?
And moreover many things are touched by heat alone
and ignite at a distance before the fire soaks them at close quarters.
Thus we must think that it also happens in that fountain.   905
As to what remains, I will begin to discuss by what law
of nature it occurs that that stone can attract iron
which the Greeks call "magnet" from the name of its native country,
since its origin came to be in the native boundaries of the Magnetes.[66]
People are amazed at this stone: for it often makes   910
a chain of little rings hang off of itself.
For indeed you can sometimes see five or more
in suspended succession, jostled by light breezes,
when one hangs down from another clinging from underneath,
and each learns from the other the binding force of the stone: 915

---

[64] Aradus is an island near the coast of Phoenicia in the eastern Mediterranean. Its fresh water spring is discussed by Strabo (16.2.13) and Pliny (*Natural History* 2.102.227).

[65] Lucretius here returns to his discussion of the spring at Dodona that he began in 879-889.

[66] The town of Magnesia that Lucretius refers to was located in Lydia (Turkey).

so penetratingly and pervasively does its force persist in its potency.[67]
In matters of this kind many things must be established
before you can give an account of the thing itself,
and it must be approached by exceedingly long and winding roads:
920 all the more I demand that your ears and mind be attentive.
First of all, from all things, whatever we see,
bodies that strike our eyes and stir up sight
must continually flow, be projected, and scattered widely.[68]
And odors flow continuously from certain things,
925 just like coolness from rivers, heat from the sun, and spray
from the waves of the sea, the gnawer of walls close by the shore.
Nor do various sounds ever cease pouring through the air.
Lastly, a salty-tasting moisture often forms in our mouths
when we spend time near the sea, but when we see wormwood
930 being diluted and mixed, a bitter taste is experienced.   (934)
So from all things each thing is carried in a flow   (935)
and is sent off everywhere in all directions;   (930)
neither delay nor any respite is given to the flowing,   (931)
since we continuously receive sensations, and it is always
     permitted   (932)
935 that we see all things, smell them, and sense their sound.   (933)
Now I will retell how all things are endowed with porous
bodies, as is made clear also in the first book.[69]
For indeed, although it is important to know this for many
things, it is now especially important to make certain,
940 in the case of this very thing that I am setting out to discuss,
that nothing is visible around us except body mixed with void.
First it happens that in caves the rocks arrayed above
sweat with moisture and trickle with flowing drops.
Likewise sweat flows out from our whole body,
945 the beard grows, and hair over all our limbs and members.
Food is distributed to all the veins, and increases and nourishes
even the tiniest fingertips and furthest extremities of the body.
Likewise we feel coldness and warm heat wend their way
through bronze, likewise too we feel them wend their way
950 through gold and through silver, when we are holding filled cups.
And then voices wing their way through the stone partitioning walls
of houses, and smell wafts through, and cold, and the heat

---

[67] Lucretius apparently coined two new Latin words in this line to describe
      the power of the magnet: *permanenter* ("penetratingly and pervasively")
      and *pervalet* ("persist in potency").

[68] 5.923-935 = 4.217-229, with minor changes.

[69] 1.329-369.

of fire, which is also accustomed to penetrate the force of iron.
And then where the corselet of the sky has its boundaries set
    up,[70]   **954a**
<the bodies of clouds and seeds of storm-clouds penetrate,>   **954b**
together with the power of disease, when it enters in from outside.   **955**
And violent storms that spring from the earth and sky
naturally retire and go away into the sky and earth,
since there is nothing that is not woven with a porous body.
In addition, not all bodies that are thrown off
from things are endowed with the same power of moving the senses,   **960**
nor are they suited in the same way for all things.
First, the sun cooks the earth and makes it dry,
but it dissolves ice and makes snow piled high
in high mountains melt away under the force of its rays.
Again, wax becomes liquid when placed in its heat.   **965**
Likewise, fire liquefies bronze and melts gold,
but it draws together and causes skin and hides to contract.
Further, the moisture of water hardens iron fresh from the fire,
but it softens hides and skin made hard by heat.
Oleaster[71] is as pleasing to beard-studded she-goats   **970**
as if it was really dripping ambrosia and was dipped in nectar;
yet there is nothing more bitter for humans than this foliage.
Further, the pig avoids marjoram and fears every
ointment, because what is bitter poison to bristle-covered pigs
is what seems at times almost to restore us to life.   **975**
In contrast, although mud is the foulest slime to us,
the very same stuff is seen to be pleasing to pigs,
so that they wallow in it from head to toe and never grow tired of it.
There also remains the following which seems to need to be said
before I commence to speak about my main topic.[72]   **980**
Since many pores are allotted to different things,
they must be endowed with natures that differ from one another
and each possess their own natures and pathways.
For indeed different senses are present in living creatures,
each of which perceives in itself its own proper object.   **985**
For we see sounds penetrate by one path, juicy
flavors by another, and rich smells by yet another.[73]

---

[70] Most editors agree one or more lines have been lost after 954. I have translated Bailey's suggested supplement.

[71] Oleaster is also called wild olive.

[72] "My main topic," i.e., the magnet.

[73] Lines 988-989 are identical to 995-996, and are therefore omitted by editors and translators.

| | Moreover, one thing is seen to ooze through rocks,[74] | **(991)** |

Moreover, one thing is seen to ooze through rocks,[74]   **(991)**
990 another through wood, yet another to pass through gold,   **(992)**
     and still another to make its way out through silver and glass. **(993)**
     For sight is seen to flow through glass, and heat to go through
          silver,   **(994)**
     and one thing to travel more quickly than others along the same
          path.   **(995)**
995 Certainly the nature of the passageways forces this to happen,   **(996)**
     since they differ in many ways, as we showed a little while   **(997)**
     before,[75] on account of the different nature and textures of
          things.   **(990)**
     Therefore, with all these things confirmed, fixed,
     and established, and prepared and set out in advance for us,
1000 for the rest we will easily give an account based on this
     and the whole cause that attracts the force of the iron will be revealed.
     First, very many seeds must flow from this stone
     or even perhaps a surge which by means of its blows pushes
     away all the air located between the rock and the iron.
1005 When this space is emptied and a large space in the middle
     becomes vacated, immediately the first beginnings of the iron
     slip forward into the vacuum and fall while connected, and it happens
          that
     the ring itself follows and so moves with its whole body.
     Nor does anything cling together more tightly
1010 right from its first elements, restricted and linked together,
     than the natural character and cool hardness of powerful iron.
     It is thus less wondrous, since it is derived from its elements,[76]
     if many bodies that spring forth from the iron are unable
     to be carried into the vacuum without the ring itself following.
1015 This it does, and it follows until it has finally reached
     the stone itself and clung on to it with invisible bonds.
     The same thing happens in all directions. On whatever
     side the space is emptied, whether off to the side or above,
     neighboring bodies are immediately carried into the vacuum.
1020 For indeed they are driven by blows from another side nor
     can they rise up into the air of their own accord.
     To this is also added this further thing to help
     it be able to happen better and give assistance to the movement,
     that, as soon as the air in front of the ring is made

---

[74] I follow Lambinus' rearrangement of lines 990-997.

[75] 6.981-983.

[76] The text of the last half of the line is uncertain. I have translated Lachmann's conjecture.

more rarified and the space is caused to be more void and empty,[77]   **1025**
it immediately happens that whatever air is located to the rear **(1033)**
pushes the ring forward, as it were, and propels it from
    behind.   **(1026)**
For the air that is placed around things is always buffeting
    them,   **(1027)**
but it happens that it propels the iron forward at such a time **(1028)**
because the space is empty on one side and it receives it into
    itself.   **(1029) 1030**
The air that I am mentioning to you subtly wends its way   **(1030)**
through the numerous pores of the iron down to its tiny parts, **(1031)**
and pushes and drives it like the wind drives ships and sails. **(1032)**
Again, all things have to contain air in their body,
in as much as they are endowed with a porous structure, and air   **1035**
surrounds and is situated next to all things.
This air, then, which is hidden deep within the iron,
is always tossed about with restless motion and therefore
doubtless strikes the ring and stirs it up from within.
The ring, of course, is carried in the same direction as where   **1040**
it has already once plunged and made an exertion into the empty space.
It also happens that the nature of iron pulls back
sometimes from this stone, accustomed to flee and follow in turns.
I have even seen iron from Samothrace[78] leap up
and iron filings go mad all at once inside bronze   **1045**
bowls, when this Magnesian stone was placed underneath,
so eagerly is the iron seen to desire to flee from the stone.
So great a disturbance is created when the bronze is interposed
because no doubt when the emanations of the bronze have seized
beforehand and occupied the open pathways of the iron,   **1050**
the emanations of the stone come afterwards and find all full
in the iron, nor do they have a path to swim through as before.
Therefore it is forced to collide with and strike the iron texture
with its wave. In this way it spews forth from itself
and agitates through the bronze that which otherwise it often ingests. **1055**
Stop wondering about this in these matters, that the emanations
from this stone are not strong enough to also move other things.
For some stand firm by their weight: gold is of this type.
But some, because they have so porous a structure that the wave flies
through intact, are not ever able to be pushed around: **1060**
things made of wood are seen to be of this type.
The nature of iron is thus located between the two,

---

[77] I follow Lambinus' transposition of line 1033 to line 1026.

[78] The "iron from Samothrace" may have been in the form of iron rings.
Samothrace is an island in the North Aegean Sea.

and when it receives a certain number of bronze particles,
then it happens that Magnesian stones repel it with their flow.
1065 Yet these things are not so foreign to other things
that I might supply only a few things of this type
which I could mention, things uniquely suited for one another.
First, you see that only mortar holds stones together.
Wood is joined together only by bull's glue,
1070 so that the grain of wooden planks more often cracks and gapes open
than the bonds of the bull's glue will relax its binding force.
Juices born of the vine are bold enough to be mixed with water
from fountains, while heavy pitch and light olive-oil cannot.
The purple color from shellfish is joined together
1075 with the bulk of wool so it can never ever be pulled apart,
not even if you set out to use Neptune's waters to restore it,
not even if the whole sea wished to wash it with all its waves.
Again, is there not just one thing that joins gold to gold,
and does it not happen that bronze is joined to bronze by tin?
1080 Now how many other things might we find? For what?
You have no need for you of such a long and winding road,
nor is it right for me to waste so much energy on this,
but it is best to deal briefly with many things in a few words.
When those things whose textures fall together so reciprocally
that the concavities of the one fit together with the convexities of the
1085   other,
and the opposite, too, among themselves, this is the best joining.
It is the case, too, that certain things can be held and joined
together, entangled among themselves, as if by rings and hooks.
This seems to be more what happens in the case of this stone and iron.
1090 Now I will explain the causes of diseases and from what source
the force of disease can suddenly arise and stir up
death-bearing destruction for the human race and herds
of livestock. First, I have shown by argument above[79]
that there are seeds of many things which are life-giving to us,
1095 and on the contrary that there must be many things flying around
that bring disease and death. When these happen by chance to have
      arisen
and caused the heavens to be disordered, the air becomes diseased.
And this whole force of disease and pestility[80] either
comes down through the sky from outside the world, as clouds
1100 and storm-clouds do, or they often come together

---

[79] 6.769-780.

[80] "Pestility" translates Lucretius' *pestilitas,* a word he apparently adapted
from the more common Latin word *pestilentia,* "plague, pestilence." The
word occurs only here and at 6.1125 and 1132 below.

and rise from the earth itself, when it is moist and becomes putrid,
struck by unseasonably heavy rains and heat spells.
Do you not see, too, that those who travel far
from their home and fatherland are badly affected by the novelty
of the climate and water because the conditions of life are so different? **1105**
For in what way do we think the climate of the Britons differs
from that in Egypt where the axis of the world slants down?
How does the climate in Pontus[81] differ from that in Gades[82]—
right on to the black races of men with their well-baked color?
Just as we see that those climates, situated at the four   **1110**
winds[83] and quarters of the sky, differ from one another,
so the color and appearance of humans are seen to differ greatly,
and diseases to hold the peoples each after their kind.
There is the elephant disease[84] that arises along the waters
of the Nile in the middle of Egypt and nowhere else besides.   **1115**
In Attica the feet are badly affected, as are the eyes within the borders
of Achaea. Hence different places are harmful to different
parts and limbs: the varying air brings this about.
So, when a sky that happens to be hostile to us sets itself
in motion and harmful air begins to creep about,   **1120**
it crawls slowly, like fog and clouds, and everywhere
it goes it perturbs and compels[85] everything to change.
It happens too that when it at last comes to our sky,
it corrupts it and makes it similar to itself and hostile to us.
And so this new destruction and pestilence either falls   **1125**
suddenly on water or sinks deeply into the crops themselves
or the other fodder of human beings and food of flocks,
or it even remains as a force suspended in the air itself
and, when we breathe and take in air mixed with it,
it too must be absorbed in equal measure into the body.   **1130**
In a similar way pestilence often also falls on
cattle, and sickness on lazy, bleating creatures,[86] too.

---

[81] Pontus was in northern Asia Minor, along the southeast shore of the Black Sea.

[82] Gades is the ancient name for Cadiz, a famous city in southern Spain.

[83] "The four winds" = the winds coming from north, south, east, and west.

[84] The "elephant disease" is elephantiasis, a disease characterized by the enlargement and hardening of the skin, especially on the legs, so that it resembles an elephant's skin.

[85] The Latin word for "compel" that Lucretius uses here and in 1161 is *coacto*, a verb he apparently coined.

[86] The "lazy, bleating creatures" are sheep.

THE PLAGUE

Nor does it make any difference whether we take a journey
to places harmful to us and change the mantle of the sky,
1135 or nature of her own accord brings a diseased sky
to us, or something else that we are not used to experiencing,
which is able to affect us badly by its fresh new arrival.
This cause of disease[87] and death-bearing wave
once rendered the fields lifeless within the borders of Cecrops,[88]
1140 made the streets desolate, and drained the city of its citizens.
For it arose and came from deep within the borders of Egypt,
traversing much air and the swimming surfaces of the sea,
and at last bore down on the whole people of Pandion.[89]
Then they were handed over in batches to disease and death.
1145 First they could feel their heads on fire with fever
and their two eyes reddening with light welling up beneath.
Their blackened throats, too, sweat with blood internally,
the path of their voice was hedged in and contracted with ulcers,
and the tongue, the interpreter of the mind, poured out blood,
1150 weakened by pain, hard to move, and rough to touch.
Then when the force of the disease traveled through the throat and
filled
the chest, flowing right into the grieving heart[90] of the sick,
then truly all the barricades of life were collapsing.
The breath circulated a foul odor outside the mouth,
1155 like the penetrating reek of rotting corpses tossed outdoors.
And straightaway the strength of the whole mind and all
the body languished, then at the very threshold of death.
To these evils, impossible to bear, anxious anguish
and wailing intermingled with groans were constant comrades.
1160 Frequent retching, often lasting all day and night,
continually compelled them to convulse their sinews and limbs,
and broke down and fatigued those already previously exhausted.
Nor were you able to discern that the top layer of the body's
top surface was burning with excessive heat for anyone,

---

[87] The description of the great plague at Athens in 430 BC that closes Book
6 closely follows the account of the Athenian plague by the Greek
historian Thucydides in his *History of the Peloponnesian War*, 2.47-52.

[88] "Borders of Cecrops" = Athens. According to legend, Cecrops was the
name of the first king of Athens.

[89] Pandion was one of the early kings of Athens.

[90] "Into the grieving heart" (*in cor maestum*) could also be translated "into
the grieving mind," since Epicureans taught that area of the chest near
the heart was the location of the mind, as Lucretius argued at the
beginning of Book 3.

follows Thucydides

but instead, it gave out a feeling of warmth to the hand   **1165**
and at the same time the whole body reddened as if branded
by ulcers, as happens when the sacred fire[91] is distributed through the
    limbs.
But the inner parts of people were burning all the way to the bones,
and a flame was burning in the stomach as if in a furnace.
There was nothing light or thin enough that you could turn it to good **1170**
use for anyone's limbs, but always wind and cold.
Some were giving over their limbs, burning from the disease,
to cool streams, hurling their naked bodies into the waves.
Many fell headlong from on high into well water,   **(1178)**
hitting the surface with their mouths wide open: **(1174) 1175**
an unquenchable, dry thirst, causing them to drench their
    bodies,   **(1175)**
made a great shower no more effective than a few drops.   **(1176)**
Nor was there any rest from their pain: their bodies lay   **(1177)**
there exhausted. Medicine mumbled in silent fear,
in as much as they rolled the orbs of their eyes, wide-open,   **1180**
burning with disease, and bereft of sleep, so many times.
Many more signs of death were then given besides:
the rational faculty of the mind was perturbed by grief and fear,
the brow was gloomy, the facial expression frenzied and wild,
and further the ears were agitated and filled with loud noises,   **1185**
the breath frequent or drawn deeply at irregular intervals,
the glistening drops of sweat running down the neck,
spit thin and scarce, and tinged with yellow color
and salty, scarcely ejected through the throat with a hoarse cough.
But the sinews in the hands did not hesitate to contract, nor the limbs **1190**
to tremble, nor cold to move up little by little
from the feet. Likewise in the end at the final moment
the nostrils were compressed, the tip of the nose sharp and thin,
the eyes retracted, the temples hollow, the skin cold
and hard, the mouth agape, the forehead tense and swollen.[92]   **1195**
And not much later the limbs lay stiffened in death.
For the most part it was on the eighth shining light of the sun
or even on its ninth illumination that they gave up their life.
If any of them, as it happened, had escaped the ruinous rites of death,
afterwards horrible ulcers and a black discharge from the bowels   **1200**
saw to it that a withering death still awaited them,

---

[91] "Sacred fire" (*sacer ignis*) was the Latin term for erysipelas, an acute
inflammatory skin condition.

[92] The text of this line is very uncertain, and many suggestions for alternate
readings have been made.

or else a large quantity of corrupted blood, often
in close conjunction with a headache, was emitted from choked nostrils:
into this the person's whole strength and substance flowed.
1205 Further, for the one who escaped the fierce discharge of foul
blood, the disease still traveled into the sinews
and limbs, and even into the genital parts of the body.
And some, fearing with great severity the threshold of death,
continued to live once their manly parts were cut off
1210 by the knife, and others yet remained in life without benefit
of hands or feet, and some suffered the loss of their eyes:
so far had the piercing fear of death come over them.
And, too, a total forgetfulness of all things
seized some, so that they could not recognize who they were.
1215 And although many bodies lay on the ground unburied
on top of other bodies, still the race of birds and beasts
either leapt far away to avoid the acrid smell
or after a taste became weak at their imminent death.
Nor yet scarcely at all in those days could any
1220 bird be found, nor would the sad generations of wild
beasts leave the forests. Most were weakened by the disease
and died. The faithful force of dogs especially was strewn
on every road and they reluctantly gave up their spirit,
for the force of the disease would wring out the life from their limbs.
1225 Deserted, empty funerals competed to be hurried up.[93]
Nor was there a sure method of cure that worked for all.
For what allowed one to inhale the life-giving
breezes of the air and gaze upon the regions of the sky,
this was destruction to others and brought them death.
1230 In these affairs this one distressing thing above
all had to be pitied, that when anyone realized he was caught
in the snares of the disease, just as if he were condemned to death,
his spirit failed and he lay down with grieving heart.
Awaiting his death, he would lose his life then and there.
1235 For indeed at no time did the contagion of the devouring disease
stop seizing upon one after another, as if

they were wool-bearing flocks and the stock of horned cattle.	**(1245)**
And this above all else heaped death on death.	**(1237)**
For whoever avoided going and seeing their own sick,	**(1238)**
1240 excessively greedy for life and being afraid of death,	**(1239)**
was punished soon after by slaughtering neglect	**(1240)**
with a foul and evil death, abandoned and without aid.	**(1241)**

---

[93] Some editors, following Lachmann, transfer this line after 1246, where
funerals are further discussed.

But those who stayed around to help died from contagion   **(1242)**
and the labor that shame then forced them to undergo,   **(1243)**
and the coaxing voice of the sick mixed with the voice of
    lamentation.   **(1244) 1245**
The most virtuous people underwent this type of death.[94]

     *   *   *   *   *   *   *   *   *   *   *   *   *

… and one upon others, striving to bury the throng of their own
dead: they returned worn out from weeping and wailing,
then for the most part they took to their beds in grief.
Nor was anyone able to be found whom disease or death   **1250**
or grief had not affected badly at so terrible a time.
Now, moreover, the shepherd and every herdsman,
and likewise the strong wielder of the curved plow, drooped
from weakness, and their bodies lay piled up deep
within their huts, handed over to death by poverty and disease. **1255**
At times you were able to see the lifeless bodies of parents
on top of their lifeless children, and conversely, you could see children
taking their last breath on top of their mothers and fathers.
This affliction flowed in no small part
from the country into the city, for the weakened and diseased band   **1260**
of farmers brought it with them as they arrived from every direction.
They filled all spaces and houses, so that all the more
with the heat death was heaping them packed together in piles.
Many bodies, prostrate from thirst and toppled over
in the street, lay strewn by the Silenus water fountains.[95]   **1265**
Their breath was choked off by the excessive allure of water.
And many you would see scattered throughout the public places
and roads, drooping limbs with bodies barely alive,
studded with muck and completely covered with rags, dying
from bodily filth, nothing more than skin and bones,   **1270**
nearly buried already by foul ulcers and scum.
At last death filled up all the holy shrines
of the gods with lifeless bodies, and everywhere all
the temples of the heavenly ones remained burdened with corpses,
which places the temple-guardians had packed with guests.   **1275**
Nor indeed any longer was reverence of the gods or their divinity
of much worth: the present grief was completely overwhelming.

---

[94] There are textual difficulties after 1246, and editors think a number of
lines may have dropped out.

[95] "Silenus water fountains" were apparently so-called because the water
gushed through the mouths of carved Silenus figures into the fountains.
Silenus figures were mythological creatures represented as men with
animal (often equestrian) features, and were thought to be musical and
very fond of drink.

Nor did those burial rites continue in the city, with which
these people before were always traditionally buried.
1280 For the whole populace was perturbed and in a panic, and each one,
grieving, buried his own dead hastily, as time allowed.[96]
The suddenness of events and poverty led to many horrible actions.
For they placed their own blood-relatives with tremendous wailing
on top of funeral pyres heaped high for others
1285 and set torches beneath them, often violently quarreling
with great bloodshed rather than desert the bodies.

---

[96] The text of 1281 is uncertain. I have translated Housman's suggested
emendation.

GLOSSARY

The purpose of this glossary is to introduce the reader to some of the key Latin terms of Lucretius' poem as well as some of Epicurus' Greek terms Lucretius was explicating. The entries will also help identify some of the important themes of Epicurean philosophy and the way in which Lucretius developed them.

accidents (*eventa*; Gr. *sumptômata*) **and properties** (*conjuncta*; Gr. *aïdia parakolouthounta*): Epicurus held that the only things that existed *per se* (through themselves) were body and space, and that all other things must be attributes of these and not have independent existence. When he discussed attributes, he distinguished between attributes that were permanent and those that were not. He used the Greek term *sumbebêkota* (from the verb *sumbainô*, "go with, happen, turn out") for the general notion of "attribute," and then distinguised two types of attributes, accidents (*sumptômata*, literally "things that fall with") and properties (*aïdia parakolouthounta*, literally "things that always accompany"). Lucretius used the Latin term *eventa* (literally "things that happened or chanced to be") for accidents, and *conjuncta* (literally, "things have been joined with") for properties. By properties or permanent attributes, Epicurus and Lucretius means those attributes which cannot be separated from the body without it ceasing to be what it is. For example, atoms have the properties of weight, size, and shape, and void has the property of yielding. At the perceptible level, compound bodies have the properties of shape, color, size, and weight. Accidents or accidental properties, on the other hand, can be changed or separated from the body without it ceasing to be what it is. For example, motion and rest are accidents of perceptible things like humans, rocks, etc. Being at rest or in motion is not essential to what they are.

application of the mind: see **mental focusing**.

atom: Lucretius never uses the term *atomus*, the Latin transliteration of the Greek term *atomos* (literally, "indivisible, unable to be cut") found in some other Latin writers. He preferred instead to use a number of different terms, stressing various aspects and functions of atoms (see 1. 55-61): "first beginnings" (*primordia, principia*) "matter"(*materies*), "generating bodies" (*genitalia corpora*), "seeds of things" (*semina rerum*), "first bodies" (*corpora prima*), "particles," "tiny bodies" (*corpuscula*), and "elements" (*elementa*). While the Greek term *atomos* stresses indivisibility and indestructibility, most of the terms Lucretius uses emphasize that atoms are the building blocks and generating principles out of which the world around us is built. Also, Lucretius' use of the term "elements" (*elementa*) for atoms allows him to stress how important the arrangement of atoms is. *Elementa* means both "elements" and "letters," and Lucretius notes in several passages (1.196-198, 823-829, 907-914; 2.688-697, 1013-1022) that just as the same group of letters (*elementa*) can be rearranged to form many different words, so can atoms (*elementa*) be rearranged to form different compounds.

chance (*fors, forte, fortuna, casus, casu*; Gr. *tuchê*): Unlike his predecessor Democritus or his contemporaries the Stoics, Epicurus taught that not all things were determined and that chance played a role in the universe. Lucretius' Latin terms for chance include the words *fors* (chance), *forte* (by chance), and *fortuna* (fortune, chance), all derived from the same root as the verb *fero*, "to bear, carry, bring on (a person)," as well as *casus* (accident, chance) and *casu* (by chance, accidentally), which derive from the verb *cado*, "to fall, fall to, happen." At the atomic level, Epicurus introduced a chance, non-determined motion of the atoms with his doctrine of the swerve (see entry on the **swerve** below). In the phenomenal world around us, Epicurus argued, we can see evidence of the swerve in the existence of compound bodies (because atoms falling downward in space at the same rate would otherwise never meet) and the voluntary movements of living creatures.

concept (*notitia, notities*; Gr. *prolêpsis*): Also translated into English as "general concept," "preconception," "conception," "notion," and "basic grasp." Epicurus taught that humans begin as children to form general concepts of things by seeing individual examples of items and generalizing them into concepts, e.g., forming a general concept of dog by observing individual instances of dogs. Epicurus' Greek term for concept, *prolêpsis*, derives from a verb meaning "to grasp beforehand, anticipate," and stresses the fact that preconceptions are something which the mind, once it has them, has before particular individual sensations and uses to measure those sensations against. *Notitia* or *notities*, Lucretius' Latin translation of *prolêpsis*, derives from the verb *nosco*, "to know," and stresses that a concept is something that is known.

death (*mors*, Gr. *thanatos*): Lucretius' poem is full of death: the chief Latin noun for death, *mors*, and its various permutations (*mortalis, mortales, mortalia, mortifer*) echo throughout the *De Rerum Natura*. Lucretius constantly reminds us that only atoms and the void will last forever. Everything else, including the various worlds, suns, planets, the earth, and everything on the earth, including our bodies, souls, and minds, are subject to death and destruction. Epicurus saw that one of the greatest fears facing humans is the fear of death, and sought to counteract that fear by showing that the human soul is mortal and will perish with the body. Book 3 is an extended meditation on the soul's mortality and its consequences, and in it Lucretius argues, following Epicurus, that "death is nothing to us."

essential properties: see **accidents and properties**.

free will: see **will**.

friendship (*amicitia*; Gr. *philia*): Epicurus praised friendship as one of the greatest goods in life and source of pleasure for all humans. Epicureans were known throughout antiquity for their close and enduring friendships, and although philosophical critics complained that true friendship could never be based on what they saw as selfish Epicurean hedonism, Epicurus talks of friendship in lofty and almost god-like terms. A few examples: "All friendship has intrinsic value, although it has its start in benefiting" (*Vatican Saying* 23); "Friendship dances around the world, announcing to all of us that we should wake up to blessedness" (*Vatican Saying* 52); and "The noble person is especially concerned with wisdom and friendship. Of these the former is a mortal good, while the latter is an immortal good" (*Vatican Saying* 78). *Amicitia*, Lucretius' Latin term for friendship is related to the adjective *amicus, -a, -um* (friendly), the nouns *amicus* (friend) and *amor* (love, affection), and the verb *amo* (to love). Although Lucretius does not use the term *amicitia* frequently in the poem, it has an important role to play. Lucretius says he is writing his poem out of friendship with Memmius (1.140-141), and he discusses how important a step it was in the evolution of human society that humans began to form friendships with one another (5.1019-1023).

god, gods (*deus*; Gr. *theos*): Lucretius uses the words "god" and "gods" throughout the poem. Epicurus taught that one of the chief sources of human unhappiness was the way humans look at the gods. Traditional Greek and Roman religion taught that the gods were involved in human affairs, punishing and rewarding humans and responding to prayers and animal sacrifices. Epicurus criticized this traditional view, and taught that the gods existed, but had nothing to do with human beings and the world in which we live. The gods, according to Epicurus, live far removed from humans, leading lives of true Epicurean pleasure. Epicurus encouraged his followers to view the gods as examples of the perfectly blessed life, and said we should model our lives of pleasure on them. Lucretius also uses the term "god" in another sense, calling Epicurus himself a god (5.1-54) because of his divine discoveries and the benefits he has bestowed on human beings by his philosophy.

grasp, basic grasp: see **concept**.

heavens, sky (*caelum, aether*), **world** (*mundus, haec rerum summa*), **universe** (*omne, omne immensum, rerum summa*): Lucretius uses a number of terms for the heavens, each with their own set of associations. Lucretius' standard term for the sky or heavens is *caelum*. Another word, *aether*, is also used in the general sense of "sky" but is also used in its more technical sense of "upper air, ether, region of space above the earth's atmosphere." Lucretius also uses a third term, *mundus*, in the sense of "sky, heavens, firmament," but *mundus* is also used to mean "world, our world." Another phrase that Lucretius uses for "our world, the world in which we live" is *haec rerum summa*, literally, "this sum of things." Lucretius, as a follower of Epicurus, taught that the world we inhabit is but one of the infinite number of worlds contained in the infinite universe, and employs a number of phrases for "the universe." They including "the all" (*omne*, Gr. *to pan*), "the immense all" (*omne immensum*), and "the sum total of things" (*rerum summa*). Lucretius taught that while individual worlds come into being and are eventually destroyed, the universe itself is eternal.

image (*simulacrum, imago, effigia, figura*; Greek *eidôlon*). The doctrine of visual and mental images plays an important part in the Epicurean analysis of vision and thought. Lucretius argues in Book 4 that all objects are constantly giving off thin "images" from their surfaces. Some of these images strike our eyes and cause us to "see" the objects that emitted them; other images that are even finer bypass our eyes and make their way directly to our minds, which use them as objects of thought. Epicurus used the Greek term *eidôlon* to refer to these images. *Eidôlon* derived from the stem *eid/id "to see,"* and meant "image, shape, insubstantial form." It is closely related to the Greek word *eidos*, "appearance, form, shape, class." The Latin terms Lucretius chose for image (*simulacrum, imago, effigia, figura*) all stress a slightly different aspect of what an image is: a copy or imitation of the object that emitted it. *Simulacrum* is related to the adjective *similis* ("similar") and the verb *simulo* ("copy, imitate"), *imago* to the verb *imitor* ("imitate"), *effigio* to the verb *effingor* ("to shape, copy, reproduce"), and *figura* to the verb *fingo* ("form a likeness of"). Lucretius, by his choice of Latin terminology for images, stresses that images are copies or imitations that faithfully reproduce the appearance of the objects that emitted them.

justice and injustice: Lucretius treats Epicurus' views on the nature and origin of justice (Gr. *dikaion, dikaiosunê*) and injustice (Gr. *adikon, adikia*) in sections of Book 5, especially 1019-1027; 1141-1160, when he discusses the development of human societies. Epicurus' view of justice was that it gradually developed as early humans realized that it was to the benefit of all to make agreements not to harm others nor be harmed by them. From this grew the concept of justice and eventually human laws. Epicurus has much to say about justice in his extant writings, especially *Principal Doctrines* 17 and 31-37. A couple of examples will give the sense of Epicurus' views. "There never was such a thing as absolute justice, but an agreement, [made] at times in different places in regards to people's dealings with each other, not to harm or be harmed" (*Principal Doctrine* 33); "Injustice is not bad in and of itself, but in the fear concerning the suspicion that it will not escape the notice of those set up to punish such things (*Principal Doctrine* 33). In the Book 5 passages in which Lucretius discusses the development of justice, he uses Latin terms for laws (*iura, leges*) and compacts (*foedera*) and the adjective *aequus, -a, -um*, meaning "just, equitable."

laws of nature (*foedera naturae*). Lucretius uses the phrase "laws of nature" (*foedera naturae*) in a number of places (1.586, 2.302, 5.310). The Latin word *foedus* (plural *foedera*) commonly has the sense in Latin of "compact, agreement, promise," so Lucretius' phrase may be more literally translated "agreements of nature." The phrase carries the connotation that nature, and the atoms and void that make it up, have reached some sort of agreement about how they should act. This can of course not be literally true, but the phrase is a vivid way to describe that the way things act is determined by the properties of atoms and the void.

limit (*finis*), **boundary** (*terminus*): The terms *finis* (limit, boundary, border) and *terminus* (boundary, boundary limit) occur frequently in Lucretius' account when he is discussing the limits beyond which something cannot go, or when he is saying that something has no limit. In Latin both terms were used literally as a "physical boundary, boundary marker, border," and were also used metaphorically, meaning a "limit, end" (e.g., *vitae finem*, "an end of life," 3.943). One of Lucretius' most memorable phrases is "deep-set boundary stone" (*alte terminus haerens*) which he uses a number of times (1.77, 1.596, 5.90, 6.66) to describe the limitations put on things because of their atomic makeup. The phrase "deep-set boundary stone" conjures up the picture of a stone marker driven deep into the ground, permanently and definitively marking the boundary between two adjacent pieces of property.

mental focusing (*animi iniectus, animi iactus*; Greek *epibolê tês dianoias*): Mental focusing is the process by which the mind focuses on a particular thought or mental image (see the term **image** above), and is one of the active processes of the mind. The root meaning of Epicurus' Greek term for the process, *epibolê*, literally means "tossing or throwing upon," used metaphorically to refer to casting the mind's attention upon a particular thought. Lucretius' Latin terms for the concept include the nouns *iniectus* and *iactus*, both from the root *iacio*, "to toss, throw," again used metaphorically for the action of mental focusing.

mind (*mens, animus,* Gr. *nous*) , **soul** (*anima,* Gr. *psychê*), **rational faculty** (*consilium,* Gr. *to logikon*): These terms, especially *mens, animus*, and *anima*, occur frequently in Book 3 when Lucretius discusses the Epicurean view of the soul. *Animus* and *anima* are the Latin words Lucretius uses for "mind" and "soul," respectively. The Latin words are closely related, *anima* deriving from a root meaning "breath, wind, soul, physical life" and *animus* derived from the same root but taken more metaphorically "mind, rational soul, courage, will." The closeness of the Latin terms *anima* and *animus* serve Lucretius' argument about the soul and mind well, because as he argues in Book 3, the soul and mind are both made up of extremely fine and mobile atoms that are intimately connected. The *animus* (mind) is located in the chest and is the center of thinking, memory, and the emotions. The *anima* (soul) extends out from the mind throughout the body, playing a role similar to the nervous system. Thus when Lucretius argues that the mind and soul are intimately connected (3.136-144), the nearly identical looking and sounding terms he uses (*animus* and *anima*) help make the point. *Mens* (mind) is a term that Lucretius uses as a synonym for *animus*, and *consilium* (rational principle) is a term he uses in a few places as a synonym and explanatory term for *animus* and *mens*.

minimal parts (*minima;* Gr. *elachista*). In Book 1. 599-634 Lucretius, following Epicurus' account (*Letter to Herodotus* 56-59), sets out the doctrine of the minimal parts of atoms. Arguing against most other ancient philosophers who taught that space and time were infinitely divisible, Epicurus maintained that when dividing space and time both physically and conceptually one would always reach what he called a minimal part (*elastichon*). In particular, although he claimed that atoms were by their very nature indestructible, he maintained that they were made up of greater and lesser numbers of minimal parts, all of which were the same size, the smallest possible. This smallest possible size corresponded to the minimal unit into which space could be divided. Lucretius' two phrases for minimal parts, *minimae partes* and *minima*, derive from superlative forms of the adjective *parvus*, "small."

nature (*natura*, Gr. *physis*): *Natura* is one of the most important words in Lucretius' poem, used over 230 times. The word is related to the verb *nascor*, "to be born, arise, be generated." Its meanings in Lucretius roughly correspond to those of the word "nature" in English. First, it is used in the phrase Lucretius seems to have intended to be the title of his poem: *On the Nature of Things* (*De rerum natura*, 1. 25), a Latin translation of the title of Epicurus' great treatise, *Peri Physeôs, On Nature*. Here *natura* can be glossed as something like "the way something is," so that the whole title could also be translated *"The Way Things Are."* Second, *natura* is also used to mean "Nature," i.e., to the Romans almost a personified force that controls the way everything in the world and universe operates (e.g., *unde omnis natura creet res*, "out of which nature creates all things," 1. 56). Third, *natura* is also used in the sense of the "character" or "quality" of a thing (e.g., *natura animai*, "the nature of the soul," 1. 112).

pleasure (*voluptas, gaudium*; Gr. *hêdonê*) **and pain** (*dolor*; Gr. *algêdôn*): Epicurus identified these as the greatest good (pleasure) and greatest evil (pain) for humans and all living creatures. The terms for pleasure that Epicurus used in Greek and Lucretius used in Latin, *hêdonê* and *voluptas*, were terms that were usually used in the two languages for bodily and mental pleasure. Epicurus' redefinition and Lucretius' account (especially at 2. 1-54) of the highest pleasure as "the absence of pain" would have at first seemed strange to their readers. As noted earlier in the introduction to this translation, Epicurus taught that the highest good in life is pleasure, defined as freedom from pain in the body (*aponia*), and freedom from anxiety and disturbance in the mind, a state he called *ataraxia*, literally, "untroubledness." Epicurus identified two types of pleasure, static pleasure and kinetic pleasure. Static or "katastematic" pleasure, as Epicurus named it, is the state an organism feels when it suffers no pain or want, all its needs are met, and it is functioning well. Kinetic pleasure, or "pleasure in motion," is the pleasure an organism feels when it is physically or mentally stimulated. Epicurus taught that katastematic pleasure, characterized by an absence of physical pain and mental distress, is the highest possible for a human being. Kinetic pleasure does not increase pleasure further, but varies it (*Principal Doctrine* 18).

pores (*foramina*): *Foramen* (singular) derives from the verb *foro*, to "pierce" or "bore through." Lucretius uses the Latin term *foramina* ("openings, pores, passageways, paths") in a broad range of physical and physiological explanations. The world Lucretius describes is one full of pores, although most pores are not visible to the naked eye: there are pores in objects that allow lightning to pass through but not ordinary fire (2. 386), in the eyes (4. 350), in glass (4. 600-601), in the body, mouth, and palate (4. 650), in the body (4. 894, 940), in the earth (5. 811, 6. 981), and in iron (6.1031-1033). The theory of *foramina* has great explanatory power, allowing Lucretius to explain why some things can pass through bodies, and others cannot.

properties: see **accidents and properties**.

reasoning, understanding, thinking (*ratio*), **wisdom** (*sapientia*, Gr. *sophia*): Lucretius uses the word *ratio* often (over 220 times). As Bailey pointed out,[1] Lucretius employs *ratio* in a number of senses: (1) "reasoning, understanding, thinking"; (2) "system, philosophy"; (3) "account, theory"; (4) "law, workings"; (5) "way, means." Lucretius thought that one of the greatest accomplishments of Epicurus was to apply rationality, philosophical thinking, and scientific thought to the world, gods, and human soul, thus gaining for human beings the knowledge of how the world works and how to live happily. Lucretius makes this clear early in the poem (1. 62-79) in his description of Epicurus' battle with religion, and in a famous passage at the beginning of Book 5 (8-12) he connects Epicurus' discovery of a *ratio* of life to wisdom (*sapientia*) and scientific method (*ars*): "...he (Epicurus) was a god, a god, illustrious Memmius, / who was the first one to discover this system (*ratio*) of life which / now is called wisdom (*sapientia*) and who by his scientific method (*ars*) / rescued life from such great waves and such great darkness / and situated it in such calm waters and such clear light."

religion (*religio*). Religion is one of the major themes of Lucretius' poem. The Romans considered themselves a very religious people, and displayed this through public and private rituals, cults, and

---

[1]   Bailey (1947) 605-606.

sacrifices. Educated Romans often contrasted religion (*religio*) with superstition (*superstitio*), praising the benefit of the former and harmfulness of the latter. Lucretius rejects this distinction, maintaining that religion as the Romans practiced it was a harmful error and, in effect, no different than superstition. The Epicurean critique of traditional religion led to a charge of atheism, but it is clear from Lucretius and other Epicurean sources that the Epicureans believed that gods existed but had nothing to do with the human world. They lived in perfect happiness, and Epicureans used them as exemplars of the blessed life.

sense perception, senses, sense organs, sensation (*sensus*): *Sensus* is a word with fairly wide connotations, and must be translated in different ways depending on the context. It is related to the verb *sentio*, "to perceive, sense, become aware of," and can refer to different components of the process of sensation, including the senses or sense organs, the process of sensation, and the resulting sensation. The process of sensation is a very active one on the Epicurean model. Objects of sensation emit atoms that strike our sense organs (in the case of sight, hearing, and smell), or our sense organs contact the atoms on the objects' surfaces directly (in the case of taste and touch). Once the atoms of the objects of sensation strike the proper organ of sensation, these motions are transmitted via soul atoms (which function like the nervous system) to the mind, located in our chests, where they are "sensed" and interpreted. *Sensus* is also closely related to an adjective that only occurs in Lucretius and nowhere else in Latin literature: *sensifer*, literally "sense-bearing," and always modifies the word *motus*, "motion" The phrase *sensifer motus* occurs six times in Book 3 (240, 245, 272, 379, 570, 924) in its various forms, and means something like "motions that cause sensations," but seems also to shade over into what we would call "consiousness," the ability to be aware and perceive things.

soul: see **mind**.

space (*spatium*, Gr. *chôra*)**, place** (*locus*, Gr. *topos*)**, void** (*inane, vacuum, vacans*; Gr. *kenon*): Epicurus and Lucretius use a number of different words to name and describe space or void, one of the two components of reality, atoms and the void. Many have charged that Epicurus did not clearly distinguish between occupied and unoccupied space, but as Long and Sedley have shown,[2] Epicurus seems to have thought carefully about the problem. Epicurus

---

[2] In my discussion of Epicurus' notion of the void I follow Long and Sedley (1987) I. 27-31.

appears to have used the term *anaphês physis* ("intangible nature," "intangible substance") for space in general, and then used other terms to differentiate unoccupied space (*kenon*, "void"), occupied space (*topos*, "place"), and space when bodies move through it (*chôra*, "space, room"). Lucretius' account seems consistent with Epicurus'. Lucretius uses *intactile* ("not subject to touch") to translate *anaphês* ("intangible"), *locus* ("place") to translate *topos* ("place"), *inane*, *vacuum*, *vacans* ("void, empty, vacant") to translate *kenon* ("void, empty space"), and *spatium* (space) to translate *chôra* ("space, room").

swerve (*clinamen*). The swerve of atoms was one of Epicurus' most controversial doctrines. As Lucretius makes clear at the beginning of Book 2, there are three types of atomic motion: downward motion caused by the atom's weight, motion in all directions caused by collisions between atoms, and the tiny swerve of an atom which was random and unpredictable. The Latin and Greek terms for the swerve (Latin *clinamen*, *declinatio*, *inclinatio*; Greek *parenklisis*) derive from a common stem *klin-*, "to incline, lean, bend, turn aside," and describe the momentary bend a swerving atom makes in its trajectory. Epicurus invoked the swerve to explain two things: (1) how, if all atoms fall downwards at equal speed in the void, collisions of atoms can occur and produce compound bodies, and (2) how, if everything, including the workings of the human mind, can be reduced to the motions of atoms in the void, anything like "free will" (*libera voluntas*) can exist. How the swerve preserves "free will" was the subject of great debate in antiquity and remains so today.[3]

things (*res*): Like the word "thing" in English, the Latin word *res* can be used in many different ways. Lucretius uses *res* in its various forms over 600 times in the poem, and one of the challenges of reading or translating the poem in Latin is figuring out how to make sense of the various occurrences of *res*. One of the forms of *res*, the genitive plural *rerum* (literally, "of things"), is used in the title of Lucretius' poem: *De Rerum Natura* (*On the Nature of Things*) (see the entry on **natura** above). (Here, as often, the plural of *res*, "things", is used in the sense of "what exists, the universe"). *Res* can have many other meanings in Latin, including "object, being, affair, event, fact, circumstance condition, reality, truth, cause, reason, account, business, law case, act" (See Lewis and Short, "*res*,"1575-

---

[3] For more on the swerve, see Furley (1967), Englert (1987), Long and Sedley (1987), Annas (1992), and Purinton (1999).

1576, O.L.D., *"res,"*1625-1626.)[4] Phrases with *res* that are particular favorites of Lucretius include: *hanc ob rem* ("on account of this thing"), *rerum natura* ("nature of things"), *semina rerum* ("seeds of things" = "atoms"), *primordia rerum* ("first beginnings of things" = "atoms"), *summa rerum* ("sum total of things" = "the universe"), *copia rerum* ("supply of things"), *simulacra rerum* ("images of things"), *species rerum* ("the appearance of things"), *nomina rerum* ("the names of things"), *natura gerit res* ("nature conducts her business"), *res in quo quaeque geruntur* ("in which all things are carried out"), and *manifesta docet res* ("the plain facts show").

tranquillity (Gr. *ataraxia*): Epicurus taught that the greatest good is pleasure, defined as freedom from pain, and the greatest evil pain. He taught that "freedom from physical pain" (*aponia*) was a great good, but that "freedom from mental or psychic pain" (*ataraxia*) was an even greater good. *Ataraxia*, literally "freedom from disturbance," but also translated into English as "tranquillity, peacefulness, calmness," was the goal of the Epicurean sage. Lucretius has no single Latin technical term to translate the Greek word *ataraxia*, but instead uses a number of phrases to explicate it. Some of his fullest discussions of *ataraxia* are in his descriptions of the perfectly blessed lives of the gods (See 1. 44-49, 2. 646-651, 2. 1093-1094). Phrases he uses in the poem, all of which get at aspects of Epicurean *ataraxia*, include: *aequo animo* ("with tranquil mind"), *summa cum pace* ("with perfect peace"), *privata dolore omni* ("free from all pain"), *privata periclis* ("free from dangers"), *mente fruatur / iucundo sensu cura semota metuque* ("...and enjoy in the mind pleasant feelings, and be far from care and fear"), (*tranquilla...pace quae placidum degunt aevum vitamque serenam* ("which in tranquil peace pass their placid age and serene life"), *pectore tranquillo* ("with a calm breast"), *vultuque sereno* ("with face serene"), *placidam ac pacatam degere vitam* ("to lead a quiet and peaceful life"), *pacata posse omnia mente tueri* ("to be able to look upon everything with a tranquil mind"), *placida cum pace quietos* ("though calm in placid peace"), *placido cum pectore* ("with placid heart").

universe: see **heavens**.

void: see **space**.

will (*voluntas*): *Voluntas*, the abstract noun Lucretius uses a number of times for "will, wish, desire," derives from the verb *volo*, "to wish, want, be willing." Lucretius discusses aspects of the will in two

---

[4] Lewis and Short, *A Latin Dictionary*, Oxford, 1879; *Oxford Latin Dictionary*, ed. P.G.W. Glare, Oxford, 1982.

passages (2.251-293; 4.877-906), and seems to view it as having an important role to play in the process of voluntary action (Gr. *to hekousion*) of humans and other living creatures, including horses (2.263-271). On the Epicurean view, every voluntary action of living creatures involves an act of desire or will, and Lucretius tells us in one passage (2.251-293) that this will is "free" (*libera*) thanks to the **swerve** (see above) of atoms. There is general agreement that Lucretius is not raising the problem of "free will" in the same terms in which it later became a philosophical issue, but Lucretius seems to be arguing, against determinism, that there is a significant difference between forced and free actions.

world: see **heavens**.

INDEX

All references are to book and line numbers of the English translation.